ClearRevise®

KS3
Computing

Complete course workbook

Published by
PG Online Limited
The Old Coach House
35 Main Road
Tolpuddle
Dorset
DT2 7EW
United Kingdom

sales@pgonline.co.uk
www.clearrevise.com
www.pgonline.co.uk
2024

ACKNOWLEDGMENTS

The questions in this textbook are the sole responsibility of the authors and have neither been provided nor approved by any examination boards.

Every effort has been made to trace and acknowledge ownership of copyright. The publishers will be happy to make any future amendments with copyright owners that it has not been possible to contact. The publisher would like to thank the following companies and individuals who granted permission for the use of their images or content in this textbook.

Images and illustrations © Shutterstock
Page 8, Spam tin image © Roger Utting / Shutterstock.com
Windows® and Excel screenshots used with permission from Microsoft
We are grateful for permission to use and distribute screenshots of the Flowol flowcharts and mimics.
Flowol is a registered trademark of Keep I.T. Easy: www.flowol.com
Scratch is a project of the Scratch Foundation, in collaboration with the Lifelong Kindergarten Group at the MIT Media Lab.
It is available for free at https://scratch.mit.edu
With thanks to AppShed

Design and artwork: Mike Bloys / Jessica Webb / PG Online Ltd
Editor: James Franklin
First edition 2024. 10 9 8 7 6 5 4 3 2 1
A catalogue entry for this book is available from the British Library
ISBN: 9781916518155

This product is made of material from well-managed FSC® certified forests and from recycled materials.
Printed by Bell & Bain Ltd, Glasgow, UK.

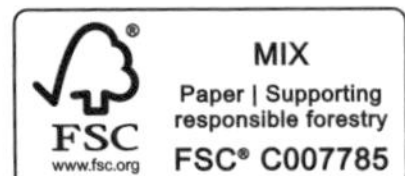

CONTENTS AND CHECKLIST

WHAT MAKES THIS GUIDE SPECIAL?

This book is a complete course workbook covering the English national curriculum for KS3 Computing.

The book covers all the content you need to know in 68 different topics. Each topic has a whole page of questions which each have 10 marks. This will help to check your understanding of the topic.

You can have a go at the units in any order, however the units do get a little harder as you go through the book.

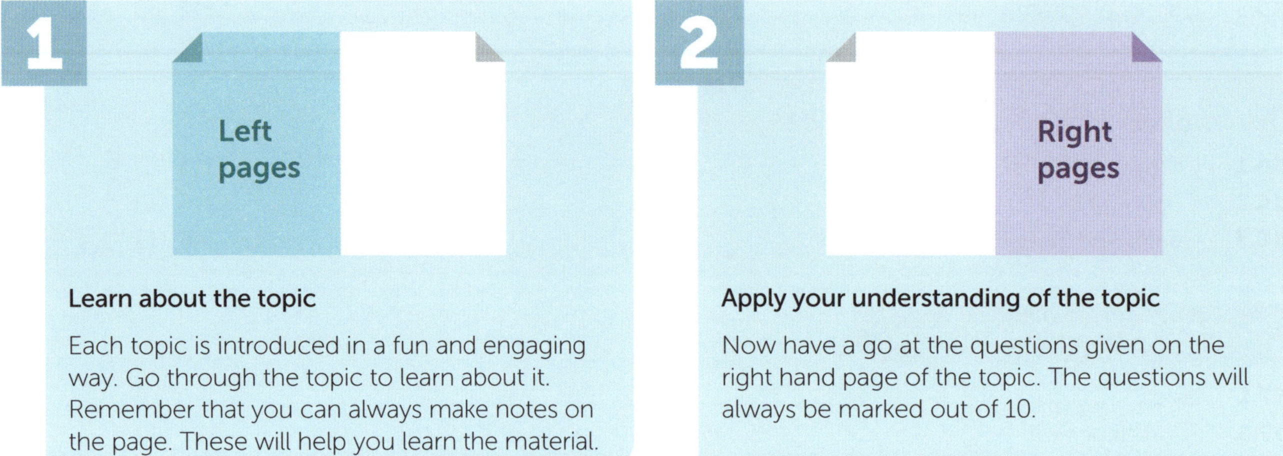

1

Learn about the topic

Each topic is introduced in a fun and engaging way. Go through the topic to learn about it. Remember that you can always make notes on the page. These will help you learn the material.

2

Apply your understanding of the topic

Now have a go at the questions given on the right hand page of the topic. The questions will always be marked out of 10.

3

Learn from the mark schemes

[1]

Mark your work using the mark scheme provided at the bottom of each page. Alternatively, if you are using this book in the classroom, your teacher may ask you to seal the answer pages with sticky tape.

At the end of the questions tick **one** box to show how confident you are at the topic.

How well do you feel you know this topic? 

4

Try the extension activity

Once you've completed the questions there is an extension activity in the **Try it** box.

These are activities which may ask you to work on a computer, a website or on paper. The icons will tell you what sort of task you'll be doing.

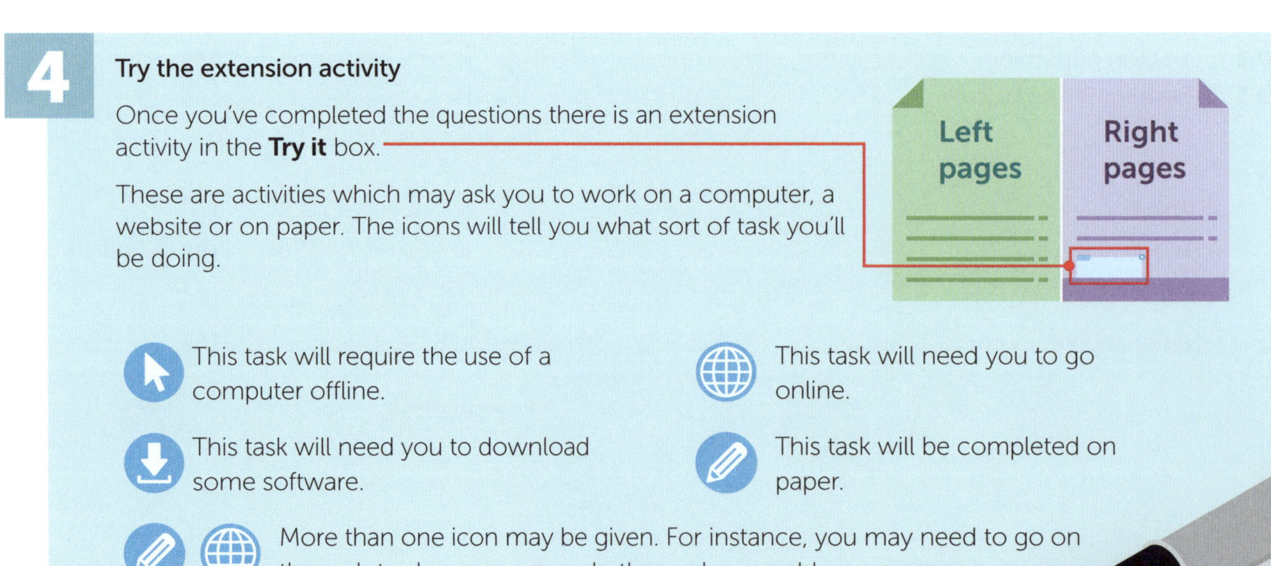

This task will require the use of a computer offline.

This task will need you to go online.

This task will need you to download some software.

This task will be completed on paper.

More than one icon may be given. For instance, you may need to go on the web to do some research, then solve a problem on paper.

COMMAND WORDS

The **command words** below are used throughout the questions in this workbook. Exam boards will typically use similar command words in examination papers given at the end of Key Stage 4. These questions therefore make great practice for the questions you will see in later years.

Command word	What you need to do
Calculate	Work out the numerical value of something. Remember to give units if appropriate.
Complete	Finish a diagram or task by adding information.
Convert	Change data from one form to another.
Define	Give the meaning of a word, phrase or concept.
Describe	Give a detailed account of a situation, event or process.
Design	Produce a plan or model.
Draw	Produce a picture or diagram using a pencil or pen.
Explain	Give the reasons or purposes.
Give	Produce information.
Identify	Provide an answer from a number of possibilities. Briefly state a distinguishing factor or feature.
Label	Add labels to a diagram, image or graph.
List	Give a sequence of brief answers with no explanation.
Name	Give the word or words that are used to refer to something.
Order	Put the responses into a logical sequence.
Show	Give the steps to solve a problem or calculation.
State	Give a specific name, value or other brief answer without explanation or calculation.
Tick	Mark (an item) with a tick or select (a box) to indicate that something has been chosen.
Write / Rewrite	Mark (letters, words, or other symbols) / write (something) again so as to alter or improve it.

PROGRESSION PATHWAY

It is up to you or your teacher in which order you complete the units in this book. You can record your marks here or in the contents pages at the front of the book.

Example

Unit: 12: Python

12.1 7/10 12.5 9/10
12.2 6/10 12.6 10/10
12.3 9/10
12.4 7/10

How do you feel about this unit?

☺ ☑ 😐 ☐ ☹ ☐

Unit:

How do you feel about this unit?

Unit:

How do you feel about this unit?

Unit:

How do you feel about this unit?

Unit:

How do you feel about this unit?

Unit:

How do you feel about this unit?

Unit:

How do you feel about this unit?

Unit:

How do you feel about this unit?

Unit:

How do you feel about this unit?

Unit:

How do you feel about this unit?

Unit:

How do you feel about this unit?

Unit:

How do you feel about this unit?

Unit:

How do you feel about this unit?

Unit:

How do you feel about this unit?

Unit:

How do you feel about this unit?

Unit:

How do you feel about this unit?

Unit:

How do you feel about this unit?

Unit:

How do you feel about this unit?

Unit:

How do you feel about this unit?

Unit:

How do you feel about this unit?

TOPIC 1.1

FILE MANAGEMENT

When working with computers, users create many **files**. These need to be well organised so they are easy to find later.

Files can be **copied**, **deleted** or **moved** to other locations within a tree structure. The top folder is known as the **root** folder.

Filenames

Files need to have **meaningful filenames** so it is easy to understand what they contain.

Meaningful filenames

- ✓ English essay 5 – War Poem.docx
- ✓ Lesson 3 Finance activity.xlsx
- ✓ Science sodium homework.pptx

Poor file names

- ✗ a.docx
- ✗ Untitled 1.xlsx
- ✗ Science stuff.pptx

Tree structure

Files are then organised into **folders** and **subfolders** in a **tree structure**.

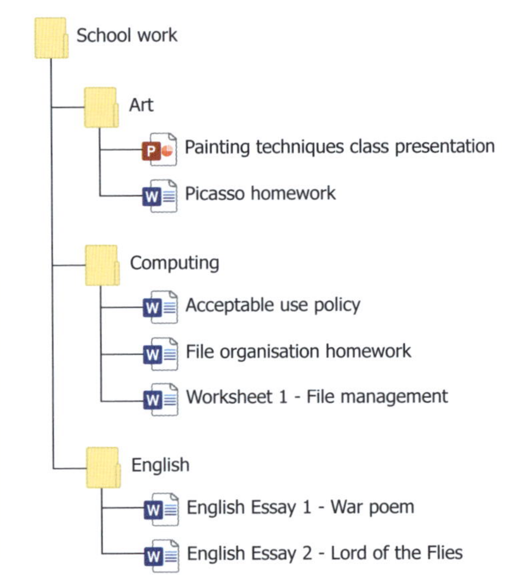

Remember

The following are **shortcuts** for managing files and folders in Microsoft® Windows®.

Shortcut	Meaning
CTRL + C	Copy
CTRL + V	Paste
DEL	Delete
F2	Rename
WIN + E	Open Windows Explorer **file manager**

Backups

What would happen if a hard drive or memory card broke?

You'd lose all the files stored on it.

Make sure you **backup** your work onto another device such as a USB stick or an external hard drive.

Path names

The **path** is the location used to identify where a file is stored. The path is made from the drive name and subdirectory names.

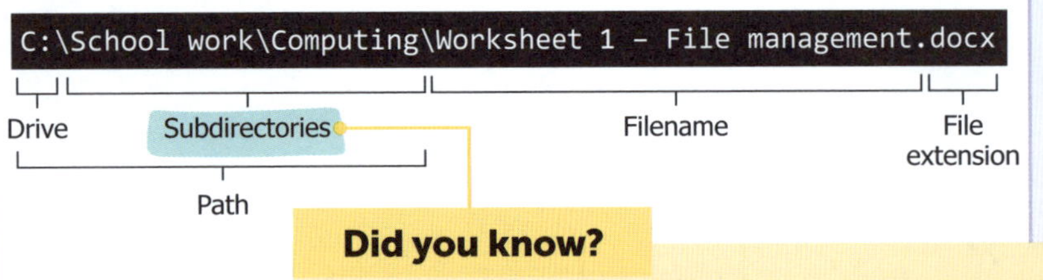

Did you know?

Folders and subfolders are known as **directories** and **sub directories** when written as text.

1. The file tree structure on the left belongs to a year 7 pupil. Look at the structure and then answer the following questions.

Write your mark here

   (a) Identify the root folder.

   .... [1]

   (b) Identify **two** subfolders of the root folder.

   ....

   .... [2]

   (c) A pupil is writing a business letter as part of their English homework.
   Give a suitable filename for the document.

   .... [1]

   (b) The year 7 pupil is now moving up to year 8. Describe how they could reorganise their folder structure.

   ....

   ....

   ....

   .... [2]

2. Sammy is working on a long essay on her home computer. The document is stored on her hard drive.

   (a) Explain why Sammy should create a backup of her work.

   ....

   .... [2]

   (b) Describe how Sammy could use keyboard shortcuts to make a backup of her work on a USB stick.

   ....

   ....

   ....

   .... [2]

Try it

Organise the files and folders on your school or home computer.

Try using the shortcut keys on the left to do this. You might find it quicker.

Total ☐ /10

How well do you feel you know this topic? ☺ ☐ 😐 ☐ ☹ ☐

TOPIC 1.2

WEB SEARCHING

The **World Wide Web** contains billions of **web pages**.

A search engine is used to find information that matches pages that contain keywords in the search **query**.

How it works

Search engines use **web spiders** to find keywords in web pages. Web spiders are programs that download the webpage and then process the text in it, storing the keywords in a **database**. When you search for keywords, the search engine looks up which pages contain those terms and selects the most relevant ones to display.

Accuracy and reliability

Anyone is able to make and upload a web page. This often leads to **inaccurate** and **unreliable** information being viewed.

Always be suspicious of information you find on the web. Some ways that help to check if a website is reliable include:

- Check the URL
- Check for a green padlock next to the **web address** (showing that the webpage is being securely transmitted using **encryption**)
- Confirm information with other websites you respect
- Check the date it was last updated

Did you know?

URL means **Uniform Resource Locator**. It's a fancy Computing term that means **web address**.

Remember

Search engine **operators** will help you when searching.

- Use a **– symbol** to exclude certain words:

entertainer -clown

- Use **speech marks** to search for a phrase:

"to be or not to be"

- To search only pages within a certain web address, use the **inurl operator**:

inurl:gov.uk

- To search only for certain filetypes, use the **filetype operator**:

filetype:pdf

Choice of search engine

There are many different search engines that are available. They will each give different results. Some of the more popular search engines include:

- **Google®**
- **Bing®**
- **DuckDuckGo®**
- **Yahoo!®**

Search engines often have **advanced searches** such as for images, shopping or books. Make use of these to improve the results.

Top tip

The following **shortcuts** are often used in web browsers to quickly bookmark pages and show the web history.

- CTRL + D **Bookmark** a web page
- CTRL + H Show the **web history**

1. State the use of each of the following types of searches.

Search query	Use
"Well done is better than well said"	
beach filetype:pdf	
fruit -apple	
map inurl:emilycollege.sch.uk	

[4]

Write your mark here

2. Give **three** ways that are used to check the accuracy and reliability of the information on a web page.

① ....

② ....

③ ....

[3]

3. (a) Google is an example of a search engine. Name **two** other search engines.

① ....

② ....

[2]

(b) Name the shortcut for bookmarking a web page in a web browser.

.... **[1]**

Try it

Most people just use the **default** search engine on their web browser. Compare results from different ones. Some popular search engines are **Google**, **Bing**, **DuckDuckGo** and **Yahoo!**

Total /10

How well do you feel you know this topic?   

TOPIC 1.3

SOCIAL MEDIA

Social media allows users to keep in contact with friends and family. This includes sharing videos, photos and commenting on them. Whilst social media may be fun, there are risks to using it, such as **cyberbulling**, **online strangers** and **inappropriate content**.

Did you know?

Cyberbullying includes any type of bullying that uses technology. It may happen via:

- Social media
- Text messages
- Email
- Photo and video sharing sites

Reducing social media risks

Cyberbullying

- Don't reply
- **Block** the sender
- Save any **evidence**
- Tell someone you trust such as a parent or teacher.

Online strangers

- Only add people who you know offline
- Tell someone you trust if you feel uncomfortable by any posts sent to you.

Inappropriate content

- Report to the website owner
- If you are upset, go to a trusted adult such as a parent or teacher. Alternatively, phone **Childline** on **0800 1111** or talk to them online.

Reporting concerns

If something concerns you, report it to one of the following:

- Report to your school
- Report to the social media owner
- Report to CEOP

Did you know?

CEOP (Child Exploitation and Online Protection Command) is run by the National Crime Agency (NCA).

CEOP allows you to make reports if someone has made you feel uncomfortable online, such as by asking you to send a nude image or pressuring you to meet them face to face.

Go to **ceop.police.uk** to make a report.

Online profiles

An **online profile** will contain lots of **personal information** such as your name, age, address and interests.

Social media sites allow you to customise your **privacy settings**. Make sure to do this. For instance, you will be safer if you just allow specific friends to see posts that you make.

1. Look at each of the scenarios in the table below. For each one, give **two** actions that could be taken to reduce the risk or deal with the situation.

Write your mark here

Scenario	Action to reduce the risk or deal with the situation
Adam is playing an online game when a stranger asks to chat privately. They keep on asking despite being told no.	1. .... 2. ....
A friend has received emails that are upsetting them.	1. .... 2. ....
Freya has seen an image online which has upset her.	1. .... 2. ....

[6]

2. Tick the correct box for the organisation that runs CEOP.

A Local council ☐

B National Crime Agency (NCA) ☐

C Social services ☐

D Your school ☐

[1]

3. (a) Give **two** examples of personal information.

① ....

....

② ....

.... **[2]**

(b) Give **one** way you could improve the privacy of your online profile.

.... **[1]**

Try it

If you use any social media sites, try going into your privacy settings and see what improvements you can make. If you don't yet have any accounts, research the risks of using social media.

Total ☐ /10

How well do you feel you know this topic?  

TOPIC 1.4

E-SAFETY

When using computers, electronic devices and the Internet, you need to understand how to keep safe. This is where **e-safety** helps. E-safety is a set of ways to act when using electronic equipment and it includes **online safety**.

Passwords

To gain access to a computer or online system you usually need to log in with a **password**. This helps to prevent hackers from **misusing** computers and services.

Secure passwords are at least 10 characters long and contain a few special characters and numbers. Basing a password on three random words can make it easier to remember, but still be secure.

Strong password examples

- aPb6Bx%3M&Rt
- phoTolionflooD*£
- advance%GearstooL$

Weak password examples

- password
- Football
- ILikeTheBeach

How it works

Hackers can find out passwords by trying every combination of letters that could be used. This is known as a **brute-force attack**.

To make this attack harder, use long passwords that contain a mixture of uppercase and lowercase letters with some numbers and **special characters** such as #)(*%^$£?.

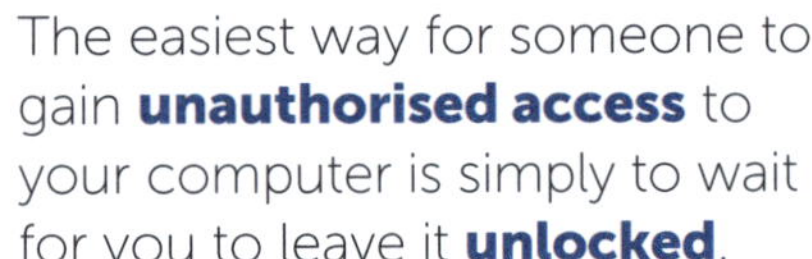

Did you know?

On Windows computers the **shortcut** WINDOWS + L will instantly lock it. Alternatively, use

CTRL + ALT + DEL and select the lock option.

On Apple Mac computers use the shortcut Control + Command + Q.

Locking computers

The easiest way for someone to gain **unauthorised access** to your computer is simply to wait for you to leave it **unlocked**.

It is very important that you **lock** your computer when you leave it, even if you are gone for just a few seconds.

Spam email

Spam is email that is sent to many users without their permission. It is often used to sell illegal products or for scams.

To prevent spam, move any junk emails you receive into a **spam folder** which will help to filter out future emails. Do not reply to it or click any links as this may result in even more spam.

Did you know?

Spam email gets its name from a Monty Python sketch in 1970 where a waitress repeatedly offers a customer spam (processed tinned ham) to eat.

Write your mark here

1. (a) Suggest **three** rules that could be used when creating strong passwords.

① ....

② ....

③ .... **[3]**

(b) Give examples of **two** special characters that could be used in a password.

① ....

② .... **[2]**

2. Ava receives a spam email.

(a) Give **one** action which should be taken once Ava realises the email is spam.

....

.... **[1]**

(b) Give **two** actions which could increase the amount of spam Ava receives.

① ....

....

② ....

.... **[2]**

3. (a) Give **one** reason why you should lock your computer when you are not sitting next to it.

....

.... **[1]**

(b) State the shortcut which is used to lock a computer.

....

.... **[1]**

Try it

Search for

How secure is my password

Use a password checking website to test the security of the passwords on the left.

Total ☐ /10

How well do you feel you know this topic? ☺ ☐ 😐 ☐ ☹ ☐

TOPIC 2.1

FLOWCHARTS

Flowcharts are diagrams that show the flow order of processes. In computing, these processes are known as **algorithms**.

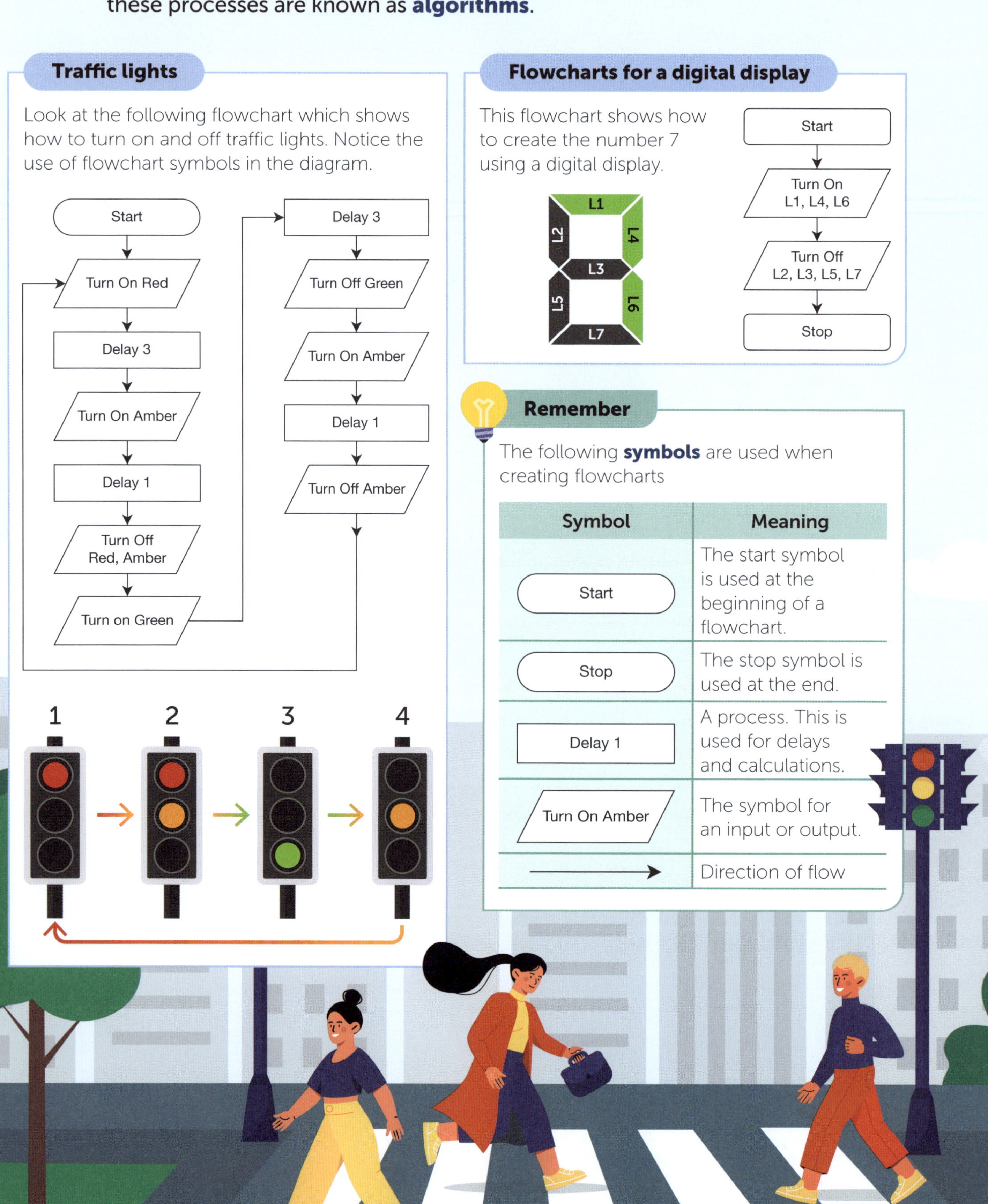

Traffic lights

Look at the following flowchart which shows how to turn on and off traffic lights. Notice the use of flowchart symbols in the diagram.

Flowcharts for a digital display

This flowchart shows how to create the number 7 using a digital display.

Remember

The following **symbols** are used when creating flowcharts

Symbol	Meaning
Start	The start symbol is used at the beginning of a flowchart.
Stop	The stop symbol is used at the end.
Delay 1	A process. This is used for delays and calculations.
Turn On Amber	The symbol for an input or output.
→	Direction of flow

1. A sports car has amber lights used for indicating a turn and white lights used for lighting the road.

Write your mark here

(a) Complete the flowchart to make Amber2 continuously flash on and off once a second. The light should remain on or off for 0.5 seconds..

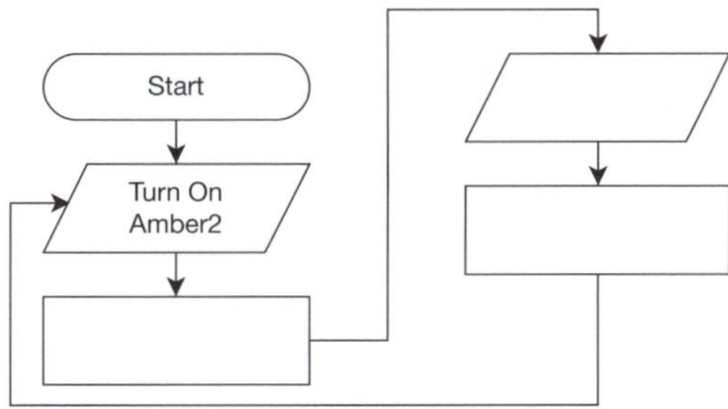

[3]

(b) When the car alarm goes off, the lights flash between both white lights and both amber lights. The white lights turn on for 0.5 seconds. They then turn off and the amber lights turn on for 0.5 seconds. Draw a flowchart to turn the lights on and off.

[7]

Try it

Flowcharts are often used in comical ways. Search for:

Funny flowcharts

Once you've read a few, try to make your own. Note that the symbols used often aren't correct.

Total

/10

How well do you feel you know this topic?

TOPIC 2.2

DECISIONS

One key aspect of flowcharts and algorithms is to be able to make decisions. In English, decisions use the word if. For instance, in a car park, *if* a car park ticket is taken, then the entry barrier will raise.

Rollercoasters

Rollercoasters make use of control systems to start and stop the ride. The safety systems are also automated.

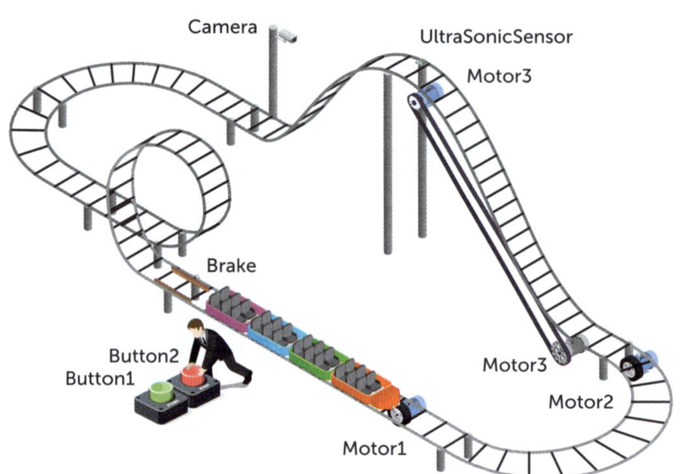

How it works

Inputs

- **Button1** starts the rollercoaster.
- **Button2** is used in an emergency to stop everything on the rollercoaster.
- The **UltraSonicSensor** is triggered when the train moves past.

Outputs

- **Motor1** moves the train around the first bend.
- **Motor2** moves the train onto the hill.
- **Motor3** moves a chain which pulls the train up the hill.
- The **Brake** clamps onto fins on the train to slow it down.

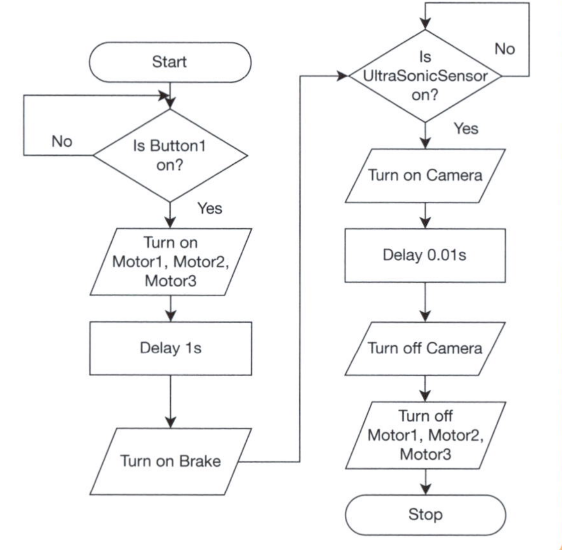

Flowchart decisions

Decisions in flowcharts use a diamond shaped symbol which contains a **condition**. There will be two arrows that come out from a decision. One will be labelled **Yes**, the other will be labelled **No**. These will be followed based on the outcome of the condition.

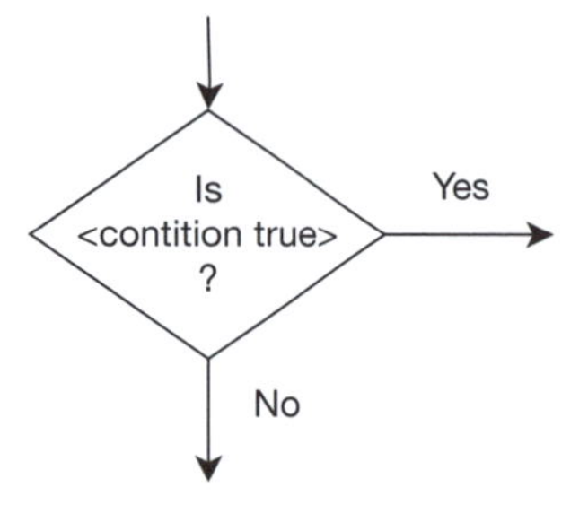

Did you know?

Ultrasonic sensors send out a pulse of **ultrasonic** sound. This is a higher **frequency** than people can hear. The sensor times how long it takes for the sound to be reflected to work out how far the object is away. This is the same system that bats use to find insects.

Write your mark here

1. When a car reverses, an ultrasonic sensor is used to detect how close it is to an object. If it is less than one metre away, then the car will make a beep sound.
Complete the flowchart below.

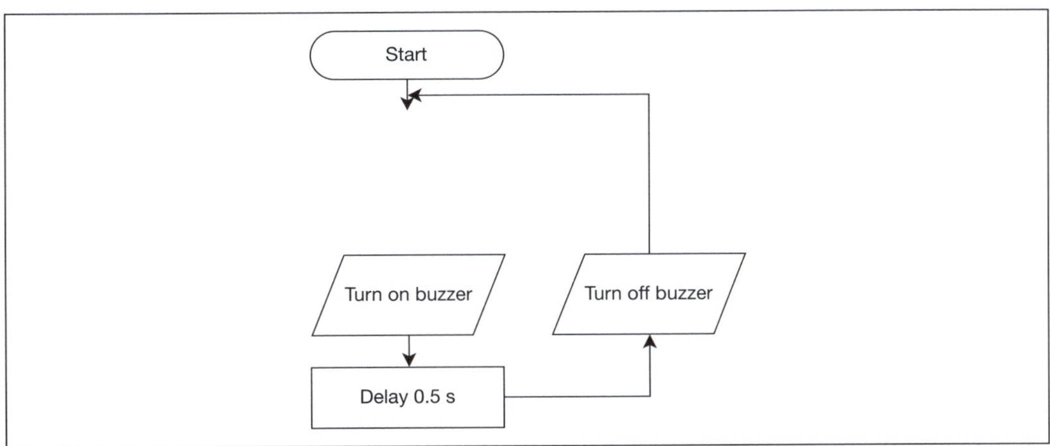

[3]

2. Look at the rollercoaster on the left.
Button2 is an emergency stop button. When it is pressed, the brake should be turned on and all the motors should be turned off.
Draw a flowchart to control the stop button.

[7]

Try it

The roller coaster could have more control system features such as:

- Automated gates
- More brakes and motors
- Lights and speakers

Make a more advanced flowchart to add these features in.

Total /10

How well do you feel you know this topic?  

TOPIC 2.3 SUBROUTINES

Flowcharts often become very long and difficult to understand. To make them easier to understand, **subroutines** are created. A subroutine is a flowchart that has its own name. Other flowcharts are then able to **call** the subroutine.

Rollercoasters

Creating subroutines is just like creating a flowchart, except that the start symbol changes to the name of the subroutine.

Sub OpenBarrier

To call the subroutine, a special subroutine box is used:

Sub OpenBarrier

Did you know?

Subroutines are used in text programming languages such as Python® using definitions (also known as functions and procedures). They are also available in Scratch™ using the **My Blocks** feature.

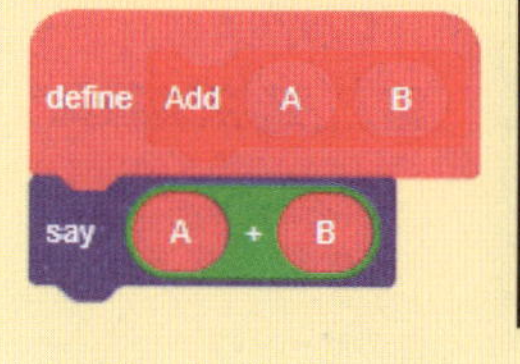

My Blocks in Scratch

```
def add(a, b):
    answer = a + b
    print(answer)
```

Python definitions

Ticket barriers

A ticket barrier has a number of different processes which make a flowchart lengthy.

To make it easier, you can break down the problem into smaller parts. This strategy is known as decomposition.

For the ticket barrier, the algorithm is:

```
Insert ticket
IF ticket is invalid THEN
  Reject ticket
ELSE
  Open barrier
  Return ticket
```

Subroutines are used to create each part of this process.

The main algorithm is shown on the right along with the first subroutine InsertTicket.

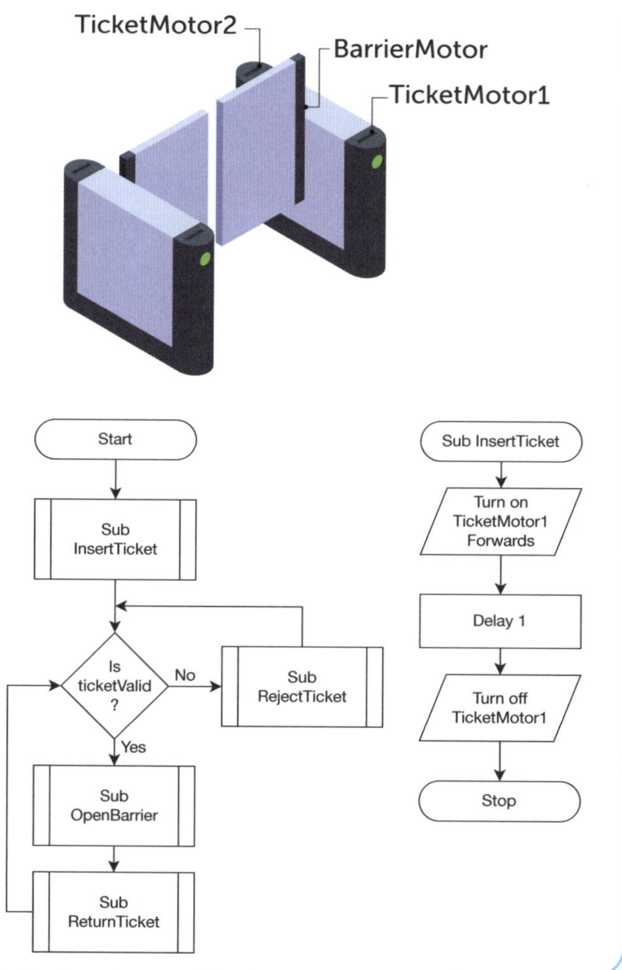

1. This question uses the ticket barriers algorithm and flowcharts on the left.

(a) Below is the RejectTicket subroutine. The ReturnTicket subroutine is very similar. Complete the ReturnTicket subroutine by filling in the missing text in three symbols. A ticket is returned using TicketMotor2.

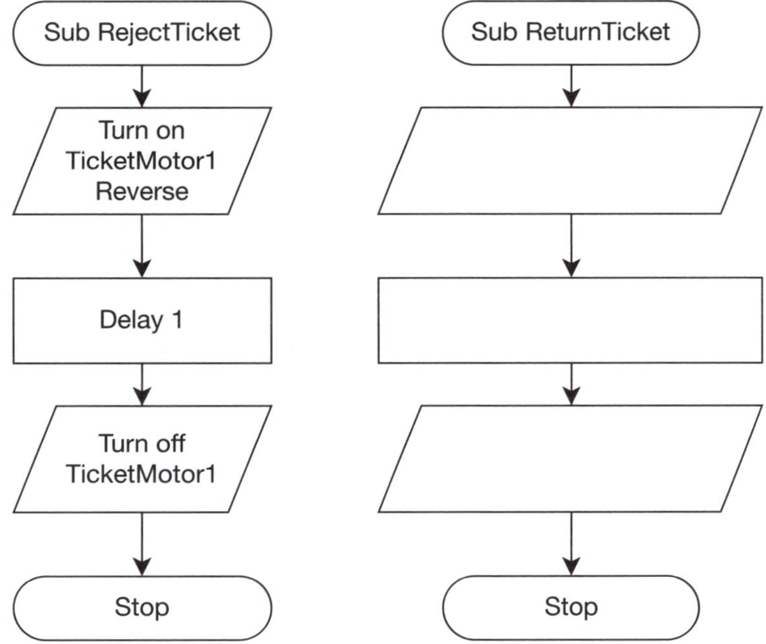

[3]

(b) Draw a flowchart for the OpenBarrier subroutine. Give two seconds for the barrier to remain open so that someone can walk through.

[7]

Write your mark here

Try it

In the ticket barrier algorithm there could be another subroutine for ticketIsInvalid. Think of other input or output devices the ticket machine would need and write a subroutine for ticketIsInvalid.

Total ☐ /10

How well do you feel you know this topic? ☺ ☐ 😐 ☐ ☹ ☐

TOPIC 2.4

VARIABLES

Variables are used to store values (numbers or text) that are to be used later on in the flowchart.

A bank ATM (Automated Teller Machine)

A bank allows users to withdraw money from ATMs. The flowchart below shows how variables could be used to withdraw money from an account.

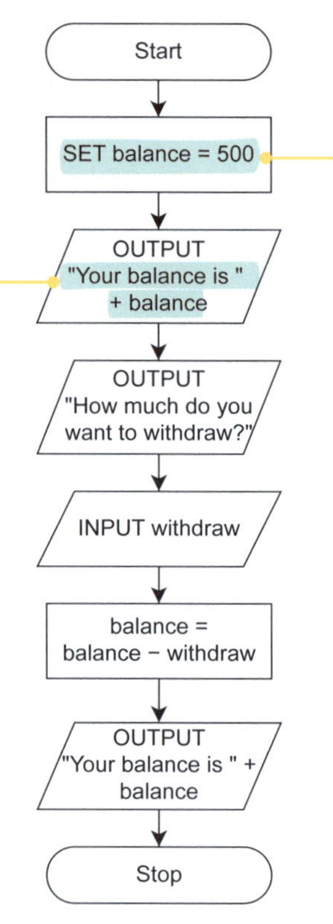


```
Your balance is 500
How much do you want to withdraw?
50
Your balance is 450
```

How it works

The variable **balance** is set to **500**. This is used to store the user's account balance.

Another variable named **withdraw** is used to store the amount which the user wants to take out of their account.

Variables in decisions

Variables are also used in decisions. The following part of a flowchart checks the user has enough money in their account before they make their withdrawal.

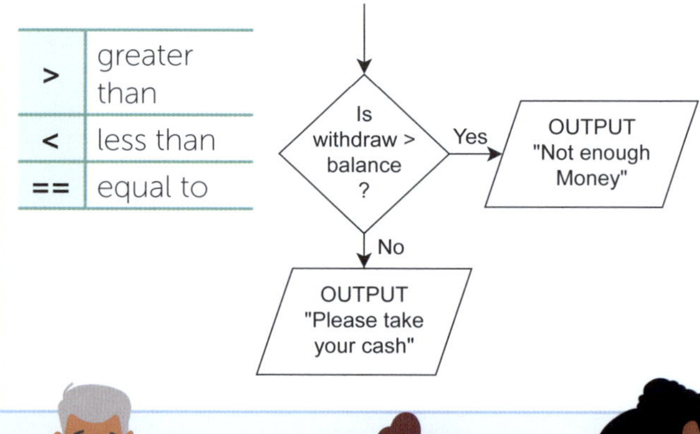

>	greater than
<	less than
==	equal to

Did you know?

The = symbol in Computing doesn't mean equals. It means **assignment**.

balance = 500 means **assign** a value of 500 to the variable named balance.

In this program, + means **concatenate**. This is a fancy word that means joining two items of text together. When + is used with numbers it means **addition**, just like in Maths.

Write your mark here

1. Look at the flowchart below.

(a) If the input numbers are 4 and 5, what will the output from the flowchart be?

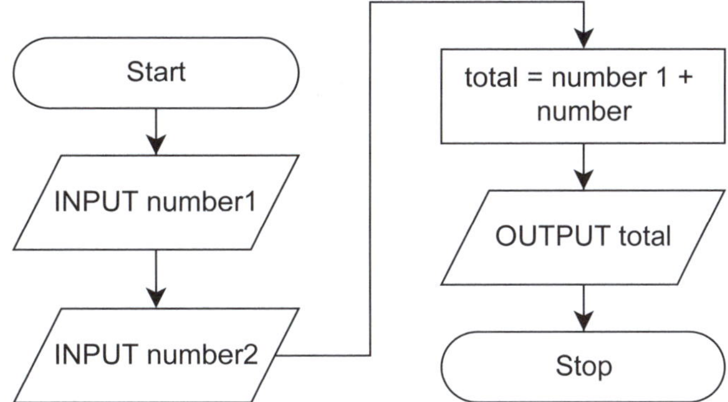

[1]

(b) Describe how the flowchart could be adapted to output the average of the two numbers after the total.

....

.... **[2]**

2. Draw a flowchart that asks the user to input two numbers. The flowchart should then output the highest of the two numbers.

[7]

Try it

A program is being made that will calculate someone's age in days when they enter how old they are in years. Write a flowchart for the program, making use of variables.

Total /10

How well do you feel you know this topic?

TOPIC 3.1

LOGICAL THINKING

Logical thinking is one part of **Computational Thinking**. It allows you to make **logical decisions** and **deductions** based on **facts**.

Venn diagrams

Venn diagrams show the logical relationship between different sets of data.

The following diagram shows the sets of people who own cats and dogs.

The ξ character is the Greek letter Xi and represents the universal set, or 'all animals'.

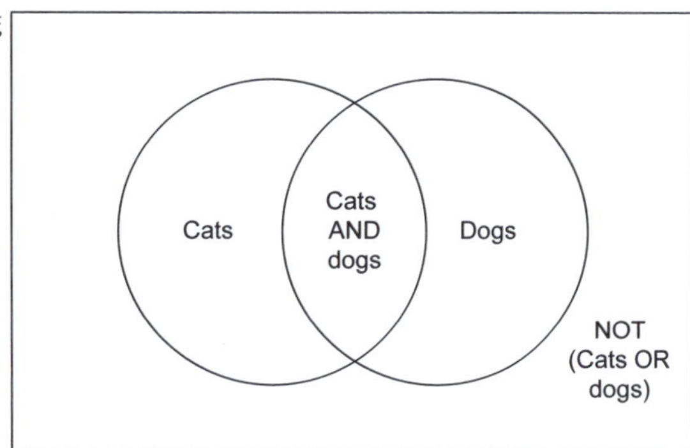

The following Venn diagram highlights the logical expression: **NOT Cats**

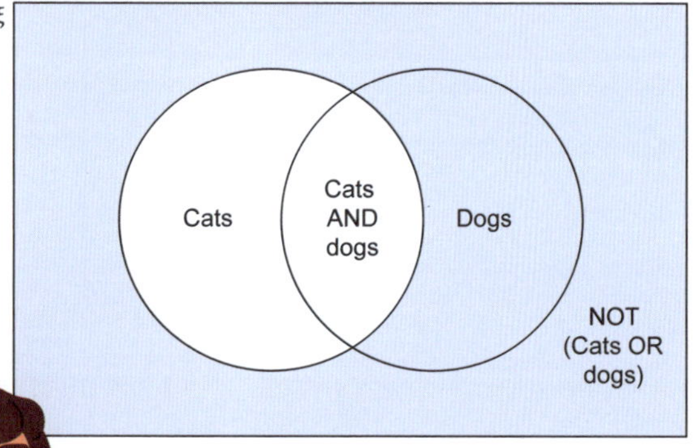

Did you know?

Computational thinking (CT) is how Computer scientists, developers and programmers think about solving problems so that they may be processed using computer systems.

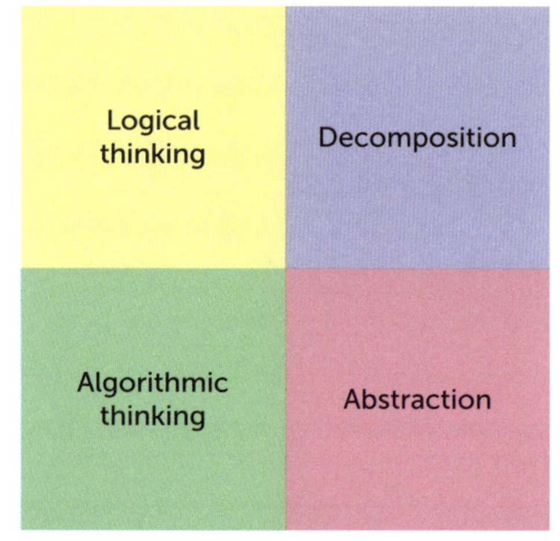

Logical operators

In computing, the operators **AND**, **OR** and **NOT** are commonly used in programming. For example:

```
IF isAdult AND hasDrivingLicence THEN
   allowToDrive()
```

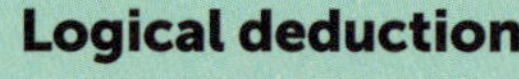

Logical deduction

Logical deduction is the process of working out if something is **True** or **False**. For example:

- All planets orbit a star
- The Sun is a star
- The Moon orbits the Earth
- The Earth is a planet

Question: Is the moon a planet?

Logical deduction: The moon is NOT a planet

Write your mark here

1. Logical thinking is one part of Computational Thinking.
   Name the **three** other parts.

   ① ....

   ② ....

   ③ .... **[3]**

2. Look at the following facts about a planetary system known as TRAPPIST-1.
   - All planets orbit a star
   - All moons orbit a planet
   - TRAPPIST-1 is not a planet
   - TRAPPIST-1b orbits TRAPPIST-1
   - TRAPPIST-1c orbits TRAPPIST-1

   Complete the table to show logical deductions for what TRAPPIST-1, TRAPPIST-1b and TRAPPIST-1c are. Tick **one** box in each row.

Name	Star (✓)	Planet (✓)	Moon (✓)
TRAPPIST-1			
TRAPPIST-1b			
TRAPPIST-1c			

[3]

3. Below are three sections of programming code. For each one, write the correct logical operator (AND, OR or NOT) in the spaces given.

(a)
```
IF inCar .......... inTaxi THEN
        mustUseChildSeat()
```
[1]

(b)
```
IF schoolAge .......... .......... sick THEN
        mustGoToSchool()
```
[2]

(c)
```
IF .......... gameOver THEN
playGame()
```
[1]

Try it

Search the Internet for:

Riddles and logic puzzles

These are fun to solve and will help with the precise thinking used when solving logical computing problems.

Total /10

How well do you feel you know this topic?  

TOPIC 3.2

LOGIC GATES

Logic gates are used in electronic circuits to determine an output based on two inputs. Computers and electronic devices make use of logic gates when running programs. The way that a logic gate affects the output is given in its **truth table**.

Did you know?

The inputs and outputs into logic gates may use True/False, On/Off or 1/0.

AND gate

An **AND gate** needs both inputs to be True for the output to be True.

A	B	Output
False	False	False
False	True	False
True	False	False
True	True	True

OR gate

An **OR gate** needs one of the inputs to be True for the output to be True.

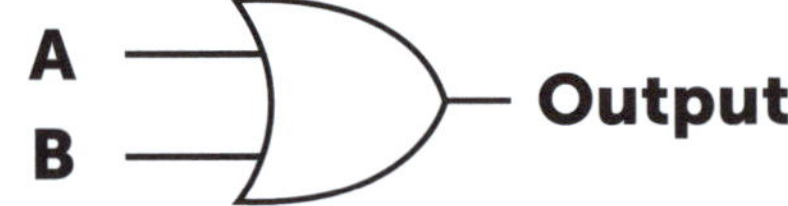

A	B	Output
False	False	False
False	True	True
True	False	True
True	True	True

NOT gate

The output from a **NOT gate** is the opposite of the input.

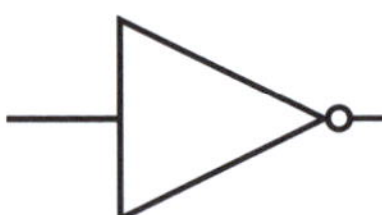

A	Output
False	True
True	False

Circuits

Logic gates may be joined together to make a circuit.

In the diagram, the yellow wires, labelled with a 1, show that the line is on and electricity is flowing through the wire.

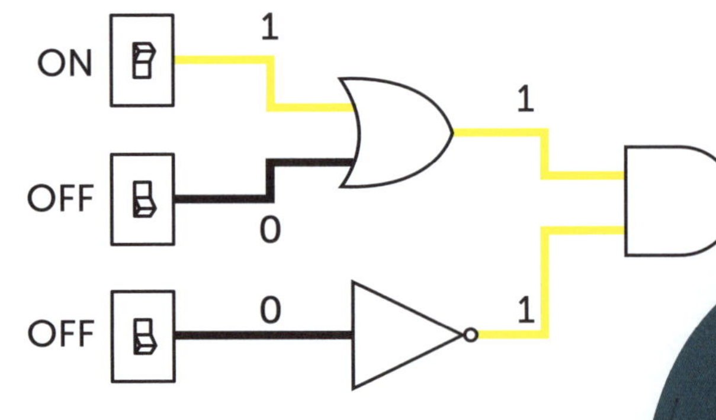

Write your mark here

1. The table below lists three logic gates. For each one, draw the symbol that is used..

Logic gate	Symbol
AND gate	
OR gate	
NOT gate	

[3]

2. Complete the truth table for an OR gate. Note that this truth table uses 0 for False and 1 for True. It also has a different order to the truth table on the left.

A	B	Output
1	1	
1	0	
0	1	
0	0	

[4]

3. Look at the following circuit. Write a 1 or 0 next to each wire to show if it is turned on or off.

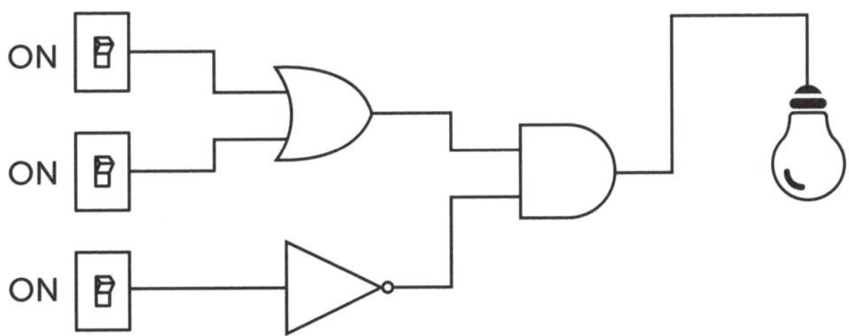

[3]

Try it

Search the Internet for:

XOR gate truth table

Now work out the truth table for the circuit on the right. What do you notice about it?

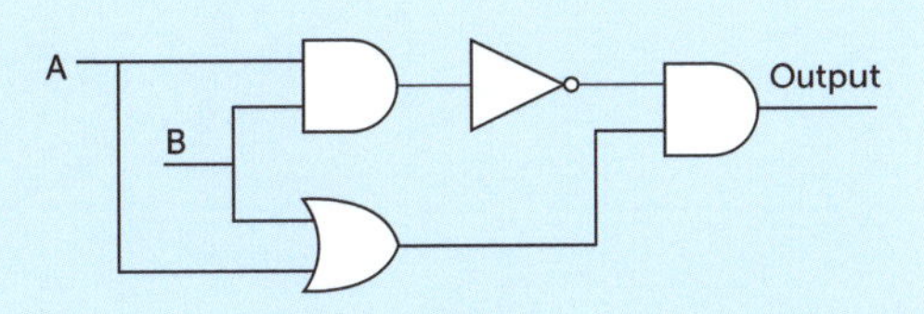

Total

/10

How well do you feel you know this topic?

TOPIC 3.3

ALGORITHMIC THINKING

An **algorithm** is a set of steps used to solve a problem. There may be many different ways to solve the same problem. The way that computer scientists and programmers consider better ways to approach an algorithm is known as **algorithmic thinking**.

A square drawing algorithm

A robot is able to use the following instructions:

```
Forward(squares)
Turn(degrees)
PenDown()
PenUp()
```

To draw a square the following algorithm would be used:

```
PenDown()
Forward(2)
Left(90)
Forward(2)
Left(90)
Forward(2)
Left(90)
Forward(2)
Left(90)
PenUp()
```

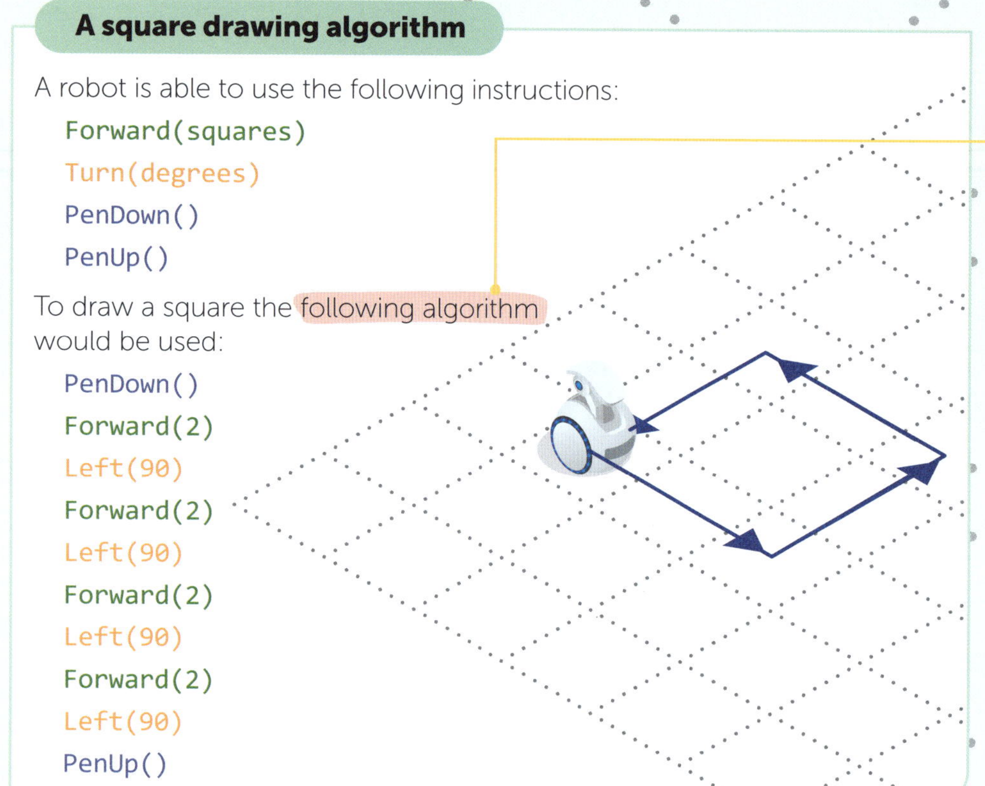

Did you know?

Instructions that are run one after the other are known as a **sequence**.

A better algorithm

The algorithm to draw a square could be written more efficiently.

Look at the following two lines in the algorithm above:

```
Forward(2)
Left(90)
```

A programmer would consider that these two lines could simply be repeated. The algorithm would now be:

```
PenDown()
REPEAT 4
   Forward(2)
   Left(90)
```

Did you know?

The **REPEAT** statement allows a **loop** to be made around the two lines.

It is possible to put a loop inside another loop. This would be known as a **nested loop**.

1. Match the computing terms with their meanings.

Algorithm	A single operation to be carried out.
Sequence	A programming structure that repeats instructions.
Loop	Instructions that are run one after the other.
Instruction	A loop inside another loop.
Nested loop	The set of steps that are used to solve a problem.

[5]

Write your mark here

2. A car is controlled by the following instructions:
   - `forward(5)` – moves forward 5 squares
   - `right(90)` – turns right 90°
   - `left(90)` – turns left 90°

   Write an algorithm to move the car along all the white squares to the finish box.

   If you need more space, use the continuation sheet page on **page 162**.

[5]

Try it

Search the Internet for:

 online logo programming

Logo is a language that controls a turtle that can draw. Go to an online site and try to make a picture using Logo.

Total /10

How well do you feel you know this topic?   

TOPIC 3.4

ABSTRACTION

Abstraction is the removing or hiding of unnecessary details to help solve a computing problem. This allows the key details to be considered more clearly.

Map abstraction

A map is one example of an abstraction of real life. Many details are ignored such as people, cars and park benches.

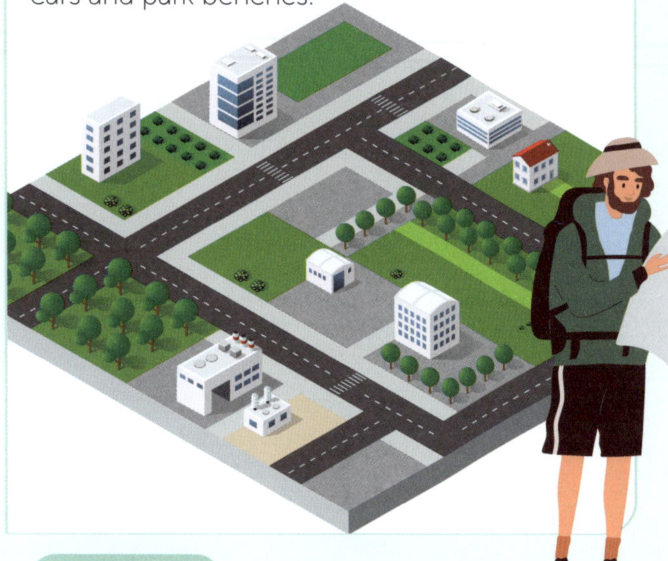

Further map abstraction

Maps are often abstracted further so that just the roads and junctions are present. This allows a route between two points to be found.

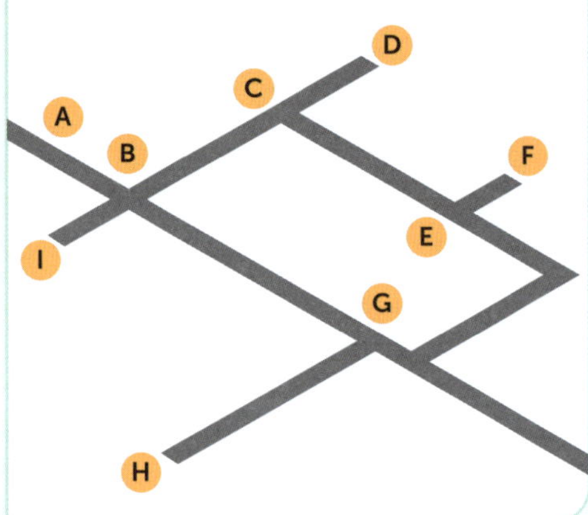

SatNavs

SatNavs are used to give directions between two points. They work by using even more abstraction.

Here, each road junction is put in a circle known as a **node**. Each connection represents a road and is known as an **arc**. The diagram that is created is known as a **graph**.

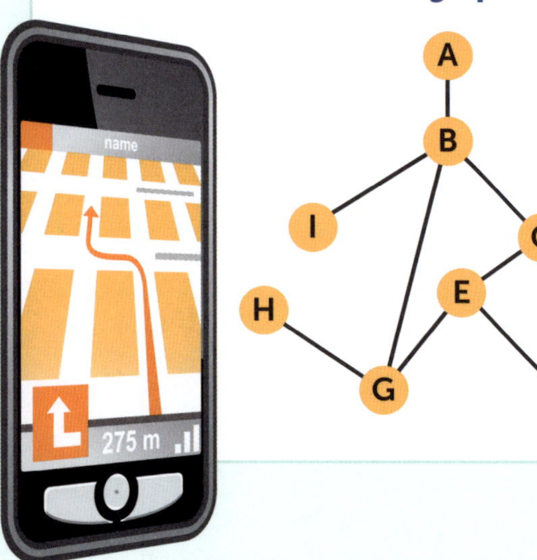

How it works

This graph can be stored in text as follows:

```
(A,B), (B,I), (B,C), (C,D), (C,E),
(E,F), (E,G), (G,H), (B,G)
```

Notice how little information is required and how much more abstract this is than the original map.

Algorithms already exist for finding the **shortest route** between two nodes in a graph. These are used to find the shortest route on mapping software.

In real software, the distance between two nodes is also stored.

Write your mark here

1. Give a definition of the term abstraction.

....

.... **[1]**

2. Use the graph on the left page to answer the following questions in the table below.

Question	Answer
Give a route to get from A to D.	
Give an alternative route to get from A to D.	
Give a route to get from H to A.	

[3]

3. A graph's arcs are stored with the following text:

(A,E), (A,G), (A,D), (E,F), (G,F), (D,C), (C,B)

(a) Draw the graph that is represented by the above arcs.

[3]

(b) Give a route to get from A to B.

.... **[1]**

(c) Give **two** routes to get from A to F.

① ....

② .... **[2]**

Try it

Search for:

Dijkstras shortest path algorithm

Study how the algorithm works. Now add some weights to the graph on the left and then use Dijkstra's algorithm to find the shortest path between two points.

Total /10

How well do you feel you know this topic?

TOPIC 3.5

DECOMPOSITION

Many problems in computing are large and complicated to solve. Imagine trying to make software such as an operating system or graphics editing software. **Decomposition** is the process of breaking down larger problems into smaller ones that are easier to solve. Even small programs are **decomposed** to make it easier for a programmer to implement each part.

Car game

A simple driving game enables a player to move a car on a road to one of three positions:

- Left
- Centre
- Right

The player can move the car left or right by touching one half of a screen.

Other cars appear on the road coming towards the player's car. If the car hits one, then the lives decrease by 1. Every tenth of a second the game is played, the score increases by 1.

Powerups, such as an extra life or turbo box alter the gameplay if the player's car touches them.

Development

Once a structure diagram has been created, it's easy to implement each part of it. For instance, moving the car left might have the following algorithm:

```
MoveCarLeft():
  IF inRightLane THEN
    MoveToCentreLane()
  ELSE IF inCentreLane THEN
    MoveToLeftLane()
  ENDIF
```

Structure diagram

Structure diagrams help to breakdown the problem into smaller problems.

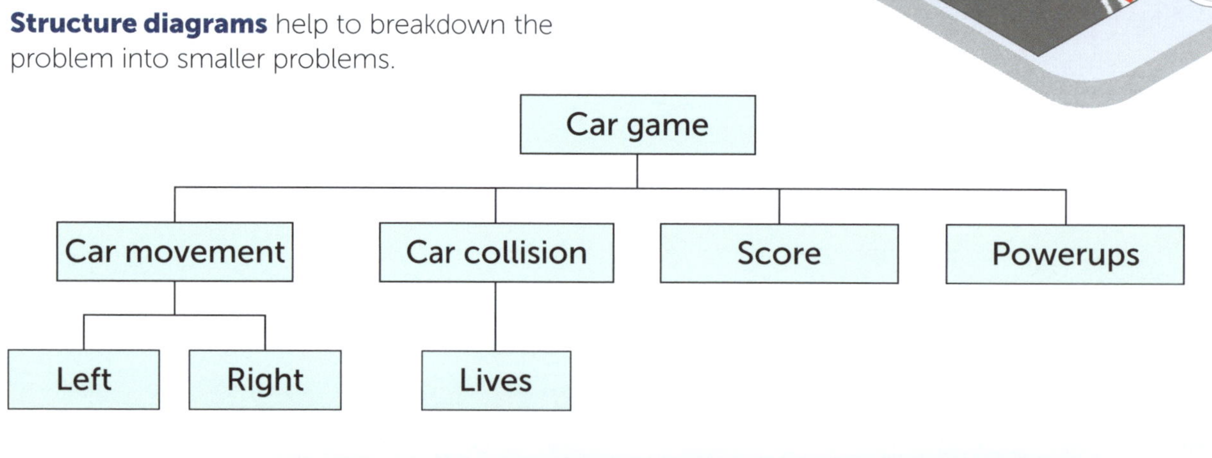

Write your mark here

1. Decomposition is being used in the development of a new messaging app.

   (a) Define the meaning of the term decomposition.

   ....

   .... **[1]**

   (b) Draw a structure diagram to decompose software for the new messaging app. You can decide what features the app should include.

   If you need more space, use the continuation sheet page on **page 162**

   [5]

2. Look at the algorithm on the left page for `MoveCarLeft()`.

   Complete the below algorithm to move the car right.

   `MoveCarRight():`

   ....

   ....

   ....

   ....

   ....

   ....

   ....

   [4]

Try it

Design algorithms for the other parts of the car game given in the structure diagram on the left:

- Score
- Car collision and lives
- Powerups

Total ☐ **/10**

How well do you feel you know this topic? ☺ ☐ 😐 ☐ ☹ ☐

TOPIC 3.6

SEARCHING

Computer systems often need to search large amounts of data. For example, to find someone's phone number on a phone, a search will be made using their name. Computers use different **algorithms** to search through data. Two algorithms are given on this page.

Linear search

In a **linear search**, each item in a list is checked in turn to see if it matches.

A search ends when the item has been found or when every item in the list has been checked.

For example, to check if 15 is in the list:

5	6	8	15	23

Check each item in the list:

5	6	8	15	23

5 ≠ 15:

5	6	8	15	23

6 ≠ 15:

5	6	8	15	23

8 ≠ 15:

5	6	8	15	23

15 = 15.

The item has been found.

If the end of the list is reached before the item is found, then the item isn't in the list.

Linear search features:

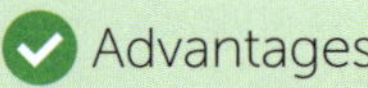

Advantages

- An easy algorithm to understand
- Easy to program
- Works for sorted and unsorted lists

Disadvantages

- Very slow for long lists as every item must be searched

Remember

The ≠ symbol means *not equal to*.

Binary search

In a **binary search**, the list must contain data that is sorted. If the list is unsorted then sorting the list will need to be completed first.

To carry out a binary search:

- Find the middle item in the list.
- If the item matches then end the search.
- Otherwise, if the item being searched for is lower than the one found, do a binary search on the left of the list. If the item being searched for is higher than the one found, do a binary search on the right of the list.
- If no more items are left to search then the item isn't in the list.

For example:

To check if the number 15 is in the list:

2	4	5	8	12	15	18

Check the middle item:

2	4	5	8	12	15	18

15 > 8

As 15 is higher, do a binary search on the right of the list.

12 15 18

12	15	18

15 = 15

The item has been found.

Binary search features:

Advantages

- Very fast to search

Disadvantages

- List must be sorted
- Harder to program

Write your mark here

1. State how many comparisons are needed in a linear search to find the number 23 in the following list:

5	6	8	15	23

.... [1]

2. Look at the following list:

2	4	5	8	12	15	18

(a) Show the steps needed for a binary search of the list to find the number 5.

....

....

.... [3]

(b) Give the minimum number of comparisons that will be needed to search the list.

.... [1]

(c) Give the maximum number of comparisons that will be needed to search the list.

.... [1]

3. Look at the following list:

18	42	6	10	97	43	80

State the algorithm which will need to be used to search this list and give a reason for your choice.

Algorithm:.. [1]

Reason for choosing this algorithm:

.... [1]

4. A dictionary contains 10 000 words. State which algorithm you would use to search this list. Give a reason for your choice.

Algorithm:.. [1]

Reason for choosing this algorithm:

.... [1]

Try it

Search for:

Linear search animation

Binary search animation

Look at how the two algorithms work. Now create a new list and show the steps to find a number in it using the two different algorithms.

Total ☐ /10

How well do you feel you know this topic? ☺ ☐ 😐 ☐ ☹ ☐

TOPIC 3.7

SORTING

Sorting algorithms put a list into **order**. Users often need data to be sorted, for example, to search phone contacts **alphabetically** or to view a price comparison site in a **numerical** order of price. Data also usually needs to be sorted for it to be searched efficiently. Two sorting algorithms are shown below.

Bubble sort

To carry out a **bubble sort**:

1. Start at the left and compare the first pair.
2. If they are out of order, then swap them.
3. Now go to the next pair (2nd and 3rd items). Compare and swap if necessary.
4. Repeat step 3 until the end of the list is reached. This is known as the first pass.
5. Now repeat steps 1-4 again as a second pass. The last item in the list is in place, so doesn't need to be included.
6. Keep carrying out more passes until a complete pass is made with no pairs being swapped.

For example, to sort the following list:

5	4	3	18	17

First pass

5	4	3	18	17	4 < 5 so swap 5 and 4
4	5	3	18	17	3 < 5 so swap 5 and 3
4	3	5	18	17	18 > 5 so don't swap
4	3	5	18	17	17 < 18 so swap 18 and 17
4	3	5	17	18	End first pass. 18 is in the correct position.

Second pass

4	3	5	17	18	3 < 4 so swap 3 and 4
3	4	5	17	18	5 > 4 so don't swap
3	4	5	17	18	17 > 5 so don't swap
3	4	5	17	18	End second pass. 17 and 18 are now in the correct position.

Third pass

Each pair is compared. As no swaps are made, the list must be in order.

Bubble sort features:

Advantages
- Easy to understand

Disadvantages
- Is very slow for longer lists

Insertion sort

To carry out an **insertion sort**:

1. Start at the 2nd item.
2. Now place this into the correct position on the left of it.
3. Now move to each item in order, placing it into the correct position on the left.
4. Once the last item is placed, the list has been sorted.

For example:

To sort the following list

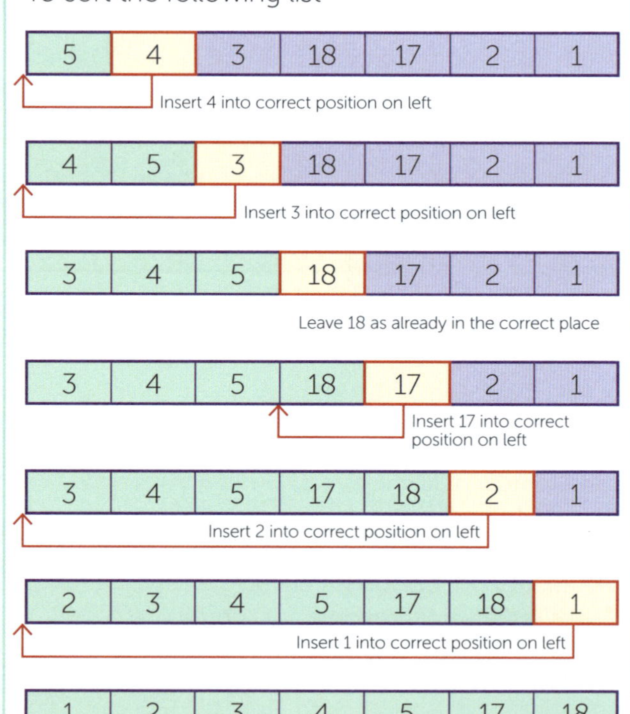

Insertion sort features:

Advantages
- Easy to understand
- It is usually faster than bubble sort

Disadvantages
- Is still slow for longer lists compared to other algorithms such as quick sort

1. Look at the following list.

8	5	7	3

(a) Show the stages of the first pass of a bubble sort for the list.

....

....

....

.... **[3]**

(b) State how the algorithm knows the list is sorted.

.... **[1]**

2. Look at the following list:

17	2	5	21	7	3

Show the stages of an insertion sort for the list.

....

....

....

....

....

....

.... **[5]**

3. Give **one** advantage of using insertion sort rather than bubble sort.

.... **[1]**

Write your mark here

Total /10

Try it

Search for:

Compare sorting algorithms animations

Look at different algorithms and how long they take to sort data. Compare the algorithms on the left with quick sort and merge sort. Which are the fastest?

How well do you feel you know this topic? ☺ ☐ 😐 ☐ ☹ ☐

TOPIC 4.1

DIGITISING SOUND

A **sound wave** is an analogue wave that is produced by a speaker. Everything that is stored in a computer needs to be stored digitally (as a number). This process is known as **digitisation**.

Did you know?

An **analogue wave** is a smooth wave. There are a **continuous** set of positions that the wave is at. The word **analogue** is used for watches where the hands move showing infinite positions between minutes. A digital watch, by contrast, only shows the time at each second.

How it works

A coil of wire, known as the **voice coil** sits inside a **permanent magnet**. When electricity is applied to the voice coil, it moves towards or away from the permanent magnet moving the speaker **cone** at the front. As the cone moves backwards and forwards it moves the air making a sound wave.

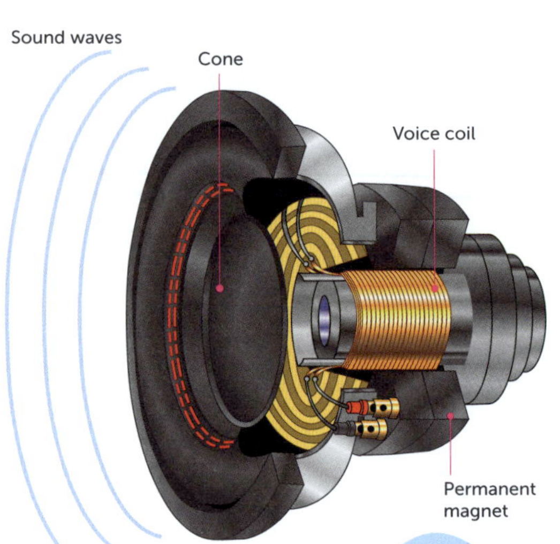

Digitising sound

To convert a sound wave to a digital format, the sound is **sampled** many times each second. This is known as the **sample rate** or **frequency** and measured in **hertz** (**Hz**). The accuracy of each sample is known as the **bit depth**.

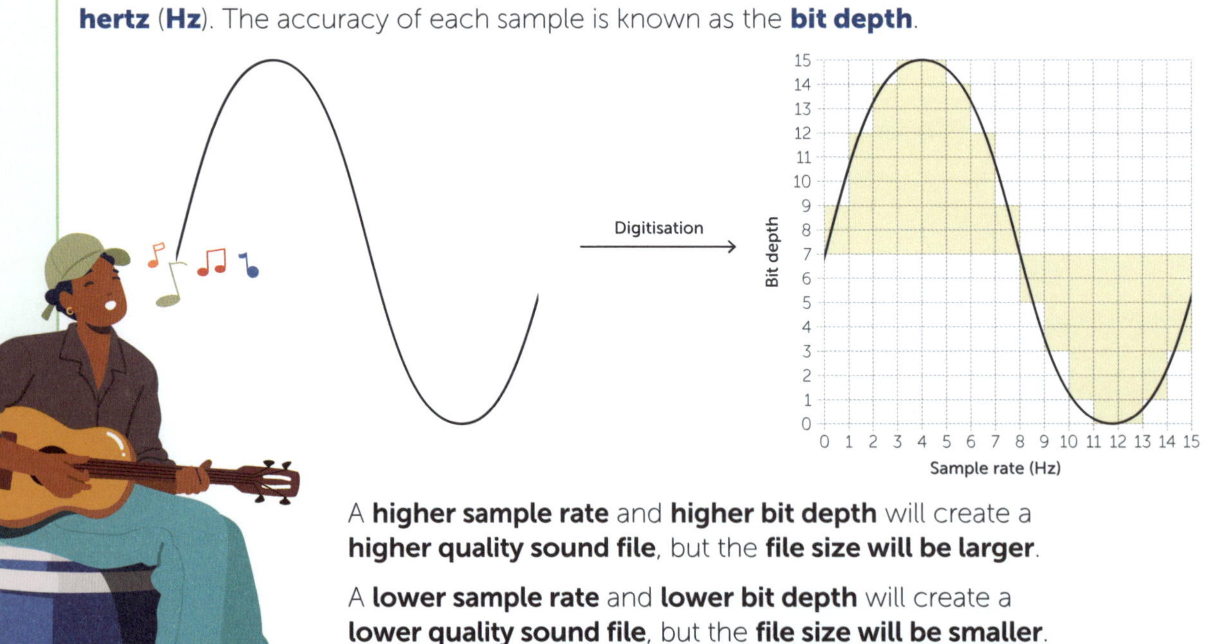

A **higher sample rate** and **higher bit depth** will create a **higher quality sound file**, but the **file size will be larger**.

A **lower sample rate** and **lower bit depth** will create a **lower quality sound file**, but the **file size will be smaller**.

Write your mark here

1. Match the Computing terms with their meanings.

Analogue wave	Moves backwards and forwards to create a sound wave.
Speaker	This causes the cone to move when electricity is passed through it.
Cone	A continuous wave.
Voice coil	An output device that produces sound.

[4]

2. (a) A compact disc (CD) has a sample rate of 44 100 Hz. Explain what this means.

....

....

....

.... **[2]**

(b) Describe how the cone position of a speaker relates to the bit depth used in a sound file.

....

....

....

.... **[2]**

(c) Describe **two** effects of reducing the sample rate of a music file.

....

....

....

.... **[2]**

Try it

The audio editing software Audacity is free to download from:
https://www.audacityteam.org/

Try recording at 44 100 Hz, then resample the recording at 8000 Hz. Describe the difference in the sound quality.

Total ☐ **/10**

How well do you feel you know this topic? ☺ ☐ 😐 ☐ ☹ ☐

TOPIC 4.2 AUDIO RECORDING AND EDITING

Audio is recorded using a microphone. An **audio technician** will be responsible for professional recordings. **Audio editing** occurs after the recording. A **sound editor** arranges recordings for a finished production.

How it works

When recording someone speaking or singing, microphones may have popping sounds with certain letters such as 'p'. A **pop filter** is used to reduce these sounds.

Microphones are placed into a **shock mount** to keep them away from vibrations in a floor or table.

Did you know?

Professional recording studios need to be **sound proofed** to prevent sounds from outside, such as emergency vehicle sirens or planes, from being recorded.

Solid walls will reflect sound and cause unwanted echoes. **Acoustic foam** is placed on walls to prevent this.

Audio editing

Audio may be recorded on more than one microphone. For instance, a microphone may be used for each singer or instrument.

Each recording is then placed on its own **audio track**.

Audio editing involves the following:

- **Mixing** the tracks together by adjusting the **volume** of each track
- **Cutting** to remove unwanted parts
- **Trimming** to remove the start or end of an audio clip
- **Fading** the audio in or out
- **Noise reduction**
- Adding **effects** such as an **echo**

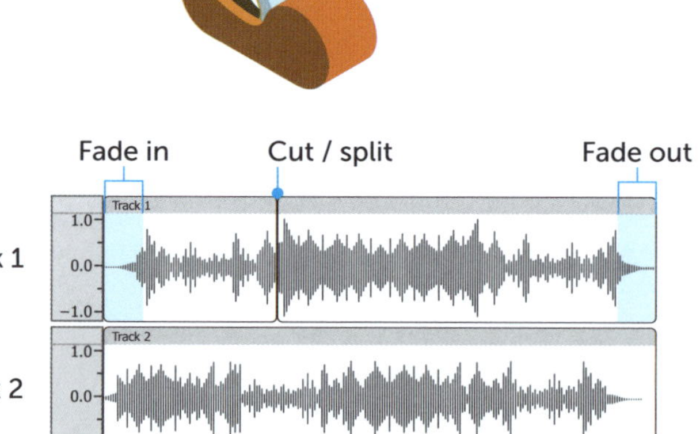

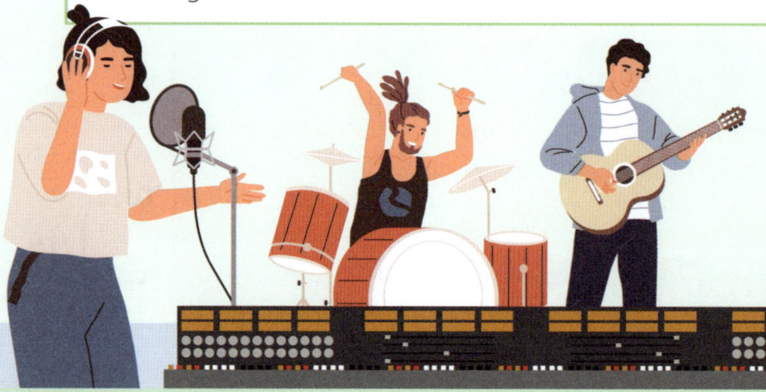

1. Liam is recording an interview for a podcast.

(a) The table below shows some problems that Liam is having when recording the interview. For each problem, write a solution.

Echoes are being heard in the interview.	
Whenever someone says a word with 'p' or 'b', a loud sound is heard on the recording.	
The microphone stand is on a table. If someone touches the table, a bang is heard on the recording.	

[3]

Once the recording is finished Liam starts editing it.

(b) The podcast has music at the start. Liam wants to reduce the volume of the music as people start talking. Give an editing feature which should be used.

.... **[1]**

(c) When editing, Liam notices a slight humming sound in the background of the track. Give an editing tool that could be used to remove it.

.... **[1]**

(d) During the interview, a mistake was made which Liam wants to remove.

Describe how audio editing software could be used to remove the mistake.

....

.... **[2]**

(e) Two microphones were used in the interview recording.

State how tracks would be used to edit the recordings for each microphone.

.... **[1]**

Liam's podcast has become very popular.

(f) Name **one** job role that could help Liam with the recording of the podcast.

.... **[1]**

(g) Name **one** job role that could help Liam with the editing of the podcast.

.... **[1]**

Write your mark here

Total ☐ /10

Try it

Try recording sound in Audacity. Now try the following editing features with your recording:

- Trim
- Split / cut
- Fade in / fade out
- Noise reduction
- Effects such as an echo

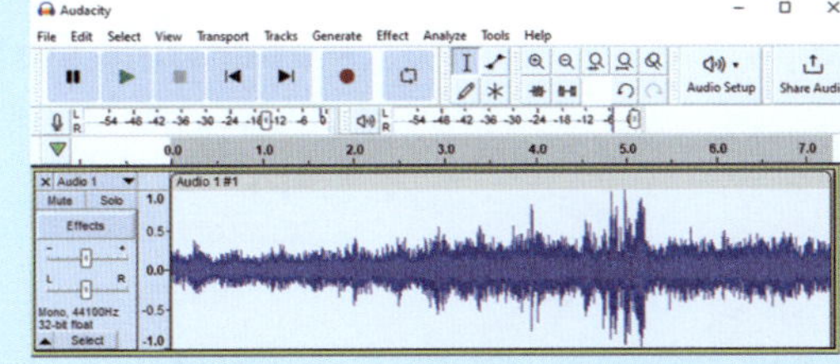

How well do you feel you know this topic? ☐ ☐ ☐

TOPIC 5.1

INPUT AND OUTPUT DEVICES

Input devices are **hardware devices** that send **data** to a **computer system**. The data is then **processed** by the **CPU** (see **page 40**). **Output devices** are hardware that **convert data** into a human understandable form and present it to the user in some way.

Input devices

Output devices

Headphones

Display

Printer

Speakers

Did you know?

A graphics tablet allows the user to write on the **tablet** with a **stylus**. The more **pressure** they apply to the stylus, the thicker a line will be, just like with a pencil.

Hardware and software

Hardware includes any **physical components** of a computer system. The CPU, input devices and output devices are all examples of computer hardware.

Software is the programs that run on the computer. It includes the:

- **operating system** (such as Windows®, MacOS®, Linux®)
- **applications** (such as a word processor, spreadsheet, computer game or web browser)

Write your mark here

1. Look at the picture of friends playing a computer game.

(a) Name **four** input devices that are shown in the picture.

① ....

② ....

③ ....

④ .... **[4]**

(b) Name **one** output device that is shown in the picture.

.... **[1]**

(c) Name another output device that could be added to allow the players to hear any background music and sound effects from the game.

.... **[1]**

2. The table below shows a selection of computer related products. For each one, tick whether it is hardware or software.

Computer product	Hardware (✓)	Software (✓)
Graphics tablet		
Microsoft Windows		
Webcam		
Racing game		

[4]

Try it

A tablet computer contains input devices and output devices as part of an enclosed computer system.

Choose a tablet and research all the input and output devices that are used inside it.

Total

/10

How well do you feel you know this topic?   

TOPIC 5.2

STORAGE DEVICES

Storage devices are used to save data on a **computer system**. If data isn't stored on a storage device it will be lost when the computer is turned off. The **CPU** (see **page 40**). will **read** and **write** to storage devices as it **processes** information.

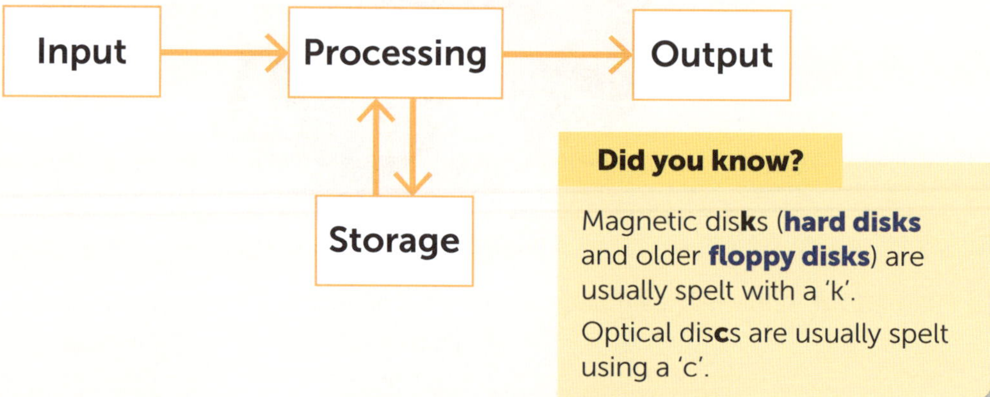

Did you know?

Magnetic dis**k**s (**hard disks** and older **floppy disks**) are usually spelt with a 'k'.

Optical dis**c**s are usually spelt using a 'c'.

Solid state storage devices

Solid state storage devices have no moving parts and lower power usage. This makes them great for **portable** devices such as **smartphones**, **tablets** and **laptops**. The technology makes it very fast to **read** data from, and **write** data to it.

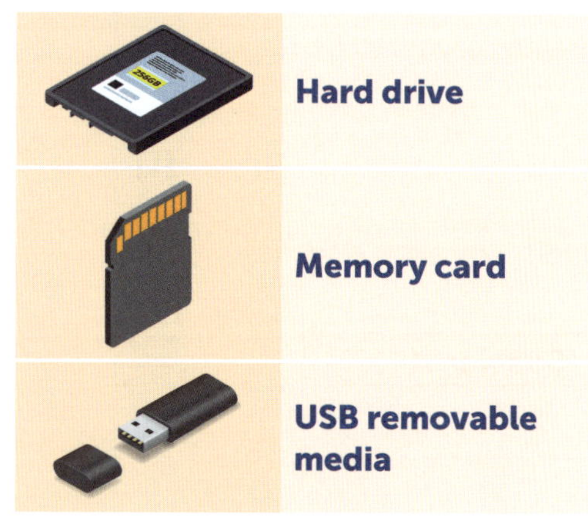

Optical storage devices

An **optical storage device** makes use of a **laser** to read a **disc**. If the discs get scratched, the drive may not be able to read them. The discs are portable and easy to share content with others. For this reason, they are commonly used for music **CDs**, and **DVDs** or **Blu-rays** that contain films.

Hardware and software

Magnetic hard disk drives spin a magnetic **platter**. A **drive head** detects magnetic changes on the disk. These disks are cheaper and usually have large amounts of storage. **Backup tapes** store very large amounts of data and are used for **backups**.

Hard disk drive

Backup tape

1. (a) The table below shows a selection of storage devices. For each one, tick whether the type of drive is solid state, magnetic or optical.

Computer product	Solid state (✓)	Magnetic (✓)	Optical (✓)
Blu-ray disc			
Hard disk drive			
Memory card			
DVD			

[4]

(b) State what 'CD' stands for.

.... **[1]**

(c) State what 'DVD' stands for.

.... **[1]**

2. Describe how a magnetic hard disk drive works.

....

....

....

.... **[2]**

3. Give **two** advantages of using a solid state drive in a laptop rather than a hard disk drive.

1. ....

....

2. ....

.... **[2]**

Write your mark here

Total /10

Try it

Different storage devices have different costs and performance.

Research different hardware that could be used in a desktop or laptop computer. For instance, the difference between using a hard disk drive and a solid state hard drive.

How well do you feel you know this topic?   

TOPIC 5.3 CPU

The **CPU** is like the brain of a computer. It is responsible for **processing** instructions. The **instructions** and **data** that the CPU needs are stored in **main memory**. The processed data is then stored back in main memory.

How it works

When you run a program or app, it is first loaded into **RAM** (**Random Access Memory**). Each instruction is then processed by the CPU and any data is stored in RAM.

Registers on the CPU are used to store very small amounts of information such as a number, letter or program instruction. The **control unit** is responsible for coordinating everything that happens on the CPU. The **ALU** (**Arithmetic Logic Unit**) is the part of the processor that **executes instructions** such as adding two numbers.

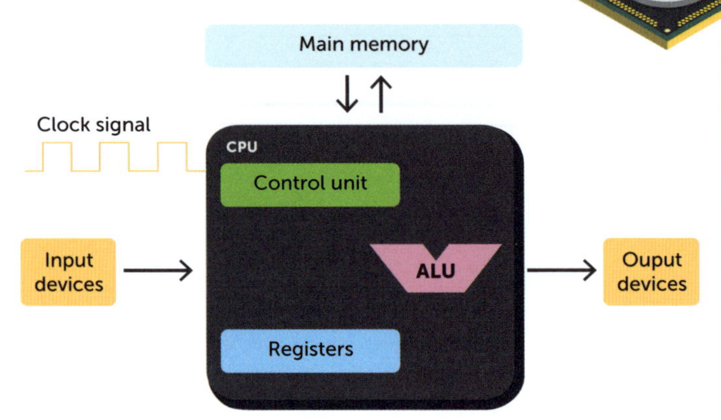

Fetch-execute cycle

To run a program, the CPU follows the **fetch-execute cycle**:

1. **Fetch** an instruction from main memory and store it in a register
2. The control unit then **decodes** the instruction
3. The instruction is then **executed** by the ALU (Arithmetic Logic Unit).

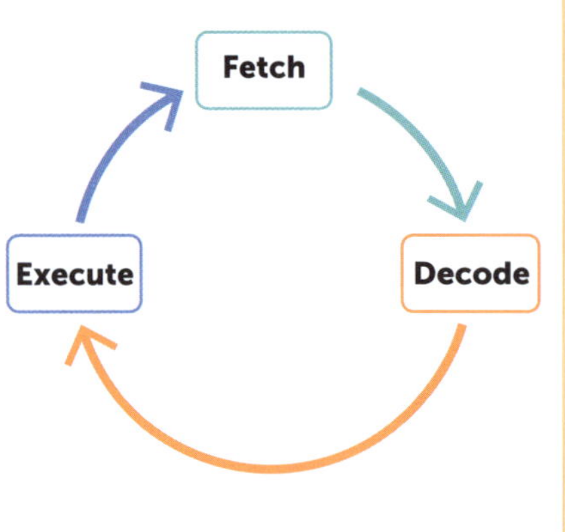

CPU clock speed

A **clock signal** is sent to the CPU. This determines how quickly the fetch-decode-execute cycle will occur.

The clock speed is measured in:

- **Megahertz** (**MHz**) – Millions of instructions processed per second
- **Gigahertz** (**GHz**) – Billions of instructions processed per second

Cooling the CPU

The CPU has a lot of work to do and so it gets hot. A **heatsink** and **fan** are often needed to help keep it cool so it functions correctly.

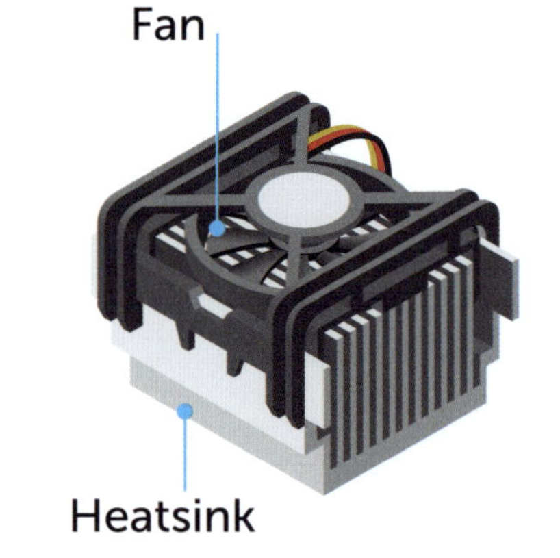

Write your mark here

1. Match the parts of the CPU with their purpose.

Control unit		Each one of these stores a very small amount of data such as one number or one instruction.
Registers		Performs operations such as addition, subtraction and comparisons.
ALU		Coordinates all the operations that are happening on the processor.

[3]

2. Give the **three** stages of the fetch-execute cycle.

① ....

② ....

③ .... **[3]**

3. Mia's mum is carrying out some video editing on her laptop computer. She asks Mia why her laptop is now 'sounding like its taking off'. Describe what is happening.

....

....

....

.... **[2]**

4. (a) Identify the faster CPU between a 4 GHz processor and an 800 MHz processor.

.... **[1]**

(b) Define the meaning of the term CPU 'clock speed'.

....

.... **[1]**

Try it

Different CPUs have different costs and performance.

Research different CPUs that could be used in a desktop or laptop computer. As part of your research find out the purpose of multiple cores and cache.

Total ☐ **/10**

How well do you feel you know this topic? ☺ ☐ 😐 ☐ ☹ ☐

TOPIC 5.4

RAM, ROM AND MOTHERBOARDS

Main memory is accessed directly by the CPU. It comes in two types – RAM (Random Access Memory) and ROM (Read-Only Memory).

RAM

RAM (**Random Access Memory**) is faster to access data from than from a hard drive or solid state drive. The CPU can both read and write to RAM. When you open a program or app, the **instructions** for it are loaded from the hard drive into RAM. As the program is running, **data** that the program or user needs is also stored in RAM.

RAM is **volatile** which means that all data is lost when the computer is turned off.

Portable devices, such as smartphones and tablets, use a small amount of power from the battery to keep the data stored in RAM.

ROM

ROM (**Read Only Memory**) is similar to RAM, but it can only be read from. It stores a small program called the BIOS.

ROM is **non-volatile**. The programs stored on it will remain there even if the program is turned off.

Did you know?

The **BIOS** is the **Basic Input/Output System** for the computer.

The BIOS stores essential hardware settings such as the hard drive that is being used and how fast the **clock speed** of the CPU needs to be. It starts the **boot sequence** of the computer which is then completed by the operating system that is installed.

Motherboard

The **motherboard** is the central place all components connect. **Chips**, **cards** and **processors** fit into **sockets** directly on the board. Input, output and storage devices usually connect to the motherboard using **cables**.

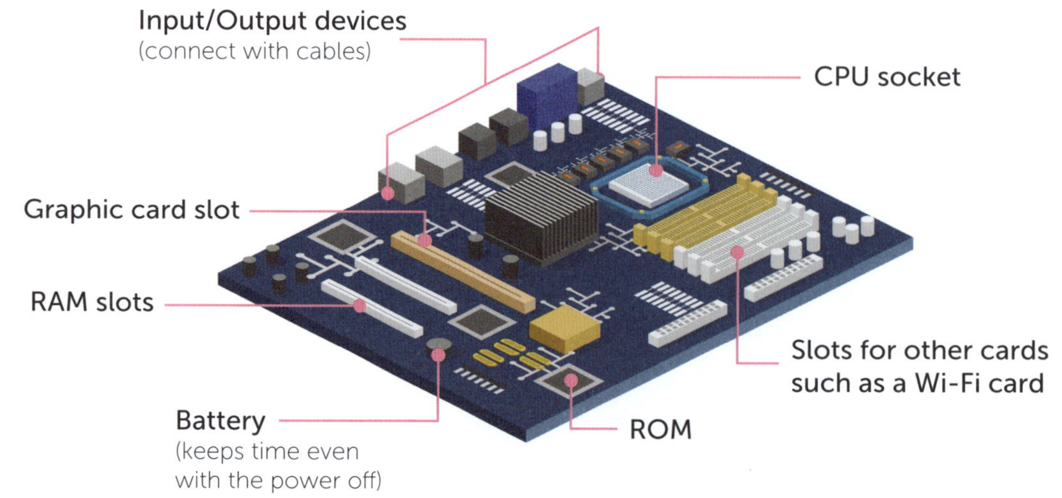

1. (a) There are two types of main memory, RAM and ROM. For each, tick whether they are volatile (lose data when the power is turned off) or non-volatile (keep data when the power is turned off).

Type of main memory	Volatile (✓)	Non-volatile (✓)
RAM		
ROM		

[2]

Write your mark here

(b) Identify which is faster to access data, RAM or a hard drive.

.... **[1]**

(c) Below are three types of data. For each one, tick whether it will be stored in RAM or on a hard drive.

Types of data	RAM (✓)	Hard Drive (✓)
A running program's instructions.		
The data being used in a running program.		
A program that isn't running.		

[3]

2. Label the parts of a computer system shown below.

Draw lines to show where they would fit or connect to the motherboard.

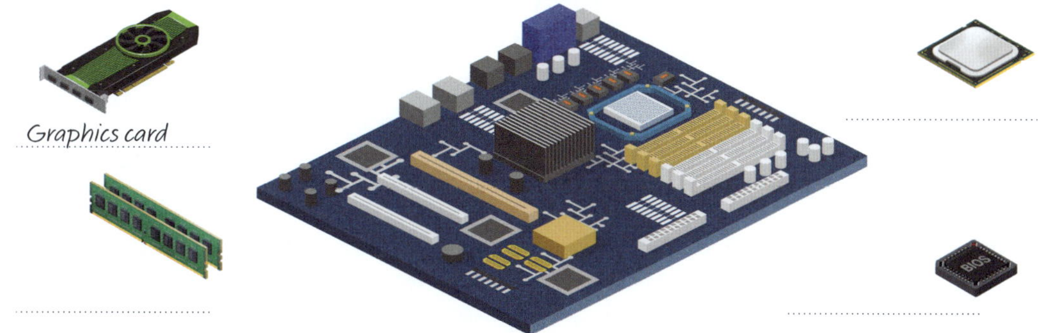

[4]

Try it

Find a photo of a motherboard. Work out where each of the components would fit onto the motherboard you have found.

Total /10

How well do you feel you know this topic?   

TOPIC 5.5

BINARY CONVERSIONS

Computers work using **switches** which have two **states**, **on** or **off**.
Binary is a number system that uses just the numbers 0 and 1.

1 represents on and **0** represents off.

Did you know?

Binary is a number system with **two numbers** (**0** and **1**) in the same way as a **bi**cycle is a cycle with two wheels.

A binary digit is known as a **bit**. Eight bits make up a **byte**.

Did you know?

The on/off symbol used on electronic products combines a binary 1 and 0.

Counting in binary

0	0000				
1	0001	6	0110	11	1011
2	0010	7	0111	12	1100
3	0011	8	1000	13	1101
4	0100	9	1001	14	1110
5	0101	10	1010	15	1111

Converting from binary to denary

Denary numbers use a units, tens, hundreds and thousands column.

1000	100	10	1
2	1	8	6

So, the number 2186 means two thousand, one hundred and eighty six .

Binary numbers use the columns 1, 2, 4, 8, 16, 32, 64, 128.

128	64	32	16	8	4	2	1	
0	1	0	0	1	1	0	1	
	1x64			1x8 +	1x4 +		1x1	=77

The number 11111111 in binary is equal to 255 in denary.

Did you know?

Denary is the counting system normally used which has **ten numbers** from 0 to 9. It comes from the Latin *denarius* which means *containing ten*.

Converting from denary to binary

To convert the denary number 39 to binary, first write all the column titles. Then ask does 128 go into 39? It doesn't, so write a zero in the column. Does 64 go into 39? Again, it doesn't so write a zero. Does 32 go into 39? It does, so write a one in the column. The remainder is 7.

Now ask if 16 goes into 7, it doesn't so write zero for this column. Does 8 go into 7? No, so again write zero in this column. Does 4 go into 7? Yes, write a one for this column. The remainder is 3. Does 2 go into 3? Yes. Write a one in the column. The remainder is 1. Does 1 go into 1? Yes. Write a one into the final column.

	128	64	32	16	8	4	2	1
	0	0	1	0	0	1	1	1
Remainder:			7			3	1	

Write your mark here

1. Denary numbers use the numbers from 0–9.
   (a) State the numbers that binary numbers use.

.... **[1]**

   (b) Use the table on the left to find the binary equivalent of the denary number 13. Write the binary number below.

.... **[1]**

2. (a) Convert the binary number 00010111 to denary using the table below.

128	64	32	16	8	4	2	1
0	0	0	1	0	1	1	1

.... **[1]**

   (b) Convert the binary number 01001010 to denary.

....

....

.... **[2]**

3. (a) Convert the denary number 18 to binary. Complete the table below to help you work out the answer.

	128	64	32	16	8	4	2	1
Remainder								

.... **[2]**

   (b) Convert the denary number 99 to binary.

....

....

.... **[2]**

4. Show the maximum value that can be stored using 8 binary digits.

.... **[1]**

Try it

The Windows Calculator has a Programmer mode. This allows you to enter binary or denary numbers. They are then automatically converted to other counting systems.

Total /10

How well do you feel you know this topic?   

TOPIC 5.6

BINARY ADDITION

Binary addition involves adding two binary numbers together. It works in a very similar way as denary addition.

Adding one digit binary numbers

In denary numbers, 1+1=2

Remember that in binary, 2 is represented as 10.

So, adding one digit binary numbers works as follows:

0 + 0 =	0
0 + 1 =	1
1 + 0 =	1
1 + 1 =	10 (2 in denary)
1 + 1 + 1 =	11 (3 in denary)

How it works

Denary addition is addition with normal numbers (also known as base 10). Each column in the number can be one of 10 different digits from 0-9.

The number is arranged into columns that are multiples of 10.

So, to add the number 347 with 292 would be carried out as follows:

	100	10	1	
	3	4	7	
	2	9	2	+
Carry	1			
	6	3	9	

Example 1:

Adding 8 bit binary numbers

Just like with denary addition, put both the numbers into columns except, as this is binary (base 2), each column is 2 times the previous one.

So, adding the numbers 10000100 + 00101010 would be carried out as follows:

	128	64	32	16	8	4	2	1	
	1	0	0	0	0	1	0	0	
	0	0	1	0	1	0	1	0	+
Carry									
	1	0	1	0	1	1	1	0	

Example 2:

Using the carry row with 1+1

If a 1+1 occurs in a column, put 0 in the column and a 1 in the carry row for the column to the left.

So, to add the numbers 01010100 + 01010101 would be carried out as follows:

	128	64	32	16	8	4	2	1	
	0	1	0	1	0	1	0	0	
	0	1	0	1	0	1	0	1	+
Carry	1		1		1				
	1	0	1	0	1	0	0	1	

Example 3:

Using the carry row with 1+1+1

If a 1+1+1 occurs in a column (because there is already a carry), then put a 1 in the column and a 1 in the next carry row.

So, to add the numbers 01110101 + 01110111 would be carried out as follows:

	128	64	32	16	8	4	2	1	
	0	1	1	1	0	1	0	1	
	0	1	1	1	0	1	1	1	+
Carry	1	1	1		1	1	1		
	1	1	1	0	1	1	0	0	

Top tip

Remember: when adding numbers, start at the right-most column.

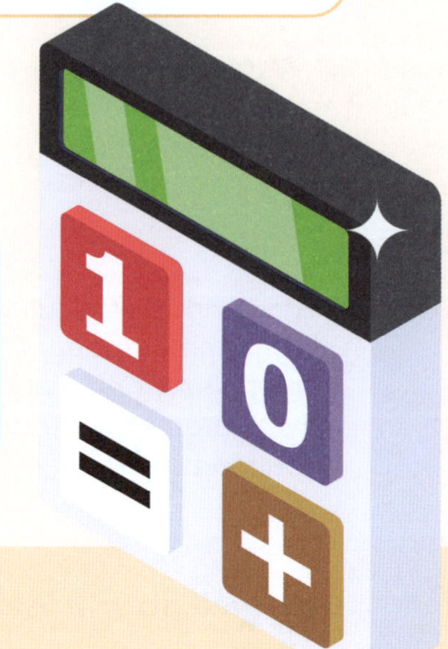

Write your mark here

1. (a) Calculate 1+1 in binary.

.... [1]

(b) Calculate 1+1+1 in binary

.... [1]

2. Complete the binary calculations.

(a)

	128	64	32	16	8	4	2	1	
	0	1	0	1	0	1	0	1	
	1	0	1	0	1	0	1	0	
Carry									+

[1]

(b)

	128	64	32	16	8	4	2	1	
	0	0	1	0	1	0	1	0	
	0	1	0	0	1	0	1	1	
Carry									+

[1]

3. Complete the column titles, then complete the binary calculations.

(a)

0	1	1	0	1	1	0	0
0	1	0	0	1	0	1	1

[1]

(b)

0	1	0	1	1	1	0	1
0	1	0	1	1	1	0	1

[1]

4. (a) Calculate 00110011 + 10101010. Show your working.

....

....

....

....

.... [2]

(b) Calculate 01011010 + 01111111. Show your working

....

....

....

....

.... [2]

Try it

The Windows calculator can do binary addition when set to programmer mode. Try checking your answers.

Now write some binary questions for a friend (or yourself). Check your answers using the calculator.

Total /10

How well do you feel you know this topic?   

TOPIC 5.7

ASCII

Computers are only able to store binary 1s and 0s. To store letters and other symbols (known as **characters**), a **binary pattern** needs to be **mapped** to each one. The mapping of binary patterns is known as a **character set**. ASCII is one way that characters are mapped to binary patterns.

Did you know?

ASCII stands for the **American Standard Code for Information Interchange**. Originally it allowed for 128 different characters using 7 bits.

Extended ASCII makes use of 8 bits to store each character and allows for 256 different characters to be stored.

ASCII table

Some of the characters from the full **ASCII table** are shown here.

Character	Decimal	Binary
a	097	0110 0001
b	098	0110 0010
c	099	0110 0011
d	100	0110 0100
e	101	0110 0101
f	102	0110 0110
g	103	0110 0111
h	104	0110 1000
i	105	0110 1001
j	106	0110 1010
k	107	0110 1011
l	108	0110 1100
m	109	0110 1101
n	110	0110 1110

Character	Decimal	Binary
o	111	0110 1111
p	112	0111 0000
q	113	0111 0001
r	114	0111 0010
s	115	0111 0011
t	116	0111 0100
u	117	0111 0101
v	118	0111 0110
w	119	0111 0111
x	120	0111 1000
y	121	0111 1001
z	122	0111 1010
Space	32	0010 0000
.	46	0010 1110

Converting to ASCII

To convert the word 'cat' into ASCII, take each letter and find the binary equivalent in the ASCII table.

c	a	t
01100011	01100001	01110100

The following binary would therefore be stored in the computer:

011000110110000101110100

Write your mark here

1. (a) Give the full name that ASCII stands for.

.... **[1]**

(b) State the number of bits that are used to store one letter in extended ASCII.

.... **[1]**

(c) Complete the table below by converting each letter into its decimal ASCII code. Use the ASCII table on the left page to help. The first row has been completed as an example.

Character	ASCII code in decimal
b	98
k	
r	
Space	
Full stop	

[4]

(d) Convert the phrase '**call me.**' to binary ASCII. Use the grid below to help give your answer.

[4]

Total /10

Try it

Another popular character set is known as Unicode. Browse some of the characters, including emoji, available at:

https://unicode-explorer.com/

Your computer or smartphone will make use of many of these characters, but won't be able to display all of them.

How well do you feel you know this topic?  

TOPIC 6.1

SCRATCH MOVEMENT

Scratch is a block-based **visual programming language**. It is used in education to make games, stories and animation.

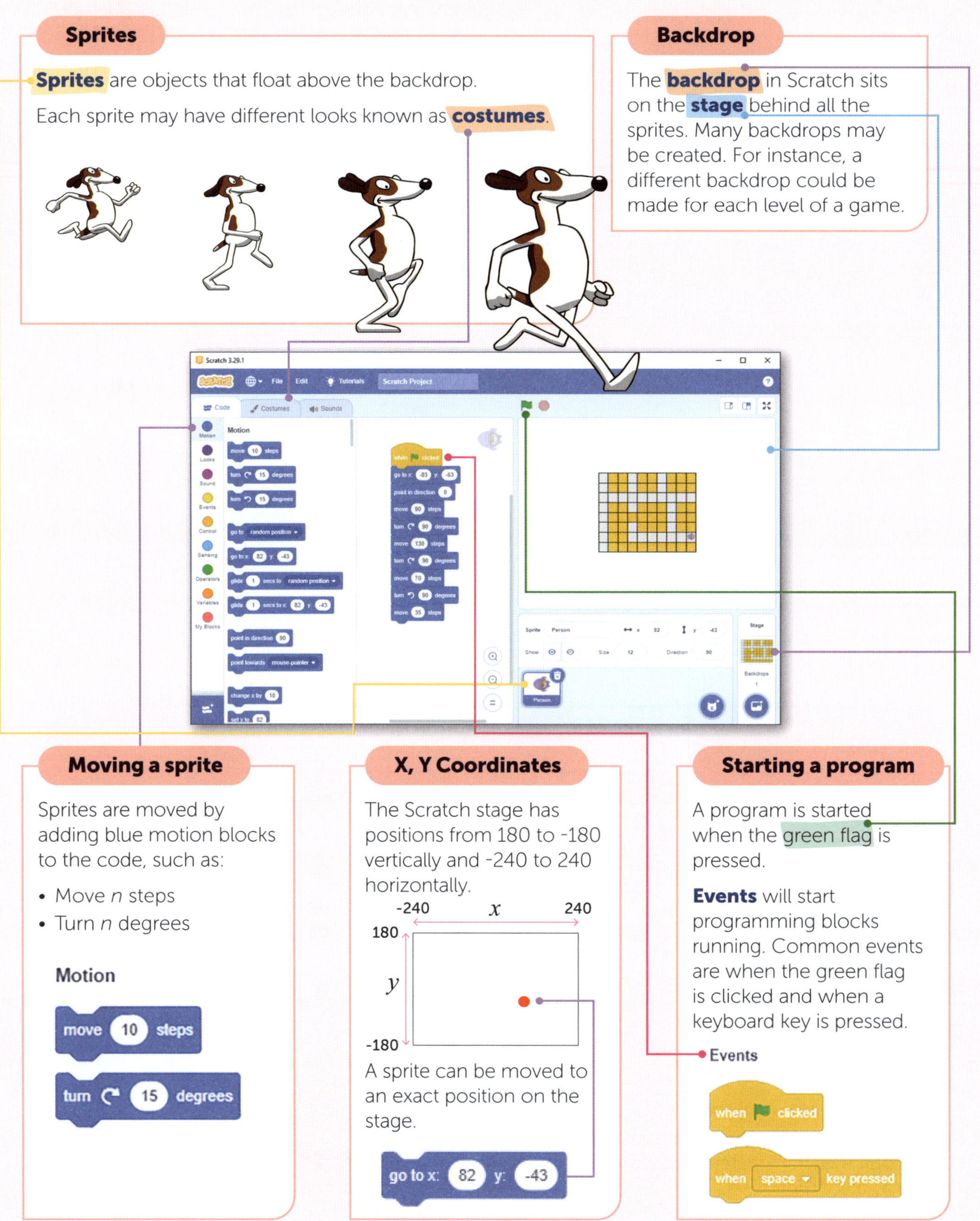

Sprites

Sprites are objects that float above the backdrop.

Each sprite may have different looks known as **costumes**.

Backdrop

The **backdrop** in Scratch sits on the **stage** behind all the sprites. Many backdrops may be created. For instance, a different backdrop could be made for each level of a game.

Moving a sprite

Sprites are moved by adding blue motion blocks to the code, such as:

- Move *n* steps
- Turn *n* degrees

X, Y Coordinates

The Scratch stage has positions from 180 to -180 vertically and -240 to 240 horizontally.

A sprite can be moved to an exact position on the stage.

Starting a program

A program is started when the green flag is pressed.

Events will start programming blocks running. Common events are when the green flag is clicked and when a keyboard key is pressed.

1. Match the Scratch terms with their meanings.

Sprite	The appearance of a sprite.
Backdrop	An object or character that floats above the backdrop.
Costume	A programming statement.
Block	The graphics displayed behind all the sprites.

[4]

Write your mark here

2. Events trigger programming blocks to start running.
Tick **two** events that are available in Scratch.

A Turn degrees ☐

B When the green flag is pressed ☐

C Go to x, y ☐

D When a key is pressed ☐

[2]

3. Mark the position on the stage of the following coordinates.
Label each point with its coordinates as two numbers.

(a) -240, 180

(b) -120, -90

[2]

4. A sprite is in the shape of a ball. It starts at coordinates (0,0) and points in the direction of 180 (south). Draw the path it takes when the following blocks of code are run.

```
when [flag] clicked
go to x: 0 y: 0
point in direction 180
move 180 steps
turn ↻ 90 degrees
move 240 steps
```

[2]

Try it

It is free to use Scratch online or to download it for offline use at **https://scratch.mit.edu/**

Use the software to start making your own programs.

Total ☐ **/10**

How well do you feel you know this topic? ☺ ☐ 😐 ☐ ☹ ☐

TOPIC 6.2

IF BLOCKS AND VARIABLES

IF blocks allow a program to take different **branches** depending on a condition. **Variables** are used to store **values** in a program.

Sprites

IF blocks are one type of control structure. They control the flow of a program.

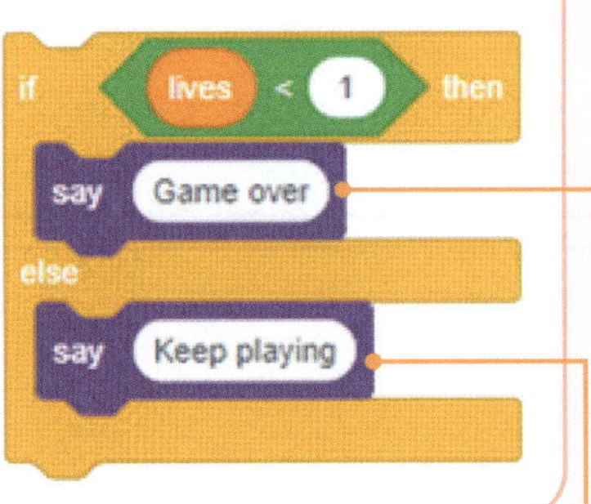

How it works

The IF block first checks a **condition**. Conditions are placed in hexagonal blocks. They either use green **operator** blocks, or blue **sensing** blocks.

If the condition is **true**, then the blocks inside the IF part of the block will be run.

If the condition is **false**, then the blocks inside the ELSE part of the block will be run.

Creating variables

To create a variable, go to **Variables**, then click the **Make a Variable** button.

Variables

Make a Variable

Name the variable. It will then appear as an option in the variable blocks.

Use the set block to give the variable an initial value.

set lives to 5

Did you know?

Variables store one value. The value may be changed when the program is running. Variable names should be short and not contain any spaces. For example:

Example variable name	Purpose
`playerName`	Store a player's name
`score`	Store a player's score
`level`	Store the level a player is currently on
`timeLeft`	Time left on a level

Changing variables

When the program is running, the value in a variable may be changed.

This could be to increase a score, change a player's name or reduce the number of lives left if they are touching an enemy.

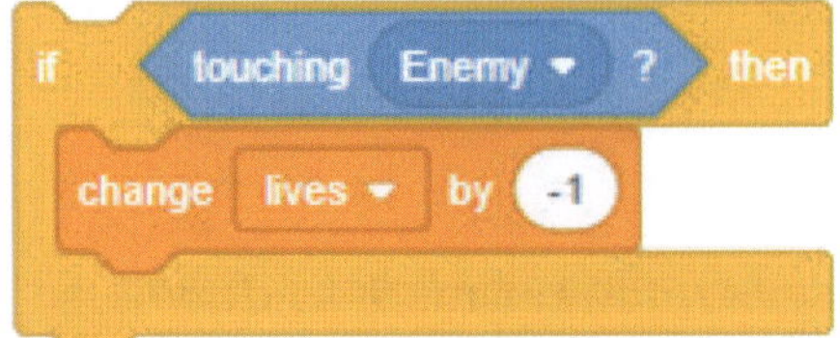

Write your mark here

1. A car racing game has two players. Both the blue and yellow cars are sprites. The blue car sprite contains the code shown to the right and the yellow car has similar code. The car track is made using a background, but the checked finish line is a separate sprite.

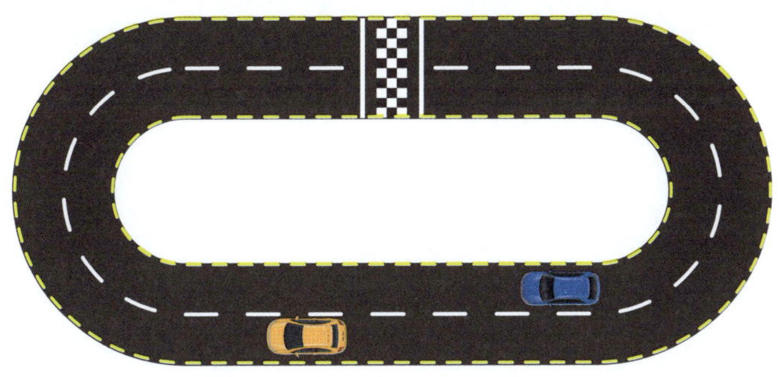

```
if <(blueCarLaps) = (3)> then
    say (You win)
else
    say (Keep going)
end
```

blueCarLaps 3

yellowCarLaps 2

(a) Match each part of the code with the correct programming component.

`laps`	Sprite
`finishLine`	Sensing block
`laps = 3`	Variable
`touching ?`	condition

[4]

(b) Identify the output for each car when they next touch the finish line.

Blue car output .... **[1]**

Yellow car output .... **[1]**

(c) Below are two other variables that are used in the game. For each one, identify a problem with the variable name and suggest a better variable name that could be used.

Current variable name	The problem with the variable name	New suggested variable name
`time to complete lap`		
`p1name`		

[4]

Try it

Try making the racing game in Scratch. Use variables to store the number of laps. Use sensing blocks to move each car when a key press is made.

Extend the game with obstacles that return the car to the start if it leaves the track.

Total /10

How well do you feel you know this topic? ☐ ☐ ☐

TOPIC 6.3 LOOPS

Loops allow parts of your code to be repeated. This could be used for an enemy's movements in a game or to repeatedly carry out code blocks in order to solve a problem.

Repeat loops

Repeat loops will repeat a section of blocks a certain number of times. The output from the code below will be "1", "2", "3".

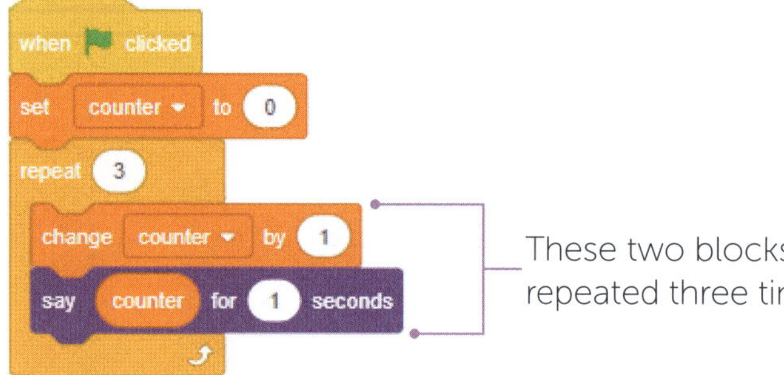

These two blocks will be repeated three times.

Repeat until loops

Repeat until loops will only repeat until the condition is true.

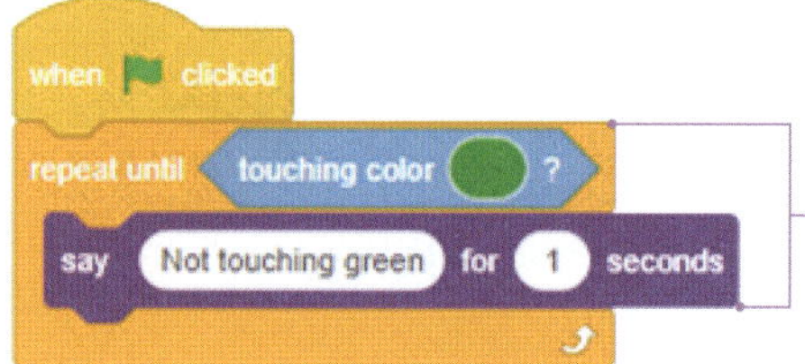

This block keeps repeating until the sprite touches something green.

Did you know?

Repeat until loops in Scratch are similar to **while** loops in Python. See **page 98** for more information about these.

Enemy movement

The movements of an enemy could be **repeated forever**. This is known as an **infinite loop**.

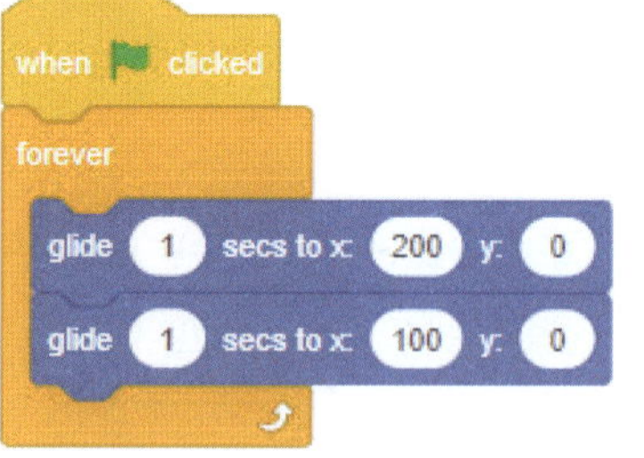

(100, 0) (200, 0)

1. From the following list, tick **three** types of loop that are available in Scratch.

A repeat <number> ☐

B while ☐

C do... while ☐

D repeat until <condition> ☐

E forever ☐

[3]

Write your mark here

2. Look at the following two sections of Scratch code and complete the table to show how many times the 'say' block will be repeated and what the final output from the 'say' block will be.

Code	when clicked set counter to 0 repeat 3 change counter by 2 say counter for 1 seconds	when clicked set counter2 to 0 repeat 3 repeat 3 change counter2 by 1 say counter2 for 1 seconds
Number of repetitions		
Output		

[4]

3. Describe what the following Scratch code does.

```
when clicked
repeat until touching mouse-pointer ?
    say Catch me
say You win
```

....

....

....

....

....

[3]

Try it

Make a Scratch maze game. The player has to move a sprite through a maze. If they touch the maze, they return to the start. Enemies automatically move and also send the player back to the start if they touch them.

Total ☐ /10

TOPIC 7.1

APP DESIGN

Before an **app** or **website** is created, a **mock-up** of the Graphical User Interface is designed. This allows any **developers** of the app to understand how it will work. It is also much easier to change a design rather than the actual final website or app.

Did you know?

A **Graphical User Interface** is also known as a **GUI** (pronounced goo-ey). It is the part of a program or app that the user interacts with. Apps, websites and **operating systems** all have GUIs.

Wireframes

When designing an app or website, standard symbols are used to represent each part. The result is an outline of the appearance known as a **wireframe**.

Images and photos

Images and **photos** are shown using a box with an X inside it.

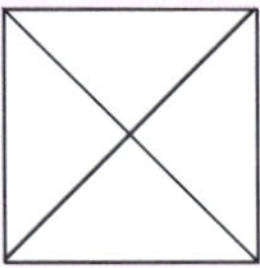

Video

Video has a box with a play button inside it.

Text

Text is represented using straight lines.

Buttons

Buttons use a box with rounded corners.

Full wireframe app screens

An app **interface** will use many different wireframe symbols to make the screen design. Occasionally text is used to help understanding. Arrows help to show how buttons link to new screens.

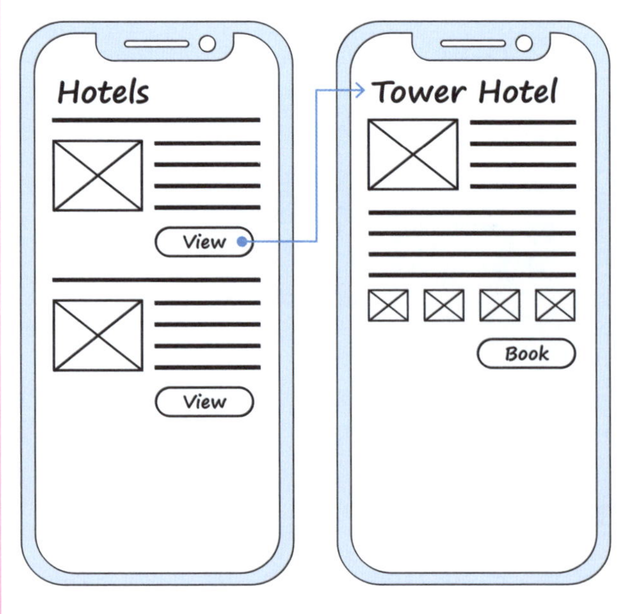

Write your mark here

1. Wireframes are used when designing apps. Name **two** other types of software that use wireframes when they are being designed.

   Software type 1 ....

   Software type 2 ....

[2]

2. The table below shows four wireframe components. For each one, state the name of the component.

Wireframe component	Name

[4]

3. Thrill Valley is a theme park that is creating a new app for smartphones. Design a wireframe mock-up for a ride or attraction at the theme park. Your wireframe needs to show:
   - The name of the ride/attraction
   - A photo
   - Other information
   - The current queue time

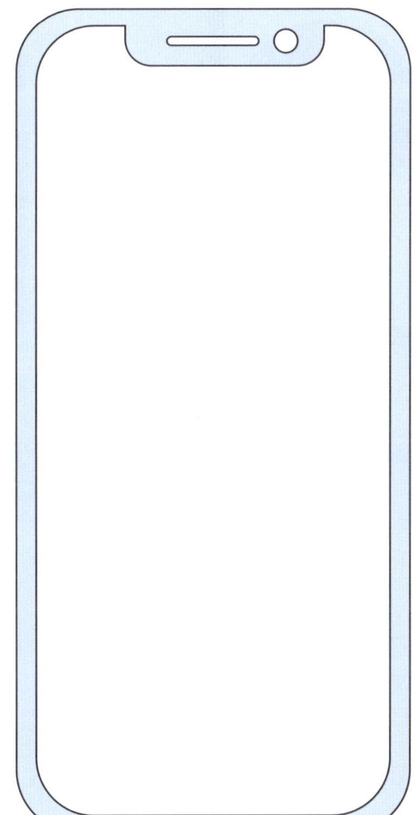

[4]

Total /10

Try it

Appshed allows you to build simple apps that run on smartphones and tablets.

There is a free version available that you might want to try.

https://appshed.com/

How well do you feel you know this topic?   

TOPIC **7.2**

DEVELOPMENT AND PUBLISHING

Once an app has been designed, it needs to be created. A **designer** will create the **graphics** and **layout** for the app. **Programmers** are responsible for writing any **computer code** that makes the app work behind the scenes. **Developers** are responsible for the whole development of the app from the wireframes all the way through to **testing** and **release**. A developer may work alone, or with many others depending on the size of the project.

Common app screens

There are many different styles of screen that designers create. Some common styles are given below.

Splash screen

A **splash screen** is displayed whilst an app is loading. It may just contain a **logo** and name of the app.

Home screen

The **home screen** is the first screen to be displayed and usually links to all of the other screens.

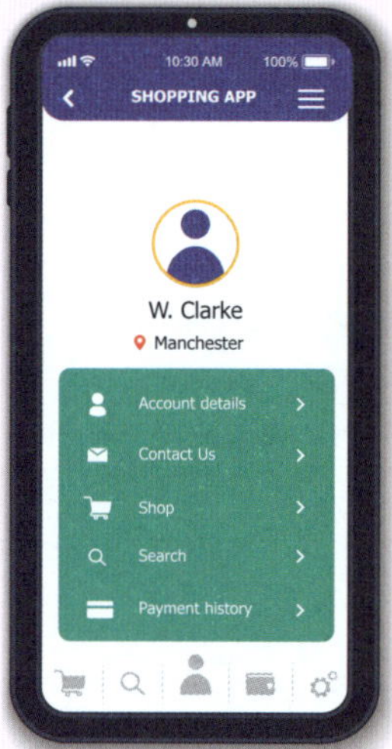

Gallery screen

A **gallery screen** allows photos to be displayed as small images called **thumbnails**. When clicked, a larger version of the image will be shown.

Common app components

Some components that are often used when developing apps include:

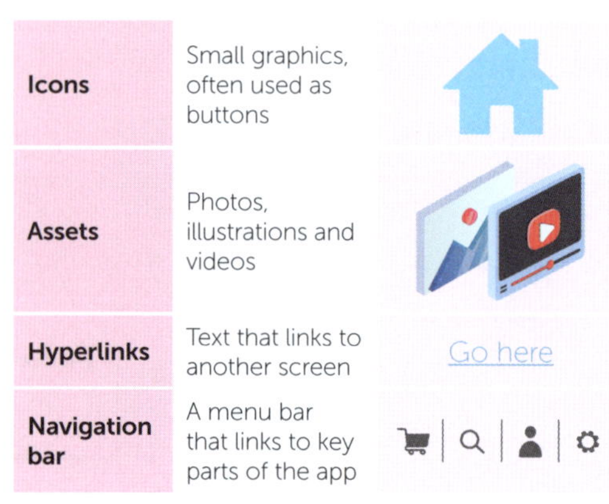

Icons	Small graphics, often used as buttons	
Assets	Photos, illustrations and videos	
Hyperlinks	Text that links to another screen	Go here
Navigation bar	A menu bar that links to key parts of the app	

Publishing

Before an app is **published**, it must be thoroughly **tested**.

Once completed, native apps are published to app **marketplaces** such as **Google Play** and the **Apple App Store**. These marketplaces deal with **distribution** of the app and **billing** customers.

Did you know?

Marketplaces only publish **native apps**. These have been developed specifically for specific smartphones or tablets that use the marketplace.

Web apps are delivered via websites. They run on any device but cannot be published on marketplaces. Appshed allows you to create web apps.

Write your mark here

1. Match the job roles on the left with their purpose on the right.

Designer	Writes and maintains computer code.
Developer	Responsible for the layout and graphics used in the app.
Programmer	Manages the app creation from the beginning to the end. May work alone on smaller projects, or with other designers and programmers.

[3]

2. A toy manufacturer has created an app that displays their products, any instructions, videos and where to buy them.

(a) Give **two** purposes of a splash screen for the app.

① ....

....

② ....

.... **[2]**

(b) Give **two** types of asset that a designer could use when creating the app.

① ....

....

② ....

.... **[2]**

(c) Once the app development is complete, a process needs to occur to check it works correctly before it can be released. Give the name for this process.

.... **[1]**

(d) The app will be released on app marketplaces. Give **two** purposes of app marketplaces.

① ....

....

② ....

.... **[2]**

Try it

Try making a simple information app in Appshed. Go through the process of designing the app, developing it, testing it then publishing it.

Total

 /10

How well do you feel you know this topic?   

TOPIC 8.1

TABLES AND FORMS

A **database** is a place where data is stored in a **structured** way in a computer.

Tables

Databases store one or more **tables**. Each table contains **fields** (columns) and **records** (rows).

Remember

One field will be the **primary key**. This field will always contain a **unique value** (usually a unique number) that identifies each record in the table.

The primary key in the Countries table is ID.

Countries table

The following table contains the fields (columns) for country, capital, population (in millions) and area (as a percentage of the world's land). The column titles are known as **field names**.

Table name: **Countries**

Field name

ID	Country	Capital	Population	Area
1	China	Beijing	1410	6.3
2	India	New Delhi	1392	2
3	USA	Washington, DC	336	6.1
4	Japan	Tokyo	124	0.2
5	France	Paris	68	0.4
6	UK	London	67	0.2
7	Australia	Canberra	26	5.2

Record

Field

Sorting

Records are easily sorted by a field. Sorting can be:

- **Ascending** (A-Z or 1-9)
- **Descending** (Z-A or 9-1)

For example, here is the countries table sorted by Area **descending**.

ID	Country	Capital	Population	Area
1	China	Beijing	1410	6.2
3	USA	Washington, DC	336	6.1
7	Australia	Canberra	26	5.2
2	India	New Delhi	1392	2
6	France	Paris	68	0.4
4	Japan	Tokyo	124	0.2
5	UK	London	67	0.2

Forms

Records may also be presented in a **form view**. This makes entering and viewing data easier as the form only displays one record. **Buttons** may also be added to help the user.

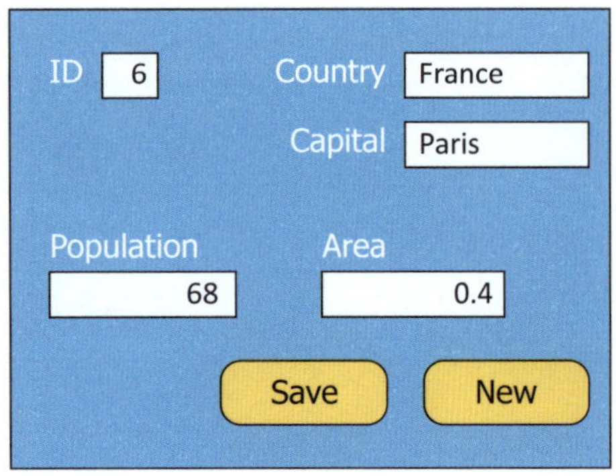

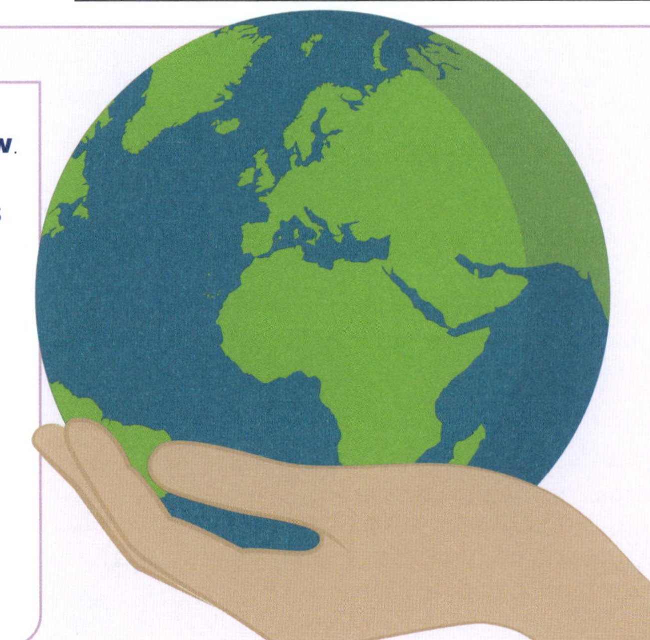

1. Use the database table on the left to answer the following questions.

Write your mark here

(a) State the number of fields in the Countries table.

.... **[1]**

(b) State the number of records in the table.

.... **[1]**

(c) Define the meaning of 'field name'

.... **[1]**

(d) Define the meaning of 'primary key'.

....

.... **[2]**

(e) List the ID numbers in order if the table is sorted by Population ascending.

.... **[1]**

(f) List the ID numbers in order if the table is ordered by Country ascending.

.... **[1]**

(g) Give **three** advantages of using a form to enter data.

① ....

....

② ....

....

③ ....

.... **[3]**

Try it

Microsoft Access is commonly used to make databases. If you don't have this software, a free alternative is LibreOffice® Base which is part of LibreOffice. Download at:

https://www.libreoffice.org/

Now use database software to create a database on a topic of your choice. For example, you could create a database of items you own, cars, sports teams or clothing.

Total

/10

How well do you feel you know this topic?  

TOPIC 8.2

QUERIES AND REPORTS

A key feature of a database is the ability to search for information. Searches are carried out using queries. The **result** from a query is a table of results which may be formatted as a **report**.

Queries

A **query** matches each record against the criteria that have been used. Fields may be shown or hidden. The result is a table (which will have zero or more records in it).

Original table

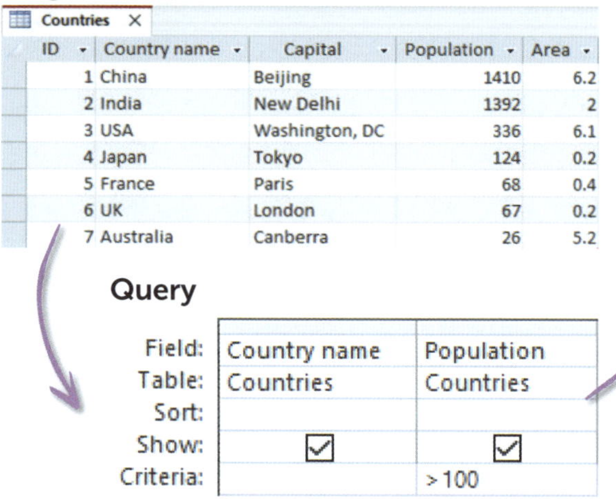

Countries

ID	Country name	Capital	Population	Area
1	China	Beijing	1410	6.2
2	India	New Delhi	1392	2
3	USA	Washington, DC	336	6.1
4	Japan	Tokyo	124	0.2
5	France	Paris	68	0.4
6	UK	London	67	0.2
7	Australia	Canberra	26	5.2

Query

Field:	Country name	Population
Table:	Countries	Countries
Sort:		
Show:	☑	☑
Criteria:		>100

This query finds all the countries where the population field is greater than 100 (which are countries with more than 100 million people).

Result

Population over 100 million

Country name	Population
China	1410
India	1392
USA	336
Japan	124

Did you know?

SQL (Structured Query Language) is a more advanced language that creates queries. SQL is written behind the scenes when creating an Access query. Here, the SQL would be:

```
SELECT 'Country name', Population
FROM Countries
WHERE Population > 100
```

Remember

The following **comparison operators** may be used in the criteria for a query:

Operator	Meaning
<	Less than
<=	Less than or equal to
>=	Greater than or equal to
>	Greater than
=	Equal to

Reports

Reports allow the tables or results of queries to be presented with better formatting and layout ready for printing.

Population over 100 million

Country name	Population in millions
China	1410
India	1392
USA	336
Japan	124
7th March	Page 1 of 4

Write your mark here

1. Write the operator that is used for each of the following:

   (a) Less than:

   .... **[1]**

   (b) Greater than or equal to:

   .... **[1]**

   (c) Equal to:

   .... **[1]**

2. A query uses criteria for the **`Area`** field in the table on the left.

   Complete the table to show how many records are returned if each of the following are used as the criteria in the **`Area`** field.

Criteria for the Area field	Records returned from query
`>6`	
`<2`	
`<=2`	
`=0.4`	

[4]

3. Name the programming language that is used to create queries.

   .... **[1]**

4. Give **two** reasons why a database report would be created rather than using the results from a query.

   ① ....

   ....

   ② ....

   .... **[2]**

Try it

If you're interested in databases, you'll need to learn SQL. Search for:

learn SQL

then choose a website to teach you SQL online. Many of these will give you challenges to carry out as you learn.

Total /10

How well do you feel you know this topic? ☺ ☐ 😐 ☐ ☹ ☐

TOPIC 9.1

HTML

Hypertext Markup Language (HTML) is the computer language that is used to make web sites. It is easier to learn than ordinary programming languages.

How it works

HTML is made up of **start tags** and **end tags** that surround text and images that need to be 'marked up' on the page.

HTML describes the content of a web page. The **web browser** then decides exactly how the content should be displayed.

For instance, to show a heading title, the following would be used:

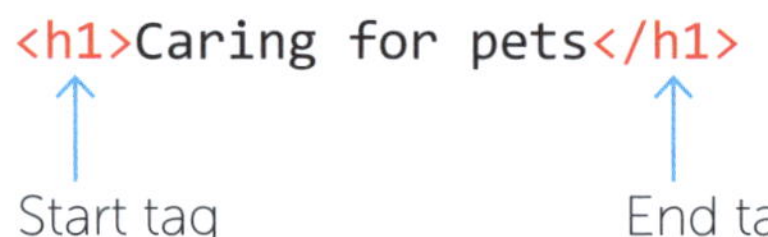

Hyperlinks

A key part of a webpage is the ability to **hyperlink** to other webpages.

The **anchor** tag is used to make a hyperlink.

```
<a href="page2.html">Go to page 2</a>
```

This will create the following hyperlink:

Go to page 2

Did you know?

Webpages have the file extension **.html**. The **homepage** of a website is usually given the filename **index.html**.

A complete web page

```
<html>
  <head>
    <title>Pets</title>
  </head>

  <body>
    <h1>Caring for pets</h1>
    <p>Make sure your pets get
       enough exercise and regular
       health checkups</p>
    <img src="vet.png">
  </body>
</html>
```

- `<html>` – Start the web page
- `<head>` – Start the **header** of the web page
- `<title>Pets</title>` – Start and end the page title which is displayed in the **tab title** or **window title**
- `</head>` – End the header
- `<body>` – Start the main **body** of the web page
- `<h1>Caring for pets</h1>` – Make a **heading** in heading 1 style
- `<p>Make sure your pets get ...` – Make a **paragraph** of text, using <p></p>
- `<img src="vet.png">` – Add an **image**. The source image is `vet.png`
- `</body>` – End the body of the web page
- `</html>` – End the web page

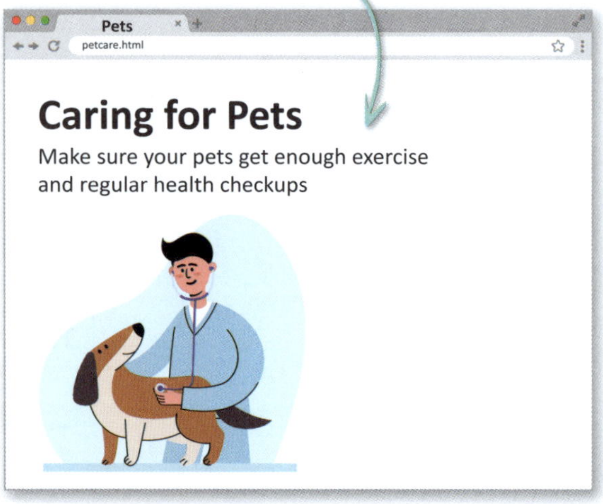

Pets
petcare.html

Caring for Pets

Make sure your pets get enough exercise and regular health checkups

Write your mark here

1. Match the HTML start tags on the left with their meaning on the right.

<body>	Begin the html for a web page.
<h1>	Start a paragraph.
<html>	Start the main part of the web page.
<p>	Begin a link to a webpage.
<img src="car.jpg">	Start heading or title.
<a href="car.html">	Show an image.

[6]

2. (a) Write the HTML which will add an image of a photo of a dog. Rearrange the blocks below to help write the HTML.

dog.jpg	>	img	<	src="	"

.... **[1]**

(b) Write the HTML which will make a hyperlink to a page about dogs. The filename for the page will be `dogs.html`.

....

.... **[3]**

Try it

Enter the HTML on the left into a text editor such as Notepad. Change the image filename to an image that you have downloaded. Save the file as `petcare.html`.

Now open the file in a web browser to test if it works correctly.

Total /10

How well do you feel you know this topic?

TOPIC 9.2

CSS

HTML describes the content of a webpage. CSS describes the style (formatting and layout) of a webpage.

Did you know?

CSS stands for **Cascading Style Sheets**. The same CSS could be used to apply styles to many web pages.

How it works

There are three ways that styles are added to web pages:

- **Inline** – with styles being added to the start tag
- **Internal** – with a `<style>` tag within the `<head>` of a web page
- **External** – with a `<link>` tag that links to an external CSS file

The examples on this page use internal styles to change the appearance of the whole page.

External CSS files allow a whole website's formatting to be changed in one place.

CSS properties

The following are some of the many properties that can be applied to parts of a web page.

The examples show the result when each **property** is applied to the HTML `<p>Some text</p>`.

CSS properties	Example
`color: green;`	Some text
`font-family: sans-serif`	Some text
`text-align: center;`	Some text
`border: 2px solid blue;`	Some text
`background-color: yellow;`	Some text

HTML and CSS example

```
<html>
  <head>
    <style>
      body {
            background-color: brown;
            font-family: sans-serif;
      }
      h1 {
          color: white;
          text-align: center;
          border: 2px dashed white;
          background-color: purple;
        }
      p {
          color: white;
        }
    </style>
  </head>
  <body>
    <h1>Elephants</h1>
    <p>The largest land animals</p>
  </body>
</html>
```

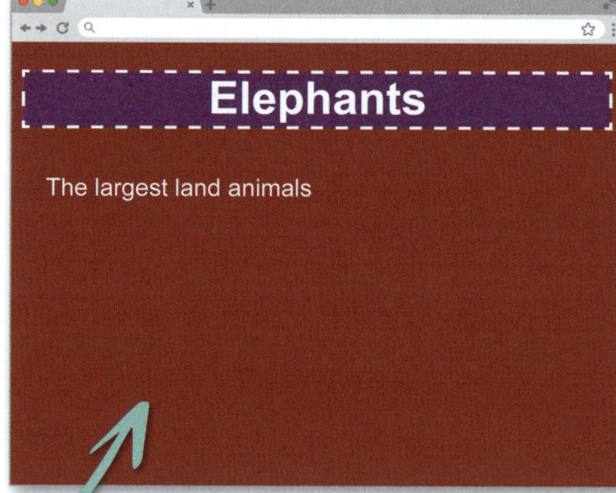

Top tip

Note that in computing, American English spellings are usually used, such as for *color* rather than *colour*.

Write your mark here

1. State what the letters CSS stand for.

....

.... **[1]**

2 Tick the correct spelling that is used in CSS for the following words.

A center ☐ **B** centre ☐ **[1]**

3. Match the CSS properties with their meanings.

color	The colour behind the text.
background-color	Make the text move to the left, centre or right.
text-align	The colour of text.
border	Set the border width, style and colour.

[4]

4. Complete the CSS below which will make the text in a paragraph have the following properties:
   - White text colour
   - Blue background
   - A solid red border with 3 pixels width
   - Centred text

```
p {
    color: ..........................................................
    ..........................................................: blue
    border:..........................................................
    text-align:......................................................
}
```

[4]

Try it

Enter the HTML and CSS example on the left into a text editor such as Notepad. Save the file as elephants.html.

Now open the file in a web browser to test if it works correctly.

Search for:

 CSS properties

View different properties and then try them out in your CSS.

Total

/10

How well do you feel you know this topic?

TOPIC 9.3

WEB FORMS

Web forms have many uses on web pages. From search engine queries to social media posts to a website enquiry. Forms allow users to submit information to the web server for the website.

Did you know?

A check mark is American English for a tick ✓. HTML uses American English words such as checkbox rather than tick box.

Form components

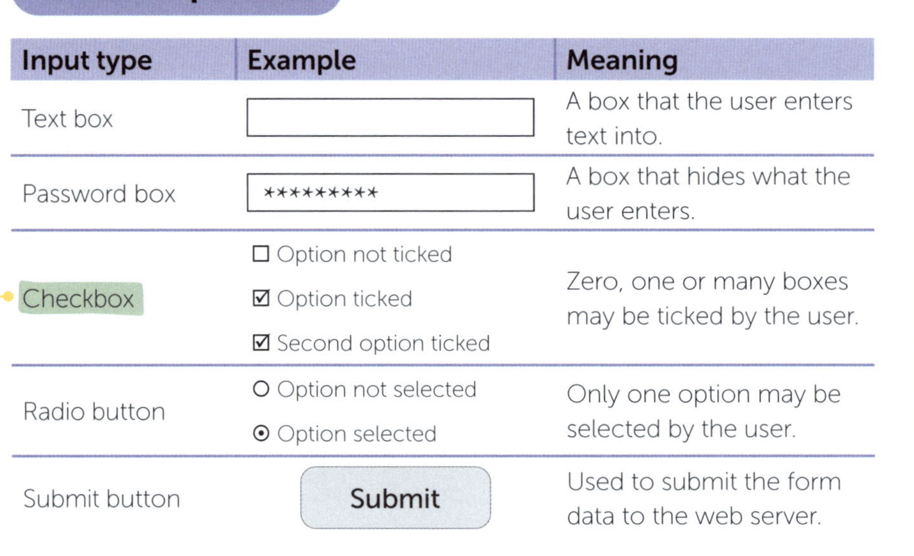

Input type	Example	Meaning
Text box		A box that the user enters text into.
Password box	*********	A box that hides what the user enters.
Checkbox	☐ Option not ticked ☑ Option ticked ☑ Second option ticked	Zero, one or many boxes may be ticked by the user.
Radio button	○ Option not selected ⦿ Option selected	Only one option may be selected by the user.
Submit button	Submit	Used to submit the form data to the web server.

HTML

```
<html>
<body>
<form action="page_to_process.php">
   Username:<input type="text"><br>
   Password:<input type="password"><br>
   <input type="submit" value="Submit">
</form>
</body>
</html>
```

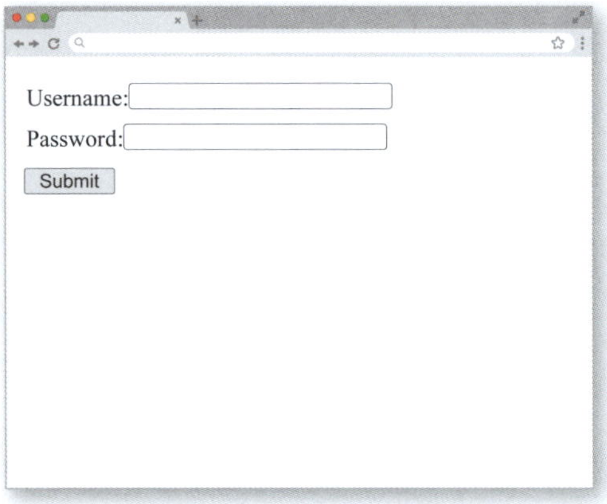

Username:
Password:
Submit

How it works

The form information will be processed by the page given here.

This makes a text box.

This makes a password box.

The <br> tag makes a new line.

This makes a submit button.

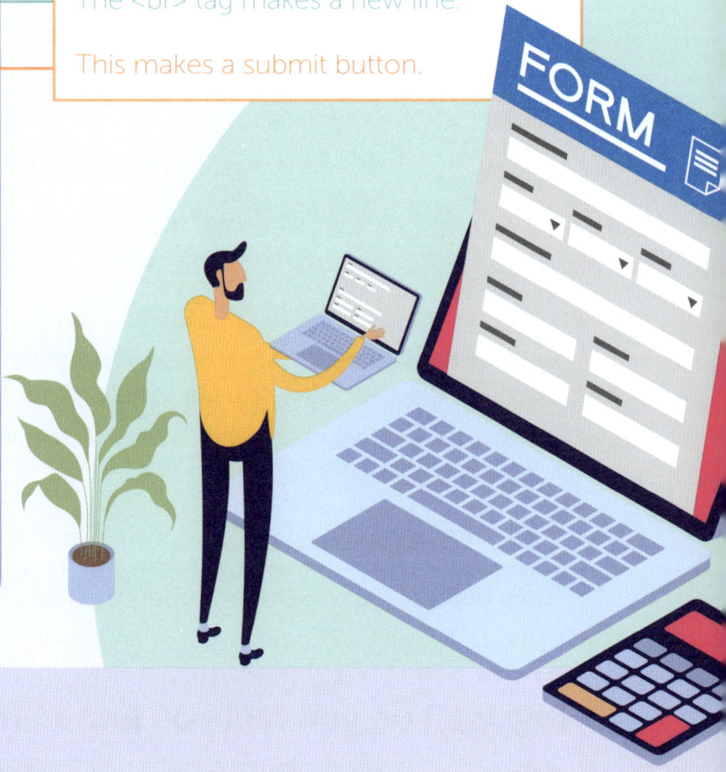

1. The form below uses four different input types. Label each input type.

Write your mark here

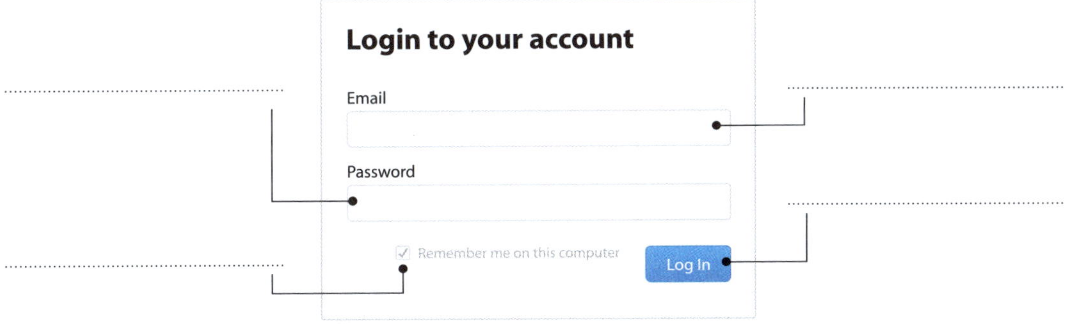

[4]

2 Describe the differences between a radio button and a checkbox.

....

....

....

.... **[2]**

3. Complete the HTML below so that it creates the web page shown on the right.

Name: [ ]
Age: [ ]
Agree to terms? [ ]
Create new account

```
<form action="page_to_process">
  Name:<input type="........................"><br>
  Age:<input type="text"><br>
  Agree to terms and conditions?
  <...................................."checkbox"><br>
  <input ...................................................="Create
   new account">
</form>
```

[4]

Try it

Enter the HTML on the left into a text editor such as Notepad with a .html extension.

Now open the file in a web browser to test if it works correctly.

Search for:

 HTML input types

then try using these in your HTML.

Total

 /10

How well do you feel you know this topic? ☺ ☐ 😐 ☐ ☹ ☐

TOPIC 10.1

NETWORK TOPOLOGIES

Networks allow many computers and other devices to communicate with each other. The layout used to connect computers together is known as the **network topology**.

Bus networks

Bus networks connect each computer, printer or server to one long cable. The cable has a **terminator** at each end to complete the cable

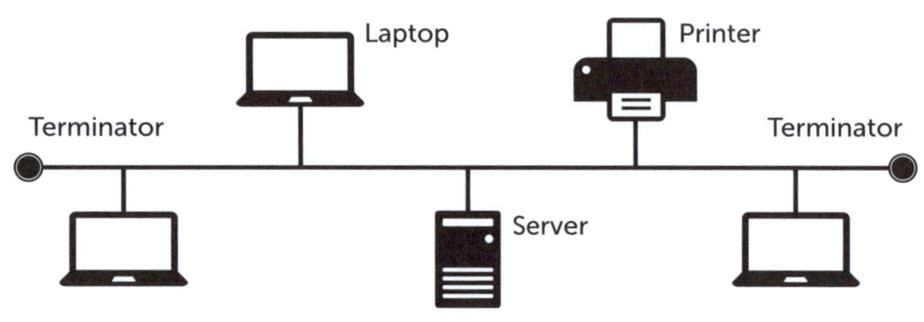

Advantages

- Only one cable is required so it is cheap to install
- Easy to connect a new computer

Disadvantages

- If the main cable breaks, then all computers lose network access
- As more computers are added, the network gets much slower

Star networks

In a **star network**, each computer, printer or server connects to a central **switch** or **hub** with its own cable. Almost all home and school networks use a star network topology.

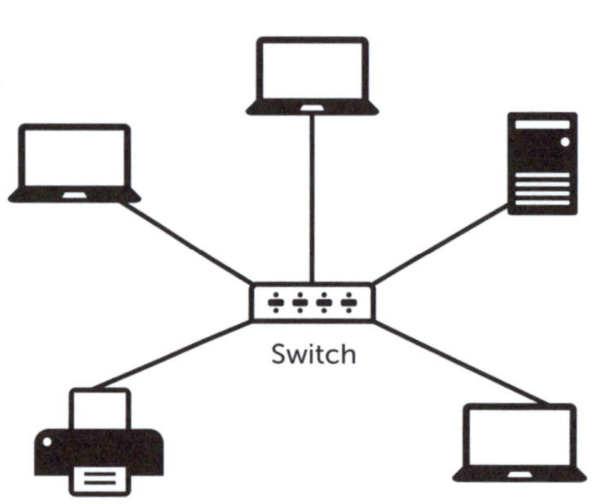

Advantages

- More reliable as if a cable breaks, it only affects one computer
- Faster performance

Disadvantages

- One cable for each computer increases the cost
- A switch or hub is needed adding to the cost

LANs and Wans

Local Area Networks (**LANs**) are networks in a small area such as a building, school, local shop or home network.

Wide Area Networks (**WANs**) Wide Area Networks (WANs) are two or more LANs that are commonly joined together by a leased line. For example, to join the network of a branch office in Manchester to the network of a head office in London. The Internet is an example of a WAN.

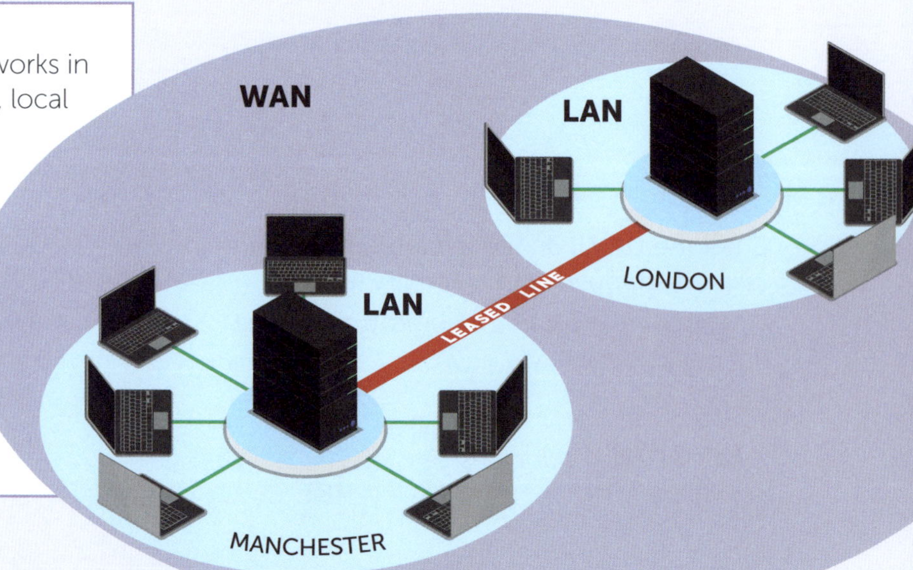

1. The table below lists hardware required to create two different types of network. For each network, tick the hardware required.

Write your mark here

	Cable(s)	Terminators	Switch
Bus network			
Star network			

[2]

2 Identify the effect of a cable being cut on each of the following network topologies.

Bus network: ....

....

Star network: ....

.... **[2]**

3. Two small classrooms, shown below, each have four computers. Some spare parts are located in a store room. The store room also contains as many cables as you need.

Complete the network diagram for each classroom topology (a bus network and star network) using the spare parts given. Label any parts that you use.

Classroom 1: **Bus network**

Classroom 2: **Star network**

Store room

[6]

Try it

Home networks usually make use of a router, switch and wireless access point. Research different home routers online and record the different features that they have.

Total /10

How well do you feel you know this topic?  

TOPIC 10.2 NETWORK CONNECTIVITY

There are different types of cable that are used to connect networks together. These have different bandwidths and costs.

Cables

Fibre optic cable

Fibre optic cables **transmit** data using **light**. The light bounces down the cable. This type of cable has a very **high bandwidth**. It is often used to connect networks to the **Internet**.

Twisted pair copper cable

Twisted pair copper cable is most commonly used to connect computers to a **switch** on a **LAN**. Bandwidth is usually quite fast, but not as fast as fibre optic cables. This cable is used in **star networks**.

Coaxial cable

Coaxial cable is slower than twisted pair copper cable. It is used when creating **bus networks**.

Did you know?

Bandwidth is the amount of data that is **transmitted** through a connection per second. It is often referred to as speed.

Wireless

Wireless (also known as **Wi-Fi**) connects laptops, smartphones and tablets to a **Wireless Access Point** (**WAP**). As no cable is used, the devices may be moved whilst still being connected to the network.

As any nearby computer is able to listen to a signal being transmitted, it is important that **encryption** is used to make the **transmission** more **secure**.

Transfer time

The time to **transfer** a file through a network connection can be calculated:

Question: A home connection has a bandwidth of 100 megabits per second (Mbps). How long will it take to transfer a 100 megabyte (MB) file?

Answer:

100 megabytes = 100 000 000 bytes

100 000 000 * 8 = 800 000 000 bits

800 000 000 bits / 100 000 000 bits per second

= **8 seconds**.

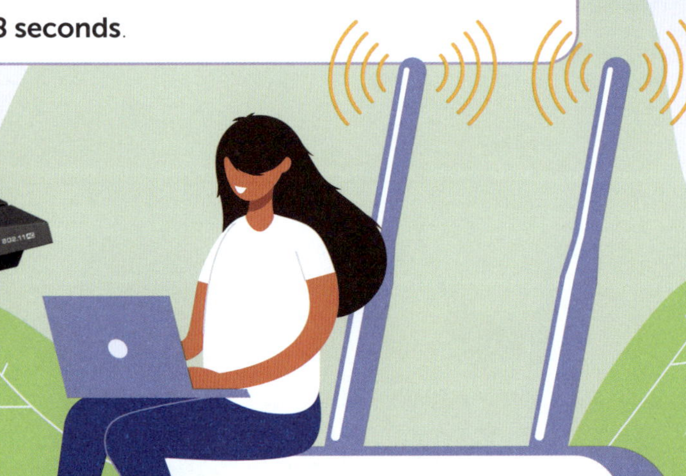

1. For each of the following network cables, state the type of cable that is shown.

Network cable	Type of cable

[3]

Write your mark here

2 For each of the following situations, identify an appropriate connection type and give a reason for your choice.

Situation	Cable type	Reason for your choice
To connect a PC to a school network.		
To connect a smartphone to a home network.		

[4]

3. Calculate the amount of time needed to transfer a 100 megabyte (MB) file using a 20 megabit per second (Mbps) connection.

....

....

....

....

....

.... [3]

Try it

List all the different devices on your home network and school network.

Name the type of connection that is used for each of the devices.

Total ☐ /10

How well do you feel you know this topic? ☺ ☐ 😐 ☐ ☹ ☐

TOPIC 10.3

THE INTERNET

The Internet is made up of a huge number of interconnected networks. Together it makes up the largest network in the world. The **World Wide Web** (**www**) is the service that is used to share web pages via the Internet.

IP addresses

Every computer and server on the Internet has a unique number known as an **IP address**. This is similar to a house number and postcode used to send letters to any house in the UK. Any information sent on the Internet will contain the **destination IP address**.

IP addresses are four numbers from 0-255 separated by dots.

For example: `52.142.124.215`

How it works

When data is sent through the **Internet** it is first divided into small parts known as **packets**. Each packet has a **packet number** along with the destination IP address. The packets may be sent through different **routes** across the Internet. They may also arrive out of order. The destination computer puts all the packets back together in the right order.

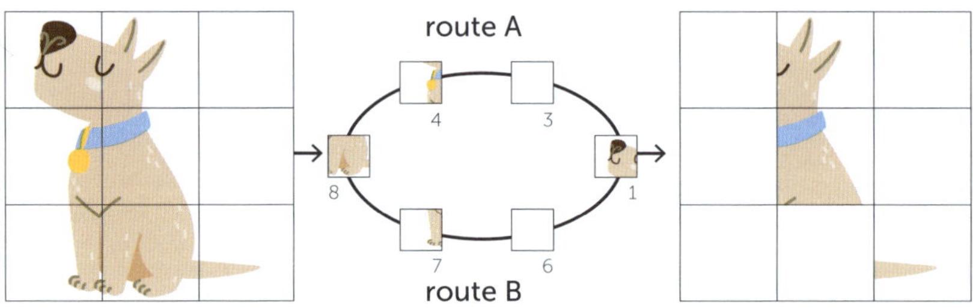

Web addresses

Web addresses are entered by users to find a particular **file** or **web page** on the **World Wide Web**. The domain name is translated to an IP address by a **Domain Name System** (**DNS**) **Server**.

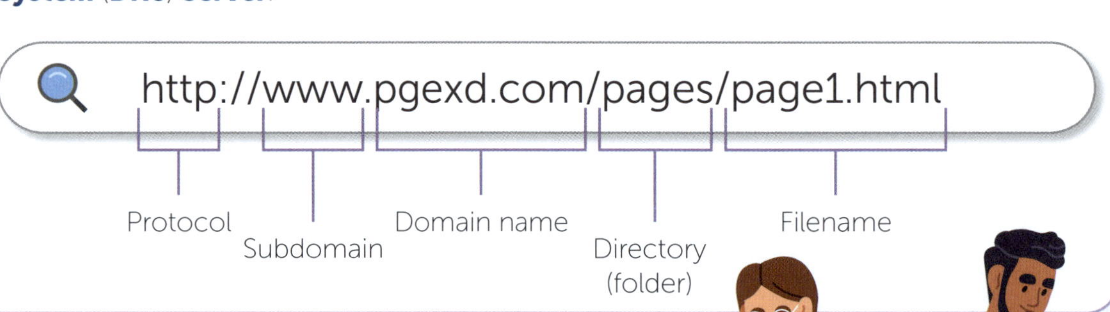

Did you know?

A **protocol** is a set of rules used by computers when communicating with each other.

HTTP stands for **Hypertext Transfer Protocol**.

Write your mark here

1. Look at the following web address:

https://social.pgexd.com/profile

(a) Identify the protocol used in the web address.

.... **[1]**

(b) Identify the subdomain used in the web address.

.... **[1]**

(c) Identify the domain name used in the web address.

.... **[1]**

(d) Identify the directory used in the web address.

.... **[1]**

2 IP addresses are given to each computer on the Internet.
Tick the valid IP addresses below.

IP address	Valid IP addresses (✓)
`74.6.143.26`	
`185.15.590.226`	
`13.107.21.200`	
`151.101.128.144.22`	

[2]

3. Describe how information is sent through the Internet.

....

....

....

.... **[3]**

4. State the difference between the World Wide Web and the Internet.

....

.... **[1]**

Try it

Search online for "Traceroute". Use this service to find all the different IP addresses that packets will travel through as they go to their destination.

Total

/10

How well do you feel you know this topic? 

TOPIC 10.4

ENCRYPTION

It is often necessary that data is kept secret from other people and other computers. This is especially true when computers communicate with each other over the Internet as this is a **public network**. Encryption is the process of converting information so that it cannot be understood without a **key** or **password**.

Caesar cipher

A **Caesar cipher** is a simple way to **encrypt** and **decrypt** a message. The Caesar cipher replaces each letter of a message with a letter further on in the alphabet. If the key is 4, then the letter A becomes E, 4 places on.

A	B	C	D	E	F	G	H	I	J
↓	↓	↓	↓	↓	↓	↓	↓	↓	↓
E	F	G	H	I	J	K	L	M	N

So, the word FAB when encrypted would become JEF.

The encryption used by computers is far harder to crack than a Caesar cipher.

How it works

Encryption

When sending information, **plaintext** is **encrypted** using an **encryption key**. The encrypted text is known as **cipher text**. The text is then **decrypted** back into plaintext using the key.

When **web browsers** request a site using HTTPS, the encryption and decryption keys are stored and dealt with by the browser and server. The user doesn't have to do anything extra.

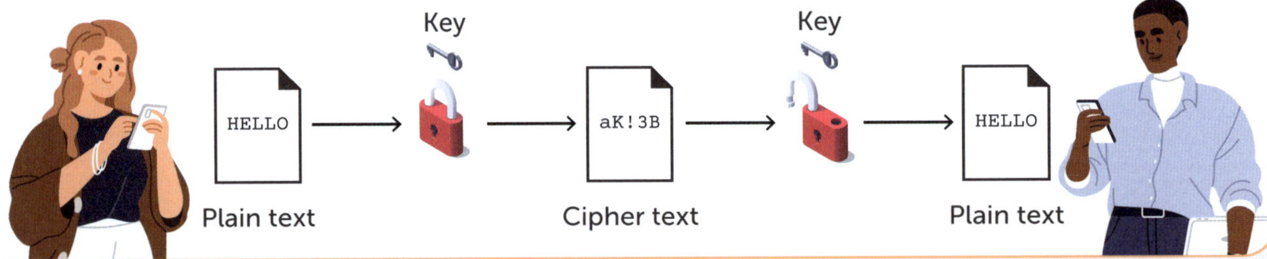

Did you know?

HTTPS is the secure version of HTTP. It prevents anyone reading information sent between a user's computer and a web server. Most websites now use HTTPS to help keep their data secure. Web browsers often use a green padlock symbol to show a webpage is using HTTPS.

1. Match the following words with their meanings.

Encrypt	The secret encrypted text.
Decrypt	The text as the user will read it.
Encryption key	Converting from cipher text to plaintext.
Plaintext	The key or password used to encrypt plaintext.
Cipher text	Converting from plaintext to cipher text.

[5]

Write your mark here

2 (a) Use the Caesar cipher on the left (with a key of 4) to encrypt the following words:

(i) IF

.... **[1]**

(ii) HAD

.... **[1]**

(iii) FEED

.... **[1]**

(b) Use the Caesar cipher on the left to decrypt the following:

JEF GLIJ FMK FIEGL

.... **[1]**

3. A website has a green padlock next to the web address.
Give the meaning of this symbol.

....

.... **[1]**

Try it

Search for:

Caesar cipher online decoder

Choose a website that carries out the cipher, then use this to encrypt and decrypt text.

Now find out how other ciphers work.

Total /10

How well do you feel you know this topic?

TOPIC 11.1

CELLS AND FORMULAE

Spreadsheets make use of tables known as **sheets**. Each sheet contains boxes known as **cells**.

Spreadsheets are used to make **calculations** just like a calculator, but spreadsheets are able to refer to **values** in other cells. When these are updated, related calculations in the spreadsheet change automatically.

Rows and columns

Rows go across the spreadsheet, just like a rowing boat.

Columns go up and down the spreadsheet, like the columns in a building.

	A	B	C
1	A1		
2			
3			
4			
5			
6			

Did you know?

Each cell in a spreadsheet is given a **cell reference** made from the column name and row number.

For example, A1 is the top left cell in a spreadsheet.

Addressing cells

When a cell with a formula in it is copied and pasted into another cell, any cell references will automatically change. This is known as **relative cell referencing**.

	A	B	C	D
1	Sweets	Price	Quantity	Total
2	Cola bottles	£0.01	10	£0.10
3	Jelly Babies	£0.02	10	=B3*C3
4	Wine gums	£0.05	5	£0.25
5			Total	£0.55

To keep a formula the same when it is copied, use $ symbols. For example, =A1 will always refer to cell A1 when it is copied. This is known as **absolute cell referencing**.

Remember

Spreadsheets use slightly different symbols to calculators.

Calculator	Meaning	Spreadsheet
+	Addition	+
−	Subtraction	−
×	Multiplication	*
÷	Division	/

How it works

The formula in **D2** is:

=**B2*C2**

This means, take the value in B2 (£0.01) and multiply it by the value in C2 (10).

=£0.01*10

=£0.10

	A	B	C	D
1	Sweets	Price	Quantity	Total
2	Cola bottles	£0.01	10	=B2*C2
3	Jelly Babies	£0.02	10	£0.20
4	Wine gums	£0.05	5	£0.25
5			Total	£0.55

Write your mark here

1. (a) Write the symbol used for multiplication in a spreadsheet.

.... [1]

(b) Write the symbol used for division in a spreadsheet.

.... [1]

2. For the following questions, refer to the spreadsheet shown below.

	A	B	C	D
1	Theme park	Quantity	Price	Subtotal
2	Adult	2	£20.00	£40.00
3	Child	2	£10.00	£20.00
4	Senior citizen	0	£15.00	£0.00
5	Student	1	£18.00	£18.00
6				
7	Total tickets	5	Grand total	£78.00

(a) State the value shown in cell C4.

.... [1]

(b) Give the cell reference that currently is showing the value £78.00.

.... [1]

(c) Complete the formula used in cell D2.

=.............................. * .... [2]

(d) The formula used in cell D2 is copied into cell D3.
Write the new formula that will be created.

.... [2]

(e) Write a formula that will calculate the value in D7.

....

.... [2]

Try it

Have a go at making the spreadsheet on the left. Some available software to make spreadsheets includes:

- Microsoft Excel (Paid)
- LibreOffice (Free)
- Google Sheets (Free)

Total /10

How well do you feel you know this topic? ☺ ☐ 😐 ☐ ☹ ☐

TOPIC 11.2

FUNCTIONS

It's very slow to add many numbers together with a calculator. Spreadsheets are able to carry out calculations, such as addition, on long lists of numbers almost instantly. Even better, they don't make mistakes. **Functions** are used to tell a spreadsheet what calculations will be required.

Rows and columns

The following spreadsheet shows weather data that has been collected over a week.

	A	B	C	D	E	F
1	Date	Rainfall (mm)	Sun hours		Max rainfall	30
2	Monday	15	6		Min rainfall	0
3	Tuesday	5	6			
4	Wednesday	30	0		Max sun	7
5	Thursday	0	6		Min sun	0
6	Friday	10	1			
7	Saturday	5	7			
8	Sunday	5	2			
9	Average	=AVERAGE(B2:B8)	4			
10		AVERAGE(**number1**, [number2], ...)				
11						

How it works

=AVERAGE(B2:B8) will find the **average** of the values in the cell **range** B2:B8. This cell range covers B2, B3, B4, B5, B6, B7 and B8.

The spreadsheet carries out the calculation

=(15+5+30+0+10+5+5)/7

=70/7

This gives the answer 10.

Did you know?

Functions will take **values** (such as numbers) as inputs and return a value.

FUNCTION_NAME(INPUTS)

Functions are also used in programming. See **page 122**.

Spreadsheet functions

The following are some useful functions used in spreadsheets.

Function	Example	Result	Meaning
=AVERAGE(range)	=AVERAGE(B2:B8)	10	Finds the **average** of the range.
=SUM(range)	=SUM(B2:B8)	70	Adds up all the numbers in the range.
=MIN(range)	=MIN(B2:B8)	0	Finds the **minimum** number in the range.
=MAX(range)	=MAX(B2:B8)	30	Finds the **maximum** number in the range.
=COUNT(range)	=COUNT(B2:B8)	7	**Counts** the number of non-empty cells in the range.

1. All the following questions refer to the spreadsheet shown on the left.

Write your mark here

(a) Calculate the result of the formula:

=AVERAGE(C2:C4)

.... **[1]**

(b) Complete the formula for cell C9.

=AVERAGE(..) **[1]**

(c) Complete the formula for cell F1.

=MAX(....) **[1]**

(d) Complete the formula for cell F4.

=...(...) **[2]**

(e) Write the formula for cell F5.

.... **[2]**

(f) Write a formula to find the number of rainfall readings that have been taken.

.... **[2]**

(g) Calculate the result for the formula:

=SUM(C2:C8)

.... **[1]**

Try it

Search for a product you are interested in buying to find its price at different shops.

Now make a spreadsheet that will calculate the average price, maximum price and minimum price.

A price comparison site works in a very similar way to this.

Total ☐ **/10**

How well do you feel you know this topic? ☐ ☐ ☐

TOPIC **11.3**

FORMATTING

Formatting allows data inside spreadsheets to be presented in a way that makes it easier to understand and more suitable for presentation.

Formatting

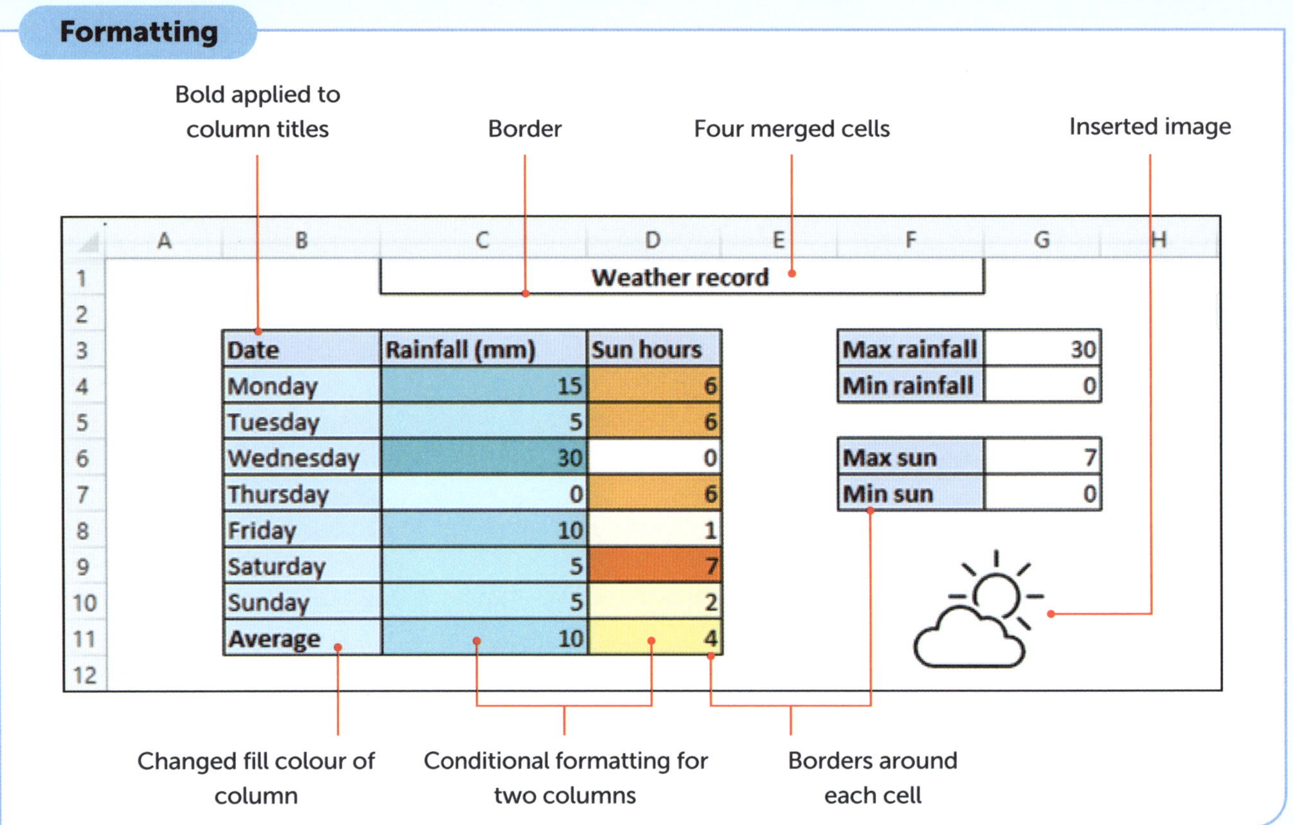

Examples

Formatting feature	Example
Fill colour	This changes the background colour of the cell.
Text colour	This alters the colour of the text in the cell.
Borders	This applies a border to the outside of the cell.
Merge cell	A B This combines two or more cells into one

Conditional formatting

Conditional formatting allows different formatting to be applied to each cell based on the **value** that is inside it. This helps to spot the larger or smaller numbers amongst others.

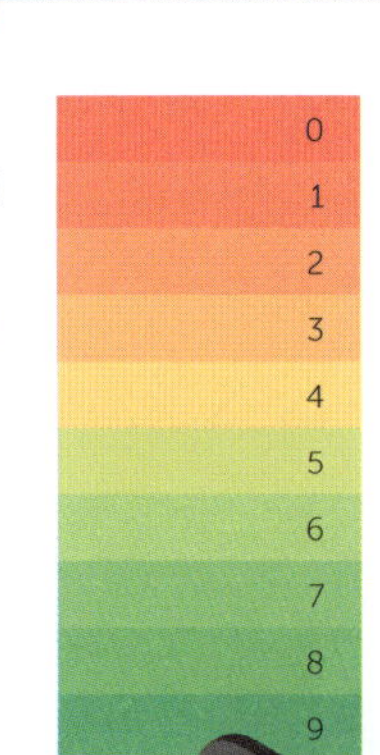

Did you know?

If you **fill** cells in a spreadsheet with white then the cell lines will disappear. This is useful for helping to make data stand out from the rest of the spreadsheet.

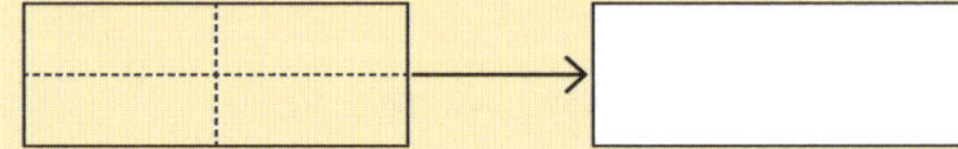

1. The middle cell in the spreadsheet below has had **three** changes to its formatting.

	text	

① ....

② ....

③ .... **[3]**

Write your mark here

2. Match the following words with their meanings.

Merge cells	Make the text thicker.
Insert image	Combine two or more cells so they act as one cell.
Bold	Add a picture, photo or illustration.

[3]

3. (a) Describe what conditional formatting does.

....

....

.... **[2]**

(b) Give an example where conditional formatting could be used other than for rainfall and sun hours.

.... **[1]**

4. Give **one** way that the thin grey gridlines in a spreadsheet could be removed.

.... **[1]**

Try it

Search for:

holiday weather averages

Find different places around the world that you would like to visit and the amount of sun they receive.

Make a spreadsheet that shows the data, using formatting and conditional formatting.

Total

/10

How well do you feel you know this topic?   

TOPIC 11.4

MODELLING

Spreadsheets are used to **model** data. **Modelling** could work out how many new schools are needed for a growing population or predict how much more wheat could be grown if a farmer buys another field. Models that deal with money are known as **financial models**.

Financial model

Fab Fast Food opened a restaurant in Birmingham last year. They are about to open a new restaurant in an airport location. They have decided to make a financial model to predict their profit for the year.

Fab Fast Food has recorded the number of people that walk past the new restaurant (known as **footfall**). They have found there is twice the footfall at the new restaurant.

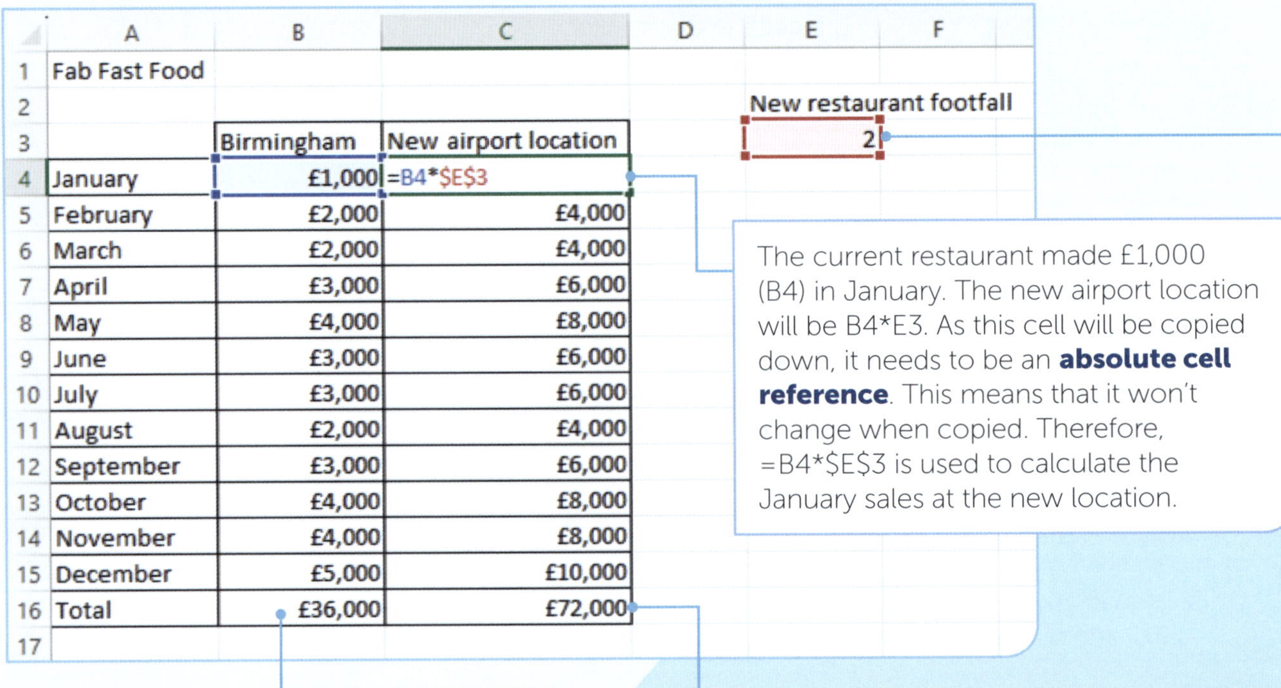

	A	B	C	D	E	F
1	Fab Fast Food					
2					New restaurant footfall	
3		Birmingham	New airport location		2	
4	January	£1,000	=B4*E3			
5	February	£2,000	£4,000			
6	March	£2,000	£4,000			
7	April	£3,000	£6,000			
8	May	£4,000	£8,000			
9	June	£3,000	£6,000			
10	July	£3,000	£6,000			
11	August	£2,000	£4,000			
12	September	£3,000	£6,000			
13	October	£4,000	£8,000			
14	November	£4,000	£8,000			
15	December	£5,000	£10,000			
16	Total	£36,000	£72,000			
17						

The current restaurant made £1,000 (B4) in January. The new airport location will be B4*E3. As this cell will be copied down, it needs to be an **absolute cell reference**. This means that it won't change when copied. Therefore, =B4*E3 is used to calculate the January sales at the new location.

The total sales are calculated by using a **SUM function** on each month's sales.

For the Birmingham store this would be:

=SUM(B4:B15)

Fab Fast Food could easily see how altering the footfall number in E3 affects the total profit that's calculated in C16.

Did you know?

Modelling is not the same as real life. It is a **prediction** of what might happen.

Models are often wrong or inaccurate. Scientists and engineers run **experiments** to help make their models more accurate.

1. The following questions make use of the spreadsheet on the left for Fab Fast Food.

Write your mark here

(a) Calculate the result that will be produced by the formula in C4.

.... **[1]**

(b) Complete the formula that will be used to calculate C5 when copied from C4.

=... * .... **[2]**

(c) Write the formula that will be used to calculate C15.

.... **[2]**

(d) Write the formula that will be used to calculate C16.

.... **[2]**

(e) The airport has told Fab Fast Food that they expect to double the number of passengers next year.
Calculate the total in C16 that will result if the footfall in E3 becomes 4.

....

.... **[1]**

(f) The formula in C4 uses two $ symbols.
Give the reason why these are used.

.... **[1]**

(g) Give **one** problem with using data from models.

.... **[1]**

Try it

Imagine that you are organising an entertainment event. It could be a special screening in a cinema, a sports competition or even a live music event.

Now create a financial model using a spreadsheet. Add all the costs to your model along with the ticket prices. How many people need to come to the event for you to make a profit?

Total

☐ /10

How well do you feel you know this topic? ☺ ☐ 😐 ☐ ☹ ☐

TOPIC 11.5

CHARTS

Charts are a way of **graphically presenting** data. This often makes **trends** and key points of the data easier to find than viewing a table of numbers.

Bar charts

Bar charts show each item of data as a bar.

The chart on the right shows the monthly sales for Fab Fast Food's Birmingham restaurant.

It is easy to identify how sales are low in January, February, March and August. They also peak in May and December.

Charts often lead to asking questions, such as:

- *Why do sales increase towards the end of the year?*
- *Why are sales very low in January?*

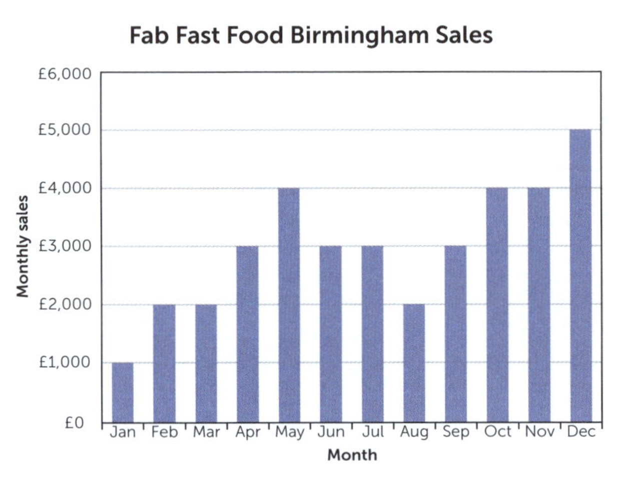

Top tip

When making charts, to make them easier to understand remember to include:

- A title
- **y-axis label**
- **x-axis label**
- A **key** if required

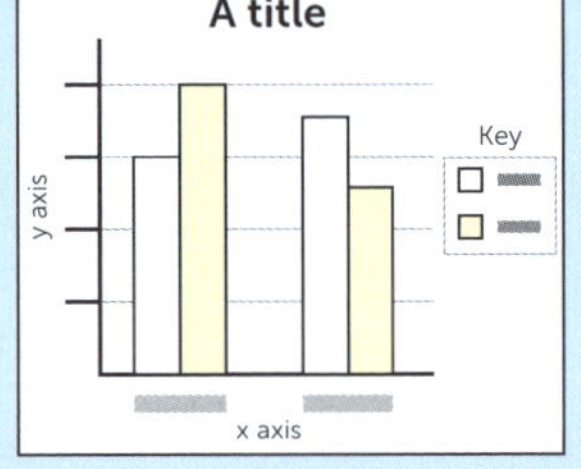

Did you know?

There are other chart options that spreadsheets offer. For instance, **line charts** are used with data such as temperature, rainfall or a person's height. Line charts are particularly good at showing changes and trends over time.

Pie charts

Pie charts give a **segment** size in proportion to the size of the whole.

This pie chart shows the same data as the left. Notice, though, that it is far harder to detect a trend or to identify the low and high sales months.

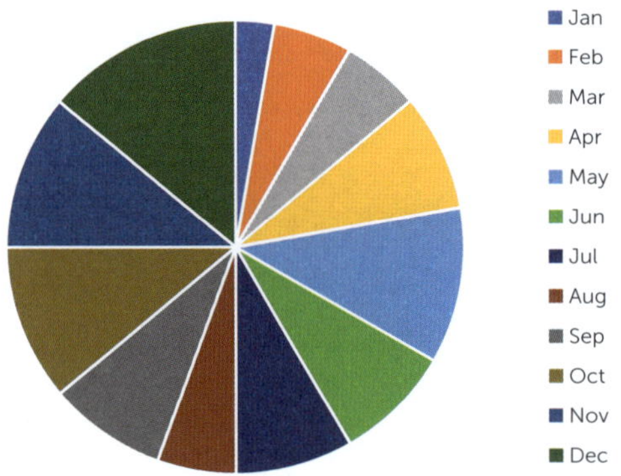

Pie charts are much easier to create in a spreadsheet than by hand as the computer will calculate each segment size.

Write your mark here

1. The following chart shows the heights of boys and girls.

Child heights • — (B)

(A) Height (cm): 200, 150, 100, 50, 0

Age • — (C): 2 3 4 5 6 7 8 9 10 11 12 13 14 15 16 17 18

(D) — • Boys — Girls

(a) Tick the chart type that has been used.

A Bar chart ☐

B Line chart ☐

C Pie chart ☐

[1]

(b) Different parts of the chart have been labelled from A-D.
Match the label with the part of the chart below.

A	Key
B	x-axis label
C	y-axis label
D	Title

[4]

(c) Give **two** key points or trends that the chart shows.

① ....

② .... **[2]**

(d) Give **two** problems with using a pie chat to show the child height data.

① ....

② .... **[2]**

2. The bar chart on the left shows low sales in January.
Give **one** reason why this may be the case.

....

.... **[1]**

Try it

Search for data on a topic you are interested in. Topics may include clothing sales, game chart sales or country populations. For example:

Game chart sales

Now put the data into a spreadsheet. Try creating different charts and see which present the data in the most informative way.

Total ☐ /10

How well do you feel you know this topic?   

TOPIC 12.1 INPUTS, OUTPUTS AND SEQUENCES

Python is a **text-based programming language**. This means that programs are written using the letters on the keyboard just as you would type an essay.

To output text from a Python program, use a print statement:

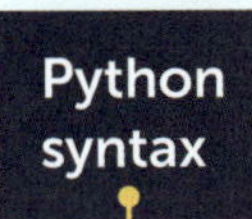


```
print("Text to output")
```

Did you know?

- Python is a **high-level programming language**. This means it uses keywords that are similar to English. If you know how to program in Python, then it will be easy to learn other high-level languages such as **C#** or **Java**.
- **Syntax** is a special word in programming which means the order in which the words and symbols need to be written. The English language also has syntax, but it is usually called **grammar** instead.

How it works

To **run** your program go to:

Run > Run Module

Or press the **F5** key on the keyboard.

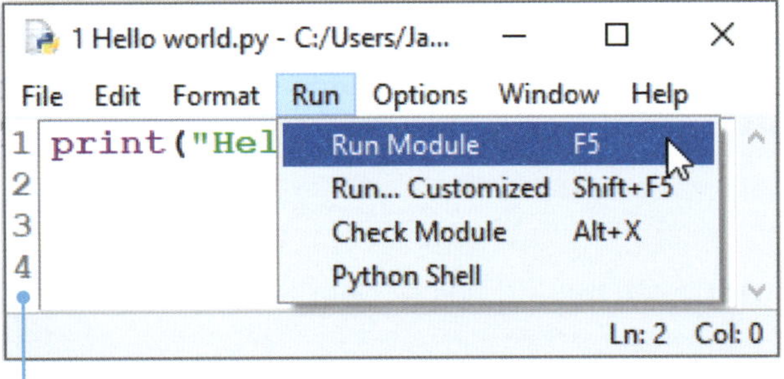

Top tip

To show the **line numbers** in Python, go to:

Options > Show Line Number

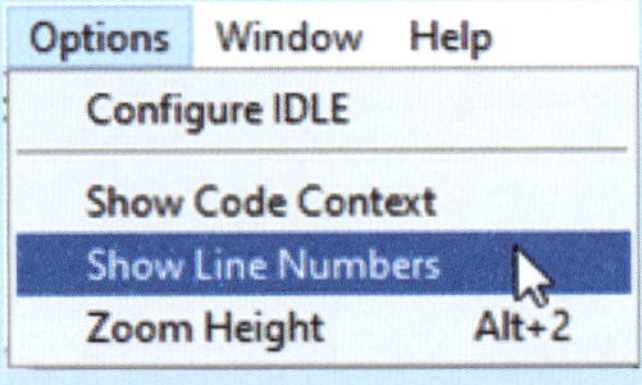

Writing code

Lines of code in a program are run in order one after the other. This type of **program flow** is known as a **sequence**.

To get input from a user, use:

Python syntax

```
input("Press Enter to continue")
```

How it works

The program **outputs** the text shown in green, then waits for the user to optionally **input** some text and press return. The text entered can be saved in a **variable** – see **page 90** for more information on variables.

The following program shows the title for an adventure game and asks the user to press enter to play the game.

Program 1: Adventure game.py

```
print("Adventure game")
print("--------------")
input("Press enter to play")
```

Program output

Write your mark here

1. (a) Match the words below with their meanings.

Syntax	Carry out the instructions in a program.
Line numbers	The order in which words and symbols are correctly placed in a programming language.
Run	Lines of code run in order, one after the other.
Sequence	A unique number given to each line of code.

[4]

(b) Complete the Python code below so that it outputs the text "Game Over!".

```
print(............................................................)
```

[1]

(c) Write **two** lines of Python code to output the following:

```
Instructions
------------
```

....

.... **[2]**

(d) Write **one** line of code that asks the user to press enter for the next level.

```
Press enter for the next level
```

.... **[2]**

(e) State the shortcut key which is used to run a program in Python.

.... **[1]**

Try it

Download Python from:
www.python.org/downloads

Now adapt Program 1 on the left to make it into an intro screen for a text adventure game of your choice.

Total /10

How well do you feel you know this topic?   

TOPIC 12.2 VARIABLES

Variables are used to store one item of data. The item could be a number or text.

To create and use a variable in Python, use:

Python syntax

```
length = 50
```

How it works

This line of code means:

- Create a variable with the name `length`
- Store the value `50` in the variable

Think of it as a box that has been labelled `length` and now stores the value `50`.

Programmers and computer scientists often use tricky words. So rather than saying 'store the value' they say '**assign** the value'.

The = symbol here is known as the **assignment operator**.

A programmer would read this line of code as "assign 50 to the length variable"

Did you know?

Programming languages call text a **string**.

Numbers are often referred to as **integers** (whole numbers) and **floating point numbers** (numbers with a decimal point).

Top tip

It's your choice what **variable name** to use. Variable names need to be meaningful and mustn't use spaces. They cannot start with a number. Examples include:

- `price`
- `firstName`
- `currentScore`

Outputting variables

The value stored in a variable is output by using print.

Program 2: Output age.py

```
age = 13
print("Age is:")
print(age)
```

Program output

```
Age is:
13
```

Storing inputs as variables

When the user inputs text, this may be stored in a variable. The text will always be stored as a string, even if it contains a number.

Program 3: Name and age.py

```
name = input("Enter name: ")
age = input("Enter age: ")
print(name)
print("You are ")
print(age)
```

Program output

```
Enter name: Freya
Enter age: 13
Freya
You are
13
```

Write your mark here

1. Complete the following text with the missing words below.

Assignment **String** **Variable**

When a program is running it needs to store values for later use. Each value is stored in a .... Values could be a .... (e.g. "Hello"), integer (e.g. 47) or floating point number (e.g. 8.72). In programming the = symbol is known as the .... operator when it is putting a value into a variable.

[3]

2 Give an appropriate variable name to store each of the items of data given in the table below. The first one has been completed for you.

Item of data	Suggested variable name
A score in a game.	score
The length of time to complete one lap around a racetrack.	
A password to log in to a website.	
Player 1 in a two player game.	

[3]

3. Look at the following code:

```
petName = input("Enter pet name: ")
print("Hello")
print(petName)
```

Write the output that the program will give if Rocky is entered into the program.

....

....

.... **[2]**

4 Complete the code below which will ask the user a question, then once they have entered an answer, it will tell them the answer they entered followed by the correct answer for them to check against.

```
city.................................. input("What is the capital of Italy?")
print("You said")
print( ...................................................... )
print("The correct answer is Rome")
```

[2]

Try it

Enter the code for Question 4 in Python. Now adapt the program so that it asks the user more questions before giving the answers.

Total ☐ /10

How well do you feel you know this topic?   

TOPIC 12.3

DATA TYPES

Variables store items of data known as **values**. Each value will be of a particular kind of data, for example a **string** or **integer**. These are known as **data types**.

Remember

The following are the most important **data types** that programmers use:

Data type	Meaning	Example
Integer	A whole number	`107`
Floating point number	A number with a decimal point	`23.568`
Character	One letter or symbol	`"A"`
String	A series of characters	`"Some text"`
Boolean	True or False	`True`

Converting data types

Data types often need to be converted from one type to another.

For instance, when a user enters a number, this will be stored as a string because all inputs are strings.

Before the number could be used in a calculation it needs to be converted.

For example:

Program 4: Age next year.py

```
age = input("Enter your age: ")
age = int(age)
age = age + 1
print("Age next year: " + str(age))
```

Program output

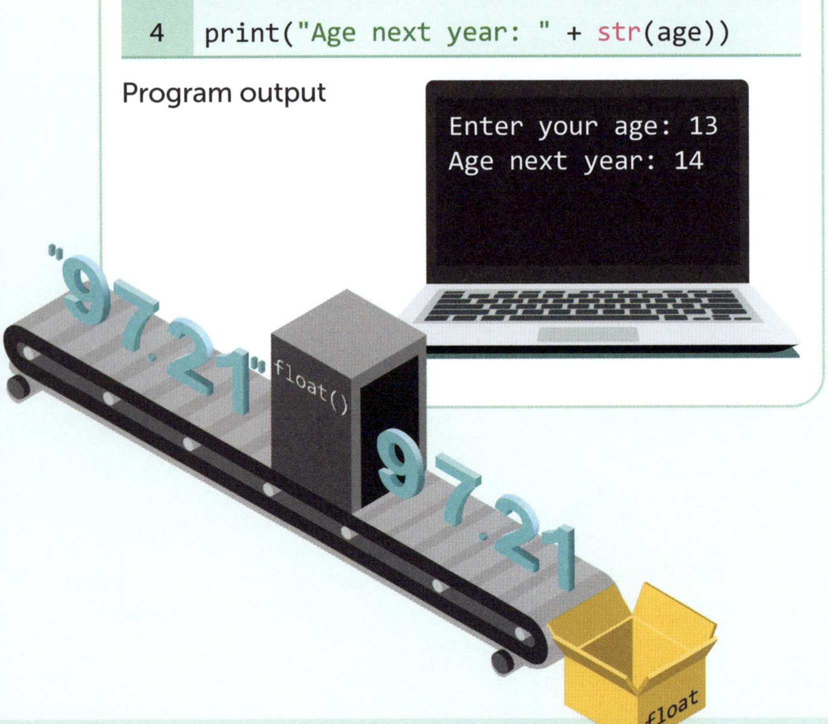

Conversion syntax

Syntax	Meaning
`int()`	Convert to an integer
`str()`	Convert to a string
`float()`	Convert to a floating point number.

Concatenation or addition?

Look at the following lines of code. Two of the lines of code use + symbols. What do you think each of these mean?

```
firstname = "Kai"
lastname = "Anderson"
fullname = firstname + lastname
score = 74
score = score + 1
```

The first + symbol is a **concatenation operator**. It is joining two strings together.

The second + symbol is an **addition operator**. It is adding 1 to the score.

Write your mark here

1. Match each of the following values with their datatype.

"Sophia"	Integer
18.3	Floating point number
14	String
False	Boolean

[4]

2 Give **two** uses for the + symbol in programming.

① ....

② .... **[2]**

3. Write the code needed to convert the string `"5.0"` to a floating point number.

.... **[1]**

4. Complete the code below which asks the user to enter the time taken to complete a race in seconds then outputs the time in minutes. Remember to check the data types that will be used and whether they need a conversion.

Note that in line 3, the / symbol means divide by.

```
1  seconds = ................................. ("Enter your race time in seconds")
2  seconds = ................................. (seconds)
3  minutes = seconds / 60
4  print("Your race time was " + ..................................... (minutes))
```

[3]

Try it

Make a Python program by entering the program for Question 4.

Now adapt the program so that it asks the user to enter the number of centimetres in a measurement. Then calculate the equivalent number of inches. There are 2.54 centimetres in one inch.

Total ☐ /10

How well do you feel you know this topic?   

TOPIC 12.4

ARITHMETIC

Computer programs often need to make calculations. The arithmetic rules are very similar to those used in maths.

Arithmetic operators

The following arithmetic operators are used in programming.

Arithmetic symbol	Meaning	Example
+	Add	`score = score + 1`
-	Subtract	`lives = lives - 1`
*	Multiply	`cm = metres * 100`
/	Divide	`metres = cm / 100`
**	Exponent power / indices	`squareArea = length**2`
()	Brackets	`tempF = (tempC * 9/5) + 32`

Did you know?

There are some differences between the **arithmetic operators** used in programming compared to those in Maths. This is because these symbols are easier to type on a keyboard.

Maths symbol	Python symbol
×	*
÷	/
length^2	`length**2`

Order of operations

The order of operations (also known as BIDMAS in maths) works the same way in Python. Calculations are carried out in the following order:

1. Brackets
2. Indices (power/exponent)
3. Divide and multiply
4. Addition and subtraction

Program 5: Calculations.py

```
score = 5
score = score + 1
print(score)

lives = 3
lives = lives - 1
print(lives)

cm = 150
metres = cm / 100
print(metres)

length = 5
squareArea = length**2
print(squareArea)

tempC = 20
tempF = (tempC * 9/5) + 32
print(tempF)
```

Program output

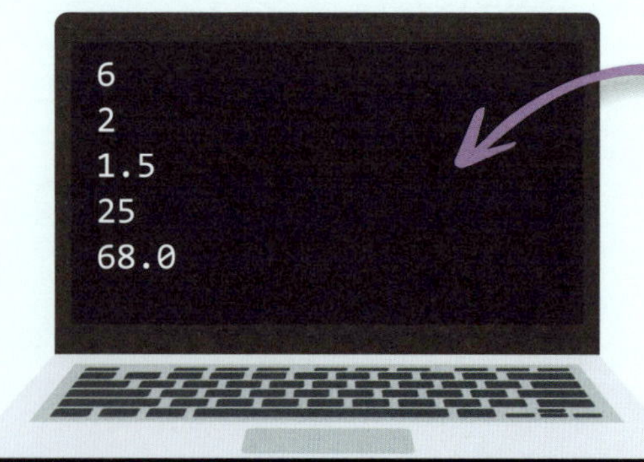

```
6
2
1.5
25
68.0
```

Write your mark here

1. The table below shows Python calculations. Write the result for each one.

Python calculation	Result
`5 + 7`	
`9 * 3`	
`12 / 4`	
`5**2`	

[4]

2. The table below shows two short Python programs and their outputs. Write the arithmetic operator needed for both programs.

	Program	Output

1	`scoreA = 50`
	`scoreB = 60`
	`teamScore = scoreA ............. scoreB`
	`print(teamScore)`
		110

2	`cash = 5.80`
	`spend = 3.00`
	`cash = cash .............. spend`
	`print(cash)`
		2.8

[2]

3. The table below shows four short Python programs. Write the output for each program.

	Program	Output

1	`mealCost = 20.00`
	`people = 5`
	`totalCost = mealCost * people`
	`print(totalCost)`	

2	`cakeSlices = 8`
	`people = 4`
	`slicesEach = cakeSlices / people`
	`print(slicesEach)`	

3	`length = 2`
	`cubicArea = length**3`
	`print(cubicArea)`	

4	`price = 100`
	`totalPrice = price + (price * 0.2)`
	`print(totalPrice)`	

[4]

Try it

Look at the code on the left from lines 13-15.

Adapt this code in Python so that it asks the user to enter a length then outputs the area of a square with that length.

Adapt the code further so that it also outputs the volume of a cube.

Total /10

How well do you feel you know this topic?   

TOPIC 12.5

BRANCHING

A key feature in programming is the ability for a program to take different branches in the code based on a **condition**.

Did you know?

Branching in programming is also known as **selection**.

Python syntax

```
if age >= 13 and age <= 19:
  print("Teenager")
elif age < 13:
  print("Child")
else:
  print("Adult")
```

Teenager
`if age >= 13 and age <= 19:`

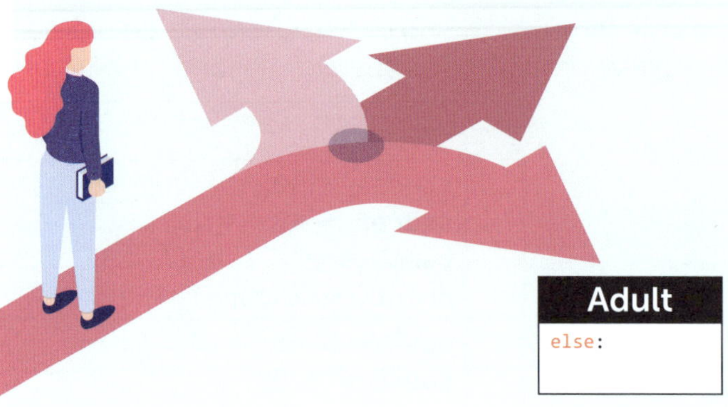

Adult
`else:`

How it works

The first `if` statement checks the condition. The age variable needs to be greater than or equal to 13 and also less than or equal to 19.

The `:` symbol (colon) shows the end of the condition. Read it as *'then'*.

The code that is indented over by one tab will be run if the condition is true.

`elif` stands for else if. This condition is checked if the first condition was false. `elif` statements are optional or there can be more than one `elif` if lots of conditions need to be checked.

The `else` code is run only if all the previous conditions are false. `else` statements are optional.

Program 6: Test scores.py

```
score = int(input("Enter score: "))
if score == 100:
  print("Perfect!")
elif score >= 60:
  print("Pass")
else:
  print("Try harder")
```

```
Enter score: 60
Pass
```

Program output

Comparison operators

Comparison operators are used in conditions to compare variables or values.

Note that == is used for **equals**. This is because = is used for assignment of variables.

Comparison operator	Meaning
<	Less than
<=	Less than or equal to
>	Greater than
>=	Greater than or equal to
==	Equal to
!=	Not equal to

Boolean operators

Boolean operators allow many conditions to be combined.

Boolean operator	Example
and	`score >= 40 and score < 60`
or	`score == 99 or score == 98`
not	`not score == 0`

Write your mark here

1. Match the parts of Python branching syntax with their meaning.

`if`	Used with an **if** or **elif** statement to determine which branch should be taken.
`elif`	A statement which will be run if all other **if** and **elif** conditions are false.
`else`	The first statement when branching is used.
Condition	An optional statement which has a condition to determine branching.

[4]

2. Complete the code below by filling in the gaps.

```
password = input("Please enter your password: ")
if password ................................ "monster15":
  print("Welcome")
................................
  print("Incorrect password")
```

[3]

3. The following program asks the user how many apples they would like to buy. If they would like to buy between 1 and 9 apples, the program outputs that they must "Buy individually". Complete the condition for the **elif** statement.

```
quantity = int(input("How many apples would you like? "))
if quantity < 1:
  print("You must buy at least 1")

elif ........................................................................................................:
  print("Buy individually")
else:
  print("Buy in bulk")
```

[3]

Try it

In Python, adapt the code from Program 6 on the left so that it takes a score out of 10 for someone's performance on the questions on this page.

Create outputs that are appropriate for the score.

Now create a quiz that asks the user to enter the answer. If they get the correct answer say "Well done.", otherwise, let them know the correct answer.

Total /10

How well do you feel you know this topic?    

TOPIC 12.6

LOOPING

Looping in programming allows instructions in a block of code to be repeated. There are two types of loop in Python. The **while** loop and the **for** loop.

> **Did you know?**
>
> **Looping** in programming is also known as **iteration** or **repetition**.

Python syntax

```
while password != "monster15":
  password = input("Enter password: ")
```

How it works

The condition `password != "monster15"` is checked at the start of the loop.

If it is true then the code within the loop is repeated until the condition is false.

Program 7: Guess number.py

```
guess = -1
while guess != 7:
  guess = int(input("Guess number: "))
print("You got it.")
```

Program output

```
Guess number: 3
Guess number: 15
Guess number: 7
You got it.
```

Python syntax

```
for i in range(0, 6):
  print(i)
```

How it works

A **for** loop is used to repeat a certain number of times. In this case, `range(0,6)` means repeat from 0 to 6 inclusive, but not including 6. The output would be:

Program 8: Five times table.py

```
for i in range(1, 6):
  fiveTimes = i * 5
  print(fiveTimes)
```

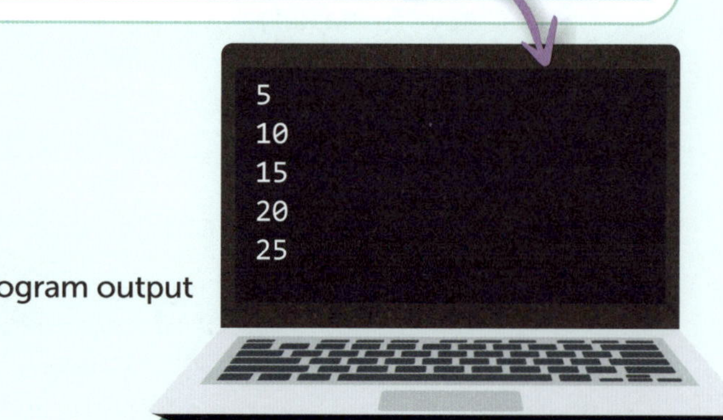

Program output

1. Tick **two** types of loop that are available in Python.

A	If loop	☐	**D**	Repeat loop	☐
B	For loop	☐	**E**	Comparison loop	☐
C	Condition loop	☐	**F**	While loop	☐

[2]

Write your mark here

2. The following code is used to work out part of the six times table.

```
for i in range(1,3):
    sixTimes = i * 6
    output = str(i) + " x 6 = " + str(sixTimes)
    print(output)
```

Give the output from this program.

....

.... **[2]**

3. The following code is for a game where the user has to guess the number the computer is thinking of.

```
target = 32
guess = -1
while guess != target:
    if guess > target:
        print("Too high.")
    else:
        print("Too low.")
    guess = int(input("Guess the number: "))
print("You got it!")
```

(a) Complete the table to show the output from the program for the different guesses that are input.

Input guess	Output
17	
-1	
33	
32	

[4]

(b) There is a problem with the program when it is run. Describe the problem.

....

.... **[2]**

Try it

Look up how to generate random numbers in Python.

🔍 Random numbers Python

Adapt the number guessing program above in question 3 so that the computer generates a random target number.

Total ☐ /10

How well do you feel you know this topic? ☺ ☐  ☐  ☐

TOPIC 13.1

ARTIFICIAL INTELLIGENCE

Artificial Intelligence (AI) is where a computer system has human-like intelligence and 'thinks' like a human with the ability to **problem solve** and **learn**.

How it works

AI relies on a **set of rules** which are used to determine which actions to take.

For example, AI in a self-driving car could be used to detect a zebra crossing. A **probability** of each object being detected could be given. Then a set of rules determines the actions to take. In the below example, there is only a 60% chance that a zebra crossing has been detected as not all of the painted lines can be seen.

Uses

Some uses for AI include:

- A computer chess player
- Non-playing characters (NPCs) in computer games
- Self-driving cars
- Robot vacuum cleaners
- Facial recognition

Ethics

Ethics deals with moral principles including the right and wrong actions that need to be taken in a given situation. The use of AI presents many ethical issues:

- *What action should be taken if facial recognition detects a suspect for a crime with only a 60% probability or certainty it was them?*
- *What happens if the AI rules are in the interests of a small number of people or large companies rather than in the interests of the majority of people?*
- *What happens to people's jobs if AI is used to drive taxis, write articles or calculate tax?*
- *What happens if AI is biased against certain minority groups or certain opinions?*

Careful consideration of these types of questions needs to be made before AI products are launched, if harmful side effects are to be avoided.

Write your mark here

1. Look at the image on the left which shows what a self-driving car has detected in front of it along with rules that it needs to use.
   Complete the table below to determine the actions of the car.

Car detection and probability	Car action
School: 100%	
Slow sign: 100%	
Girl: 90% **AND** Zebra crossing: 60%	
Zebra crossing: 100% **AND** girl: 0% **AND** boy: 0%	

[4]

2. Give **two** rules that could be given to a robot vacuum cleaner.

   ① ....

   ....

   ② ....

   .... **[2]**

3. AI is currently being used to create written text for people. For instance, this could be for a magazine or newspaper article, or the text used for an advertisement.
   Describe some ethical issues with this use.

   ....

   ....

   ....

   ....

   ....

   ....

   ....

   .... **[4]**

Try it

Think of a set of rules that could be created to control a robot vacuum cleaner.

Now consider if the vacuum cleaner could use a grid as a map of the house. It would be able to mark what furniture is stored in the house and where the vacuum had cleaned.

Improve the rules you have created for the vacuum cleaner to follow.

Total ☐ /10

How well do you feel you know this topic?    

TOPIC 13.2

MACHINE LEARNING

Machine learning (**ML**) is one way in which **artificial intelligence** is created. In machine learning, a computer system works out the rules that will be used for itself.

How it works

In **machine learning**, a computer system is given **training data**. It then uses this to create the **rules** that will be used.

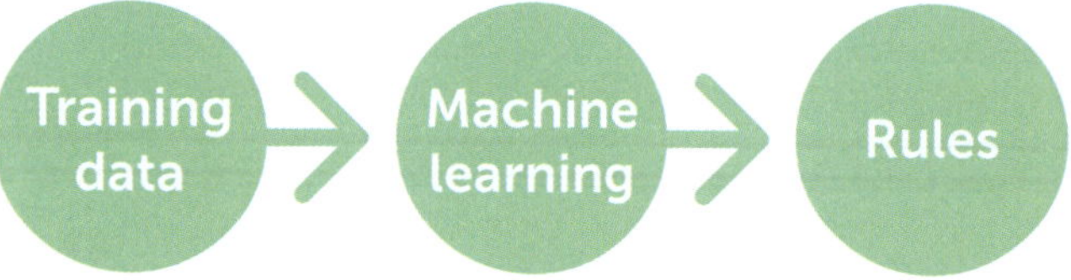

Machine learning is good at finding patterns in **unstructured data**. Structured data is organised, such as the sender of an email, or a log in time. Unstructured data is not organised. Such as the main text of an email.

Uses

Some uses for machine learning include:

- Detecting spam email
- Classifying inappropriate social media posts
- Facial recognition
- Screening medical scans

Training data

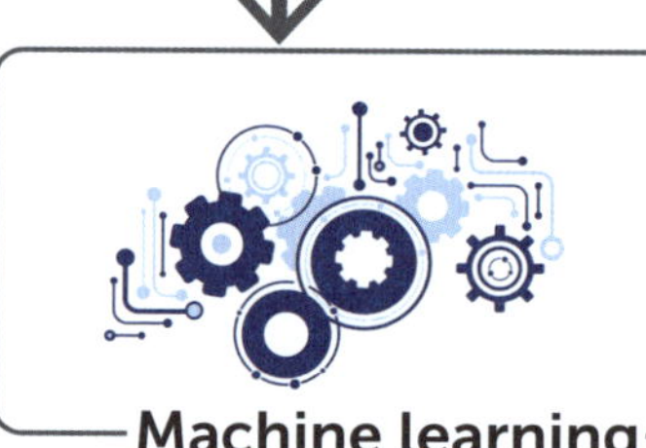

Machine learning

Rules

- Cats have two open eyes
- Cats have whiskers
- Cats have tails
- Cats have four legs when standing and two legs when sitting

Strengths and weaknesses

The following are some of the strengths and weaknesses of machine learning.

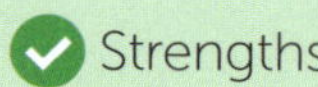

Strengths	Weaknesses
• It finds patterns that humans don't realise are there • It handles unstructured data • It improves, the more training data it is given	• It requires lots of good quality training data • Errors are hard to detect • Results may need interpreting • If the training data is misclassified it could lead to bias

1. Match the words below with their meaning.

Training data		Data that hasn't been organised in a specific way. For example, the main text in a letter.
Machine learning		The output that results from machine learning, used to make artificially intelligent decisions.
Rules		The data and information which is input into the machine learning and used to help it learn.
Unstructured data		The programs and algorithms which make use of training data to create rules.

[4]

2. Look at the following image of a cat and the training data and rules shown on the left.

(a) Explain **one** reason why the image might not be classified as a cat with the rules generated by machine learning.

....

....

.... **[2]**

(b) Explain how this problem could be fixed.

....

....

.... **[2]**

(c) Describe how machine learning could be used in medicine to detect broken arms from x-rays.

....

....

.... **[2]**

Write your mark here

Total ☐ **/10**

Try it

Research different ways in which machine learning is being used.

For each of the different ways you find, write down the different training data that would be needed.

How well do you feel you know this topic? ☺ ☐ 😐 ☐ ☹ ☐

TOPIC 14.1

BITMAPS AND VECTORS

There are two different types of computer graphics. Bitmap graphics and vector graphics. Each have different properties and uses.

How it works

Bitmap images work by dividing up an image into small squares known as pixels.

Black and white images

Black and white images use 1 bit for each pixel. 0 means black and 1 means white.

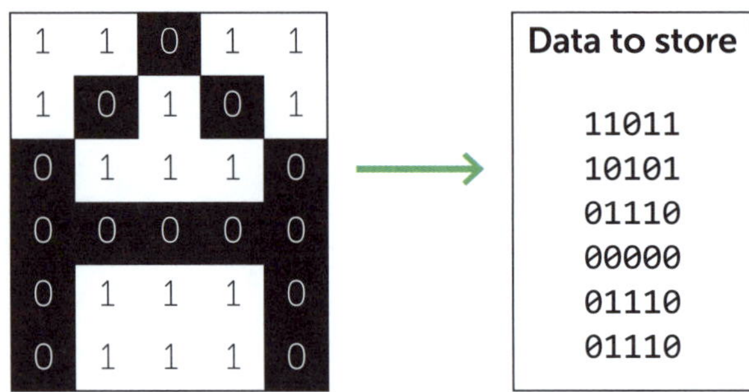

Colour images

Colour images will have different a number of bits to store the colour for each pixel.

A **2-bit image** uses 2 bits for each pixel and allows for up to four colours to be used in the image using codes 00, 01, 10 and 11.

A **colour map** is also stored which shows the colour which each bit pattern corresponds to.

11	11	11	11	11	11	11	11	11	11	11	11	11
11	11	00	00	11	11	11	11	11	11	11	11	11
11	00	01	01	00	11	11	11	11	11	11	11	11
00	01	11	10	10	00	00	00	00	00	00	00	00
00	01	10	10	10	10	10	10	10	10	10	10	00
00	01	10	10	10	00	00	01	00	00	00	01	00
11	00	10	10	00	11	11	00	11	11	00	01	00
11	11	00	00	11	11	11	11	11	11	11	00	11
11	11	11	11	11	11	11	11	11	11	11	11	11

Colour map

00	
01	
10	
11	

Did you know?

Vector graphics are made from **lines**, **curves** and **fills** (coloured in parts). Vector graphic files tend to be smaller in file size than their bitmap equivalent.

If a vector graphic is expanded in size, then the quality remains the same. If a bitmap graphic is expanded, it becomes **pixelated**.

Vector image

Bitmap image

Did you know?

The word **pixel** is an abbreviation of **pic**ture **el**ement. If more pixels are used in an image it has a **higher resolution** and creates an image with higher quality.

Bit depth

Bit depth is the number of bits used for each pixel. High quality images often make use of **24-bits** for each pixel. This allows for a choice of 16.8 million colours and is known as **true colour** as the colours appear to be natural.

1. (a) Use the binary data below to complete the bitmap image.

Data to store

```
00000
11100
11001
10011
00111
00000
```


[2]

(b) State the letter that is being stored in the bitmap image.

.... **[1]**

2. Match the words on the left with their meaning on the right.

Pixelated	Shows how each bit pattern relates to each colour.
Vector image	An image that uses a single 1 or 0 for each pixel.
Bitmap image	An image that appears blocky.
Colour map	An image made from shapes, lines and curves.
1-bit image	An image made up of a grid of pixels.

[5]

3. Tick **two** of the following methods that will result in higher quality images.

A Using image compression ☐

B Using a higher resolution ☐

C Making each pixel larger ☐

D Using a higher bit depth ☐ **[2]**

Write your mark here

Try it

Pixel art graphics are created by editing each individual pixel.

Create your own original pixel art either on a sheet of graph paper or using the pencil tool in image editing software such as Microsoft Paint or Adobe® Photoshop®.

Total ☐ /10

How well do you feel you know this topic?  

TOPIC 14.2

IMAGE EDITING

Images are created and altered using **image editing software** such as Adobe® Photoshop®, Serif® Affinity® Photo and GIMP. Different images and photos may be combined to make a **composite** image.

Image resolution

The **resolution** of an image is the number of pixels it contains.

For **digital images**, the **pixels per inch** (**PPI**) shows the number of pixels contained in each inch of the screen. Digital images typically need to be **72 PPI** or higher to be clear.

Printed images use **dots per inch** (**DPI**) to show the number of ink dots which will be contained in each inch of the page. Typically, images need to be **300 PPI** or higher to be printed sharply.

Did you know?

Higher resolution images have larger file sizes.

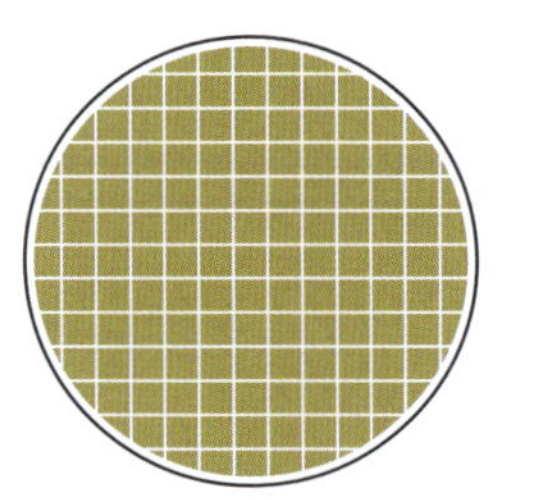

72 PPI

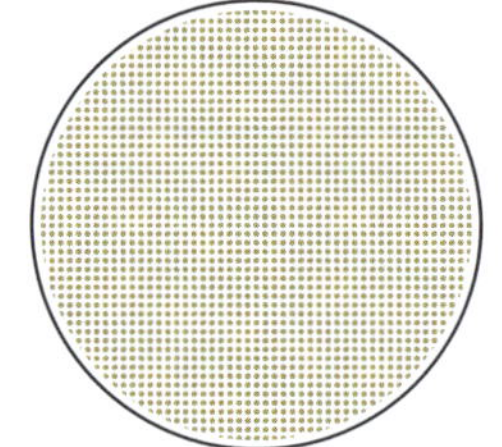

300 DPI

Layers

When editing images, different parts of the image are placed on different **layers**. This allows each layer to be altered without affecting others. Layers may also be **hidden**.

Editing file with layers

Final graphics file

Editing tools

A number of **editing tools** are available in image editing software.

Editing tool	Purpose	Example
Paintbrush Tool	Creating **brush strokes**.	
Paint Bucket Tool Gradient Tool	Applying a **fill** or **gradient** to a shape or background.	
Text Tool	Adding **text**.	Some text

Transform

Image editing software is able to transform parts of an image in the following ways:

Transformation	Example
Rotate	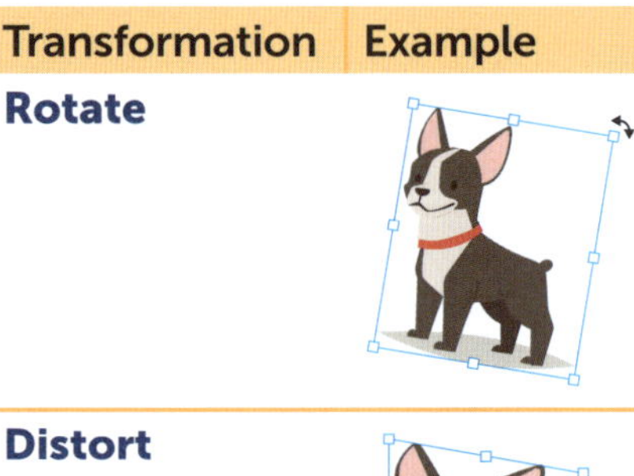
Distort	
Resize 	

Write your mark here

1. Tick the correct resolution to be used in each of the following:

Use	Resolution			
	300 PPI	300 DPI	72 PPI	72 DPI
A photograph for a magazine				
A photograph for a website				

[2]

2. Look at the following image then state the **two** transformations that have been applied to it.

Original image	**Image 1**	**Image 2**
State the transformation that has been used.		

[2]

3. Label each part of the image with the **three** editing tools that have been used to create it.

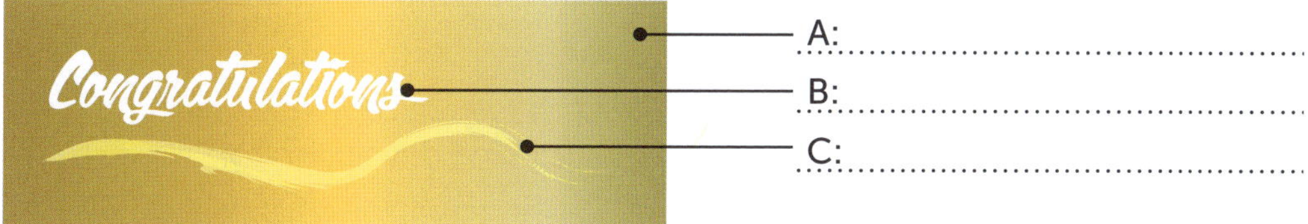

A: ....

B: ....

C: ....

[3]

4. (a) Give **one** advantage of using layers when image editing.

.... **[1]**

(b) Give **one** advantage and **one** disadvantage of using a high resolution for a photo.

Advantage: .... **[1]**

Disadvantage: .... **[1]**

Try it

GIMP is free image editing software.
Try downloading it at:
https://www.gimp.org/
Now try using layers to make a composite image with tools similar to those given on the left.

Total

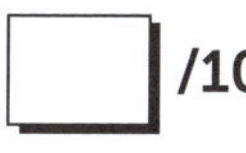

/10

How well do you feel you know this topic?

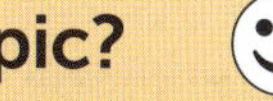

TOPIC **15.1**

SPRITES AND PROPERTIES

GDevelop is a game engine which allows PC, mobile and web games to be created. It makes use of **visual programming** which is easier than programming with text languages such as Python.

Sprites

Sprites are **objects** which sit above the **background** and are a key component in GDevelop. For instance, in a tennis game, the players, the net and the tennis ball would each be sprites.

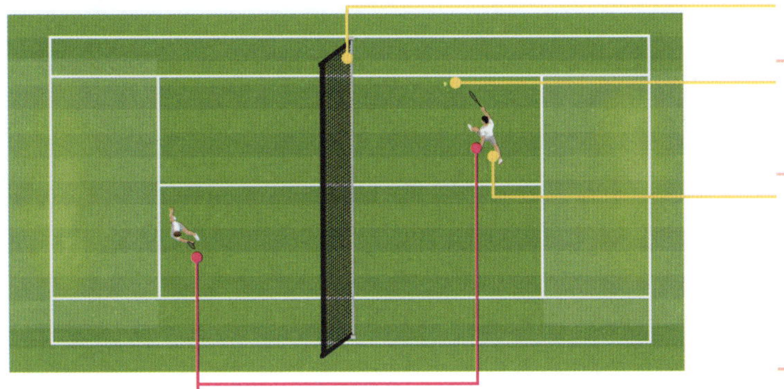

Sprite name	Sprite
Net	
Ball	
Player	

These two sprites are two **instances** of the Player **object**.

If the graphics for the Player object are changed, then they will be changed for both instances.

Sprite properties

Each sprite has its own **properties**. Some common ones are given in the table below.

Properties	Meaning
X	**x-axis** position
Y	**y-axis** position
Angle	The rotated angle (from 0 to 360)
Z Order	The order of objects on the **z-axis**
Layer	The name of the **layer**
Width	The **width** of the sprite
Height	The **height** of the sprite

GDevelop coordinates

The top left **pixel** on the screen is (0,0). The coordinate order is (x,y), the same order as in maths.

The pixel coordinates are the size of the screen the game is being developed for.

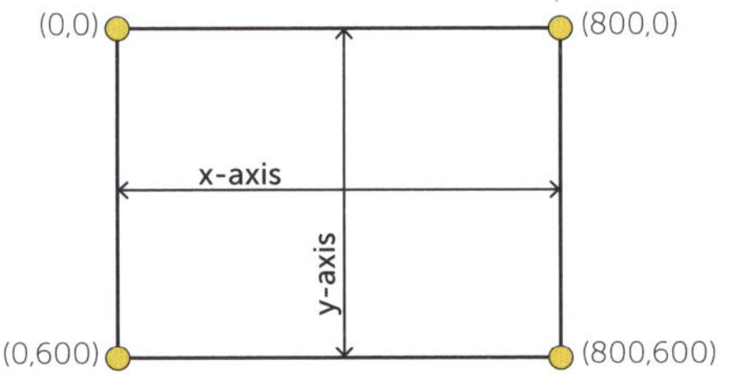

Layers

Sprites can be placed on different **layers**. Those on the top layer appear above those on layers beneath.

Within each layer, each sprite has a **Z Order** number. Sprites with a higher number appear above those with a lower number.

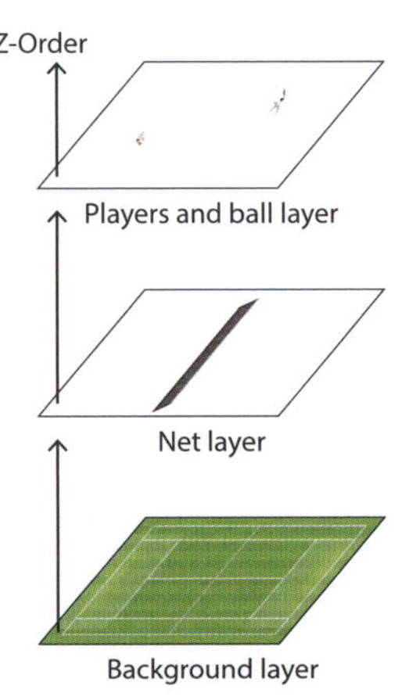

Write your mark here

1. Each sprite in a game will have its own properties. Match each of the properties below with their meaning.

X	The orientation of the sprite in degrees.
Y	The width of the sprite.
Width	The position of the sprite on the horizontal (left-right) axis.
Angle	The position of the sprite on the vertical (up-down) axis.

[4]

2. Litter Picker is a game being developed for young children. The player controls a person in the game who picks up any litter they find. They have to pick up as much litter as they can within 1 minute. Sometimes they are able to collect sweets from neighbours. If they eat the sweets they go faster.

Two sprites needed for the game are the player and litter. Name **two** other sprites that will be needed.

Sprite 1: ....

Sprite 2: ....

[2]

3. Complete the text with the words below.

Properties **Objects** **Instances**

When creating a game, a number of .... need to be made. An object, such as litter will be created which is for a general item of litter. Different .... of this litter are then created which may have different ....

[3]

4. Litter randomly appears in the game. Newer litter has a higher Z order. Two items of litter appear with the same X and Y properties.

Tick the correct box to show what happens in this case.

A Two instances of the same sprite cannot appear at the same point. ☐

B The newer litter has a higher Z order so appears below the older litter. ☐

C The newer litter has a higher Z order so appears above the older litter. ☐

[1]

Try it

GDevelop is free to download and use to create simple games. There is an online version or it can be downloaded from:

https://gdevelop.io/

There are lots of help guides and example games to look at on the website.

Total ☐ **/10**

How well do you feel you know this topic? ☐  ☐ 

TOPIC 15.2 GAME DESIGN

Game design is the first stage of game development. It is the process of creating the theme, objectives and rules of the game along with the designs for the characters.

Themes

The **theme** of a game is important for helping to immerse the player. Some examples of themes include:

- Space
- Pirates
- Fantasy
- Sports (car racing, football)
- Superheroes
- Science fiction

The **setting** of a game gives specific parts of the theme such as:

- The location
- The time period (modern, historical)
- The imaginary environment (if not based on reality)

Objectives

The **objectives** of the game are what the user has to achieve to progress and complete the game.

Common objectives include:

- Carrying out a task as quickly as possible
- Collecting coins
- Collecting keys to open doors
- Winning a race
- Solving a puzzle
- Carrying out a mission

Each game will have **rules**. For instance, in a platform game there may be a rule that if the player sprite falls off a platform it returns to the start of the level.

Did you know?

GDevelop allows you to import graphics for a new sprite or to create new original graphics using the **Piskel editor**.

GDevelop also allows sprites to use **animation**. A new image is imported or created for each frame of animation.

Sprite properties

Characters and other key parts of a game's look are firstly designed using **concept art**. These are often **sketches** that are used by designers or 3D modellers to create the actual characters.

1. A computer game allows a player to race different cars against other player's cars or computer controlled cars. A screenshot from the game is shown. The game takes place in a futuristic city environment.

Write your mark here

Identify each of the following:

(a) The theme of the game:

.... **[1]**

(b) The setting of the game:

.... **[1]**

(c) The objective of the game:

.... **[1]**

(d) Identify **three** possible rules that the game could have.

Rule 1: ....

.... **[1]**

Rule 2: ....

.... **[1]**

Rule 3: ....

.... **[1]**

2. A spy themed game asks the player to undertake missions.

(a) Explain the purpose of concept art for the main player in the game.

....

.... **[2]**

(b) Explain how the sprite could be made to appear to walk.

....

.... **[2]**

Try it

First choose a theme for a game then design the concept art for the main character in the game.

Use GDevelop's Piskel editor (or another graphics editing program) to create the design for the main character. Then add the sprite to a new GDevelop game.

Total

/10

How well do you feel you know this topic? ☺ ☐ 😐 ☐ ☹ ☐

TOPIC 15.3

GAMES PROGRAMMING

Games programming is the technical side of making games. Games programmers are responsible for adding all the rules of the game that make it work correctly. A good understanding of advanced mathematics, physics and programming is usually required.

Did you know?

The rules of games are often programmed using **behaviours** and **events**.

Behaviours

Behaviours allow many rules to be given to objects or sprites with just one click.

They are added within objects in the behaviours tab.

Some common behaviours include:

Behaviour	Meaning
Platform	A platform prevents sprites from falling through it.
Platformer character	Makes a sprite move when keys are pressed or fall down if it isn't on a platform.
Draggable object	Makes a sprite possible to pick up and drag.

Objectives

The programming of rules in GDevelop is carried out with **events**.

Below is a game called Dino Coin. The player controls the dinosaur to collect coins.

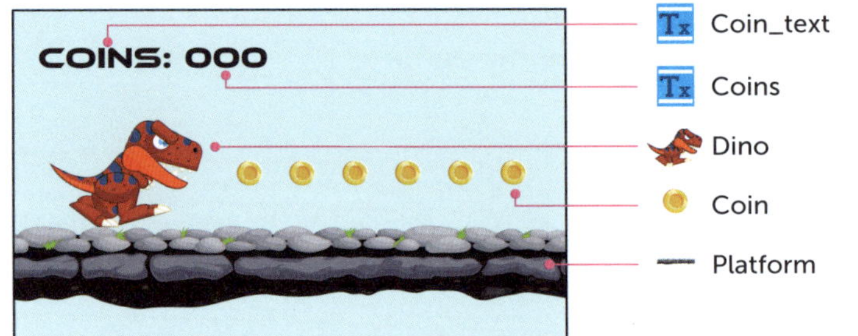

The **Platformer Character behaviour** has been applied to the dinosaur and the **Platform behaviour** has been applied to the platform.

Events are added by first going to the **Events tab**.

Each event contains a **condition** and an **action**. When the condition is met, the action(s) will be run.

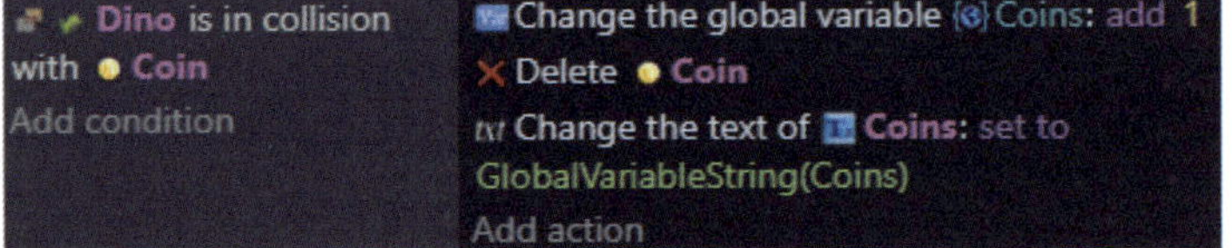

As games are developed, the **Preview** button allows the game to be tested.

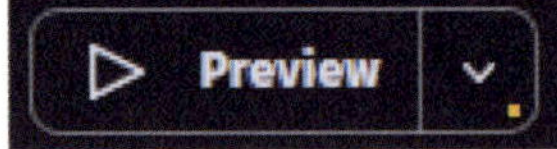

1. Match the words below with their meanings in GDevelop.

Behaviour	An expression which will result in True or False. This determines whether code will be run or not.
Event	The code that is run if a condition is True.
Condition	A set of events which are easily added to an object, such as making a sprite a Platformer Character.
Action	A condition and the action which will occur if it is true.

[4]

Write your mark here

2. Look at the screenshot of the Dino Coin game on the left.

(a) The dinosaur sprite starts at position (450, 288).
Describe what the following code does.

Condition	Actions
The y position of Dino > SceneWindowHeight()	Change the x position of Dino: set to 450 Change the y position of Dino: set to 288

....

....

....

.... **[2]**

(b) A developer of the Dino Coin game wants to add an enemy sprite to the game.
Tick the suitable behaviour that they should apply to the enemy sprite.

A Platform ☐ **C** Draggable object ☐

B Platformer character ☐ **D** No behaviour should be applied ☐

[1]

(c) When the dinosaur touches the enemy, it returns back to (450,288).
Write an event for this.

Event	
Condition	Action

[3]

Try it

Build a simple platform game like Dino Coin. Remember there are lots of tutorial videos and web pages to help online.

Total ☐ /10

How well do you feel you know this topic? ☺ ☐ 😐 ☐ ☹ ☐

TOPIC 16.1 COMPUTER MISUSE

Computer misuse is the name given to **illegal activities** involving computers such as gaining **unauthorised access** to computer systems or files, **preventing or hindering access** to computer programs or data, or **impairing the operation** of programs or data.

Did you know?

The **Computer Misuse Act** makes these activities illegal. **Computer misuse** can result in fines or a prison sentence.

Computer misuse is often carried out by guessing **weak passwords** or tricking a user into installing malware which has a **backdoor**. The backdoor allows a hacker access to the system.

Hacking

Hacking is illegally accessing a computer or data without permission. A **hacker** may be motivated by one or more of the following:

- The challenge of breaking into a system
- Money
- To steal or modify information
- To expose wrongdoing
- For political reasons
- To embarrass people

Malware

Malware is the name given to **mal**icious soft**ware**. These are programs which cause damage to data or cause a computer system not to work correctly.

Malware examples include:

Viruses	These **replicate** to **infect** more and more computers. They then delete or damage files and software
Adware	These show the user unwanted adverts, usually with pop-up tabs or windows.
Ransomware	This type of malware **encrypts** the data on a hard drive so it cannot be read unless a ransom is paid.

Protecting against malware

To protect against malware and computer misuse, make sure to do the following:

- Update software and apps
- Use strong passwords
- Only download files from websites you trust
- Never visit or download from illegal sites such as those sharing copyrighted music, films or software.

Strong passwords

It is important to use **strong passwords** to protect computer systems. Strong passwords should have:

- At least 10 characters
- A mixture of uppercase and lowercase letters
- At least one number
- At least one **special character** such as !£$%&~#

Making use of three different words with the above rules helps to make a strong password that is easier to remember. For example:

froGphone5%tongue

1. Match the words below with their meanings.

Virus	Software that causes unwanted adverts to appear on a computer.
Malware	Encrypts data on a hard drive until a fee is paid to be able to read the data again.
Ransomware	Any type of software that is created to harm a computer, software or files.
Adware	A type of malware that damages files and software.

[4]

Write your mark here

2. (a) Four passwords are given below. Tick the **two** strong passwords that are shown.

A maGazine4tooth&queen ☐ **C** Football25 ☐

B birthdayinsect ☐ **D** fq=FNrTThi+5 ☐

[2]

(b) One way to protect a computer from misuse is to use a strong password. Give **two** other ways to protect against computer misuse.

① ....

....

② ....

.... **[2]**

3. The following is an example of a weak password.

dramaHair

Give **two** reasons why it is a weak password.

① ....

....

② ....

.... **[2]**

Try it

Search for:

Check password strength

Then use a site you find to test the quality of the passwords given above. Now try checking other passwords you think up. Don't use real passwords as you don't want the website or other people to see them.

Total ☐ /10

How well do you feel you know this topic? ☺ ☐  

TOPIC 16.2

COPYRIGHT

Copyright is a way of protecting creative works from being copied without permission. This allows authors, musicians, actors and photographers to control how their work is used or reproduced.

Copyright statements

Copyright statements are usually placed at the start of books and magazines and at the end of the final credits in films and TV programmes.

The law which covers copyright is known as the **Copyright, Designs and Patents Act**.

Did you know?

A **work** is the name given to a product that can be copyrighted. Examples of works include:

- Films
- Books
- TV programmes
- Magazines

Ideas cannot be copyrighted. So, for example, a mathematical formula will not have copyright protection.

Length of copyright

Copyright protection starts as soon as a work is created. Once the protection ends, anyone can use or copy the work for free.

The length of time the copyright lasts for in the UK depends on the type of work.

Type of work	Length copyright lasts
Books	70 years after the author's death
Music	70 years after it's first published
Films	70 years after the last death of the director, script writer or composer of the music
TV/Radio broadcast	50 years from the date of first broadcast

Is it legal?

The following are examples that would be **legal** and **illegal** under copyright law.

Legal

- Storing video on a tablet for offline use in an app for a streaming service that allows this.
- Add a copyrighted photo to a website after getting permission from the photographer.

Illegal

- Paying to download a music track with a personal licence, then sharing the track with a friend.
- Adding a copyrighted image from the web to a work presentation without having a licence or permission to do this.

Write your mark here

1. Sam Heath published his book "Learning to Fish" in 2024.
Complete the below copyright statement which should be printed in the book.

.... Sam Heath .... **[3]**

2. Tick **two** examples of works that could be copyrighted.

A	A film	☐	**C**	An idea	☐
B	A mathematical formula	☐	**D**	A book	☐

[2]

3. Name the law which covers copyright.

.... **[1]**

4. The table below shows two scenarios. For each scenario state how long the copyright will last for.

Scenario	How long the copyright lasts for
① A book that has just been published.	
② A TV programme that has just been broadcast for the first time.	

[3]

5. Look at the following scenario and tick the correct box.
Scenario: Anika has paid for a soundtrack. When buying the track, the terms and conditions say that it is for personal use. Anika adds the track to a video she has made and then uploads this to YouTube.

A This is legal ☐
B This is illegal ☐
C This is legal as long as Anika credits the person who wrote the music ☐

[1]

Try it

Photo libraries provide photos that can be used by paying a fee. Some libraries are free.

Search for:

Photo library

Try some paid for and free photo libraries. Find out the conditions or cost to using the photos. Also look at the quality of photos they provide for topics you are interested in.

Total

☐ /10

How well do you feel you know this topic?   

TOPIC **16.3**

HEALTH AND SAFETY

When using computers and electronic equipment, it is important that people are kept safe from any danger or long term health effects. Health and safety is an important consideration for employers, but it should also be carefully considered for home and school users.

Reducing eyestrain and headaches

Looking at screens all day may cause **eyestrain** and **headaches**. Use the following tips to reduce these:

- Look away regularly
- Adjust the lighting in the room
- Reduce the amount of time looking at screens (**screentime**)
- Take regular breaks from using screens
- Have regular eye checkups and use glasses or contact lenses if needed

Did you know?

Health and safety includes the following aspects:

- User posture
- Training in how to use equipment safely
- Correct lighting
- Removing **trip hazards**
- Regular **electrical testing**
- Suitable **fire extinguishers**
- Access to fire escapes

Health and safety regulations

These regulations cover the setup of computers in workplaces. Computers should be set up so that they have:

- **No flickering** from the display
- An ability to **tilt** and **swivel** the display
- No **reflections** or **glare** from the display

Top tip

Devices such as smartphones, tablets and computers emit **blue light**. This may disrupt sleep patterns.

To reduce this problem, make use of **nighttime settings** on computers, smartphones and tablets. This will reduce the amount of blue light emitted and make the screen have a warm orange tint.

Posture

This diagram shows good posture for using a computer. Notice each of the following:

A: **Adjustable screen** – slightly below eye level

B: Elbow angle between 90°-120° (here the angle is around 100°)

C: **Wrist support** on the keyboard

D: **Adjustable seat**

E: **Lumbar support** (for lower back)

F: Feet touch the floor or a **footrest**

G: Straight back

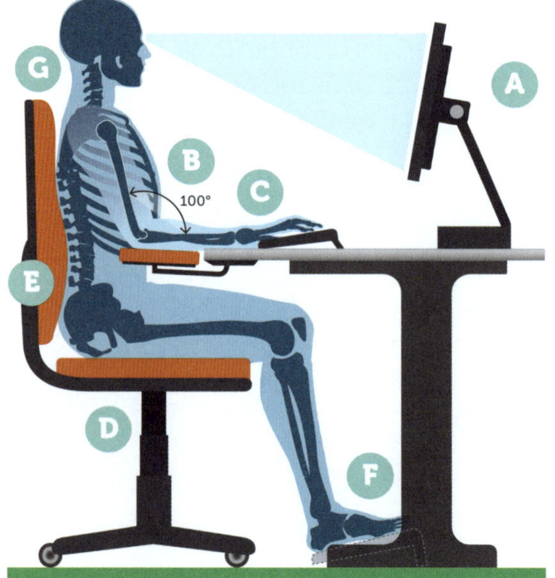

Write your mark here

1. Screen use can impact health.

   (a) Give **one** negative effect of using screens that emit blue light in the late evening.

   .... **[1]**

   (b) Give **one** way that blue light could be reduced on screens.

   .... **[1]**

   (c) Tick **three** points that are covered in the health and safety regulations for the use of computer displays.

A	The display doesn't have any reflections on it.	☐
B	The display must make use of a colour filter	☐
C	The display must be high definition (HD)	☐
D	The display can be tilted up and down.	☐
E	The display doesn't flicker.	☐
F	The display size must be at least 14".	☐

   [3]

2. The diagram shows a user sitting at a computer. The user is experiencing pain due to poor posture.

   Give **four** issues with the user's posture.

   ① ....

   ....

   ② ....

   ....

   ③ ....

   ....

   ④ ....

   [4]

3. Other than posture and blue light, name **one** other aspects of health and safety that should be considered when using computers.

   .... **[1]**

Try it

Consider any screens or displays you use at home. Write a list of improvements you could make to your posture when using them. Also write a list of any other health and safety improvements you could make whilst using computers or other electronic equipment.

Total ☐ /10

How well do you feel you know this topic? ☺ ☐ 😐 ☐ ☹ ☐

TOPIC 17.1

LISTS

Lists are used in Python to store a number of data items using just one list name.

Five pupils have taken a test. To create a list to store the five test results in Python, use:

Python syntax

```
results = [93, 86, 62, 74, 82]
```

Remember

Make sure you understand Unit 12 Introduction to Python **pages 88-98** before completing this unit.

Did you know?

Other programming languages may use **arrays** instead of lists. Arrays have a **fixed length** (number of items) and only allow items with one **data type**.

Lists allow items to be appended or removed from the list.

How it works

This line of code means:

- Make a list named `results`
- Store the values 93, 86, 62, 74 and 82 in the list

The diagram to represent this is:

Results →

93	86	62	74	82
0	1	2	3	4

Each item in the list is known as an **element**. The list length is 5 as there are 5 elements in it.

Each element has a **list reference**. These start at 0.

Appending to a list

Use **append** to add an item to a list. For the results list:

`results.append(15)` would append 15 to the end of the list.

Referencing list elements

Each element in the list is accessed using square brackets.

The first pupil was given an extra mark. The following program shows how to update the result in the list.

Program 9: Class results.py

```
results = [93, 86, 62, 74, 82]
print(results[0])
print(results)
results[0] = 94
print(results)
```

Program output

```
93
[93, 86, 62, 74, 82]
[94, 86, 62, 74, 82]
```

Referencing list elements

FOR loops are often used to loop through each element of a list.

All pupils in the class are given an extra mark. The following program shows how a FOR loop could be used to add a mark to each of the elements of the results list.

Program 10: Update class results.py

```
results = [93, 86, 62, 74, 82]
for i in range(0, 5):
    results[i] = results[i] + 1
print(results)
```

Program output

```
[94, 87, 63, 75, 83]
```

Write your mark here

1. Complete the line of code below to make a list of three names, Olivia, Noah and Ali. Remember that each name will be a string.

   `names =` .... **[3]**

2. The following code creates a list named **`results`** which stores five values.

   ```
   results = [8, 7, 9, 10, 6]
   ```

   Complete the table below to show the output for each line of code.

Line of code	Output
`print(results[0])`	
`print(results[3])`	
`print(results)`	

[3]

3. The following code is meant to find the average result for five pupils. Complete the code.

```
results = [8, 7, 9, 10, 6]
total = 0
for i in  ..........................................................................:
    total = total +  ..........................................................................
average = total / 5
print(average)
```

[4]

Try it

Enter the code for Question 3 above into a Python program.

Test your code to make sure it works.

Now adapt the code so that it finds the average of the following list of results:

`[7, 2, 5, 10, 1, 8, 5, 6, 7, 9]`

Total /10

How well do you feel you know this topic?   

TOPIC 17.2

SUBROUTINES

Subroutines allow sections of code to be given a name. They can then be re-used many times in the program. Both **procedures** and **functions** are types of subroutine. Functions **return** a value, whereas procedures do not.

The code below shows a function named area which takes two numbers, `width` and `height` and returns the `totalArea`.

Python syntax

```
def area(width, height):
    totalArea = width * height
    return totalArea

floorArea = area(5, 4)
print(floorArea)
```

```
20
```

How it works

`def` means **define** and is used to create a new subroutine.

`width` and `height` are known as **parameters**. They allow values to be **passed** to the subroutine. There can be any number of parameters (or none).

To use a Python subroutine as a function, use `return`. This allows one value (usually in a variable) to be returned to the calling function.

`area(5,4)` **calls** the function area with two **arguments**: `5` (for the width) and `4` (for the height). The two numbers are then multiplied together and returned by the function. The result of `20` is then assigned to `floorArea`.

Procedure

The following procedure outputs a menu for a game. The same procedure can be called anywhere in the program when the menu needs to be displayed.

Program 11: Menu.py

```
def showMenu():
    print("1. Play game")
    print("2. Show high scores")
    print("3. Exit game")

showMenu()
```

Program output

```
1. Play game
2. Show high scores
3. Exit game
```

Function

The following function has one argument, a distance in inches. It then converts this distance to cm and returns the result.

Program 12: InchToCM.py

```
def inchToCM(inches):
    cm = inches * 2.54
    return cm

oneFoot = 12
oneFootInCM = inchToCM(oneFoot)
print(oneFootInCM)
```

Program output

```
30.48
```

1. The following program shows a program which is used to calculate the volume of a pyramid.

```
def pyramidVolume(length, width, height):
    volume = (length * width * height) / 3
    return volume

volume = pyramidVolume(3, 3, 2)
print(volume)
```

Complete the table to answer each of the following questions about the code.

Question	Answer
Give the reason why **pyramidVolume** is a function not a procedure.	
How many arguments does **pyramidVolume** have?	
Give the output from the program.	
Give the result of the following function call: **pyramidVolume(3, 1, 1)**	
Give the result of the following function call: **pyramidVolume(5, 3, 2)**	

[5]

Write your mark here

2. The following program is used to find the average of two numbers.

(a) The function is incomplete. Complete the code.

```
def average(..........................................):
    result = (a + b) / 2
    ..........................................................
print(average(10,2))
```

[3]

(b) Give the output of the completed algorithm.

.... **[1]**

(c) Write the code needed to call the function to find the average of the numbers 15 and 5.

.... **[1]**

Try it

Enter the code for Question 1 above into Python and check it works to find the volume of a pyramid.

Now write another function that finds the volume of a cube. Test the function by calling it with a length of 3. The volume for the cube should be 27.

Total ☐ /10

How well do you feel you know this topic? ☺ ☐ 😐 ☐ ☹ ☐

TOPIC 18.1

FILMING TECHNIQUES

Before a film, TV programme or advert is created, various different shot types, camera angles and camera movements are planned in the production process.

Shot types

A **shot type** is how the person or object is framed. Different shot types are achieved by moving the camera or zooming in or out or using different camera lenses.

Close up
This shot shows the face clearly. It allows expressions to be easily seen.

Mid shot
This shot is from the waist up.

Long shot
This shows people in their surroundings

Camera angles

The **camera angle** is the direction in which the camera is pointing.

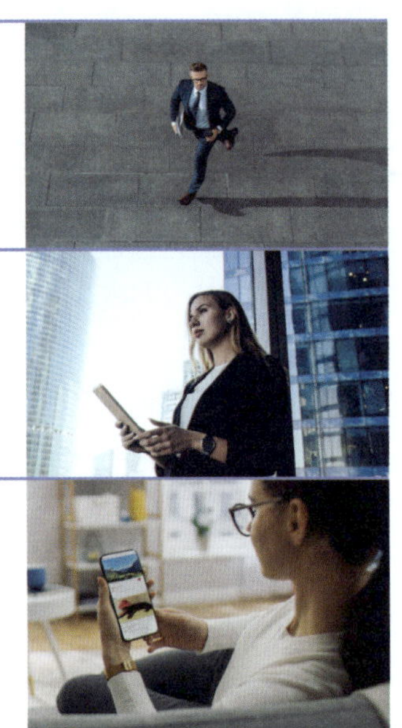

High angle
This helps to make characters appear weak or vulnerable.

Low angle
This helps to make characters look larger, authoritative or intimidating.

Over the shoulder
This helps to show a character's point of view or to show the contents of a phone or screen.

Camera movement

Tripods are used to keep a camera steady whilst filming. When on a tripod, movement is made by **tilting** the camera up and down or **panning** the camera left and right.

If a camera follows or tracks a character it is known as a **tracking shot**. The camera may be placed on a **dolly** which moves along a **track**. This is known as a **dolly shot**.

Other types of camera movement use **cranes**, **drones** and **helicopters**.

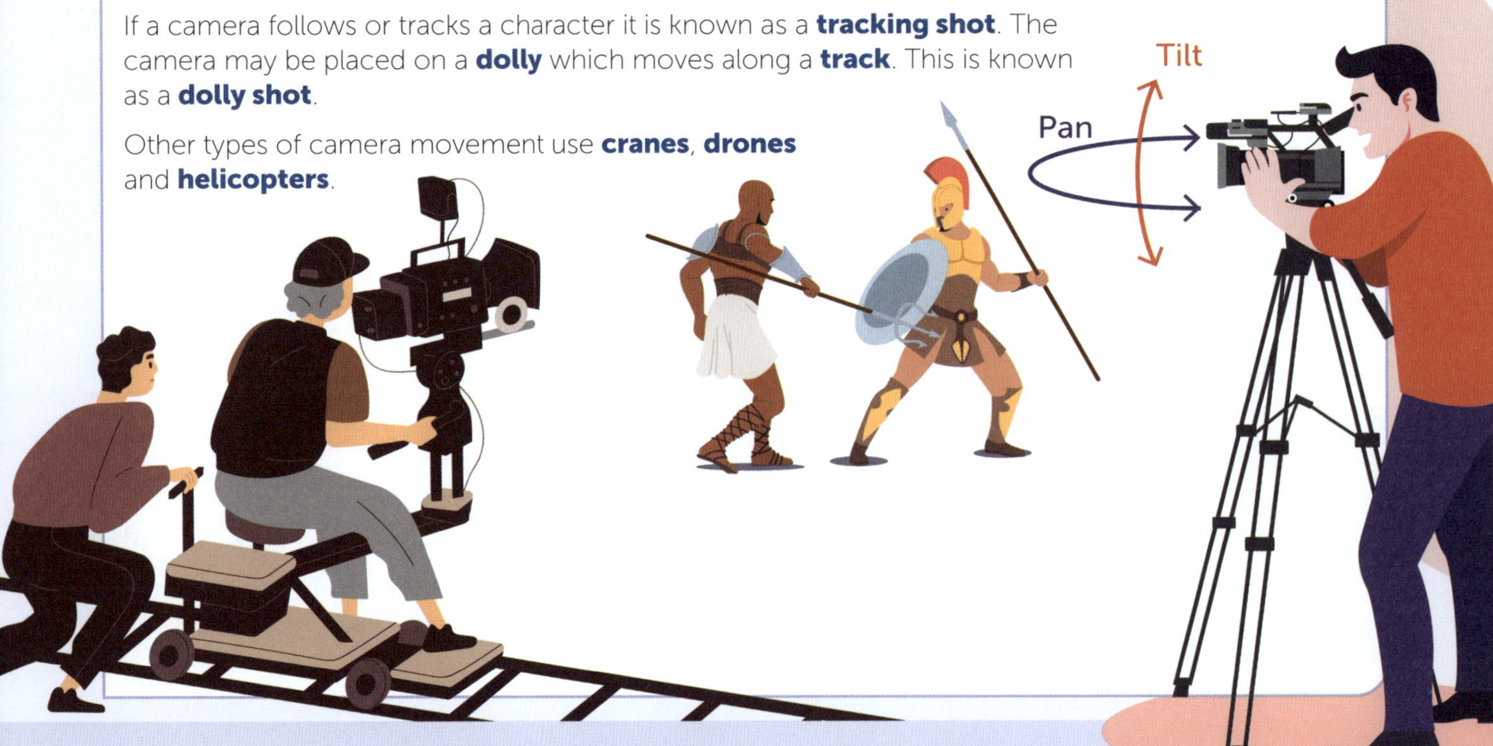

1. Match each of the following shots to their shot type.

Write your mark here

Long shot
Close up
Mid shot

[3]

2. Match each of the following camera movement terms to their meanings.

Pan	Move the camera up and down.
Tilt	Move the camera side to side.
Tracking	Move the camera along a predefined route.

[3]

3. A soap opera is filming a scene where a teenager has just been given a new bike by their parents. Name a suitable shot type to use to help show the joy of the teenager, then give a reason for choosing this type of shot.

Shot type: ....

Reason for choice: ....

.... **[2]**

4. A spy film is being made. A scene will show the spy in a room feeling alone and worried. Give a suitable camera angle that could be used and a reason for choosing this.

Camera angle: ....

Reason for choice: ....

.... **[2]**

Try it

Find a scene from a film, TV programme or advert.

Identify some key shots used. For each one, write down the shot type, camera angle and any camera movement. Explain why you think these were used for each shot.

Total ☐ **/10**

How well do you feel you know this topic?   

TOPIC 18.2

SCRIPTS

Scripts are the first part of creating a film or TV programme. They contain the **dialogue** that actors will say along with other useful information such as the **location** and **shot type**.

```
EXT. SKATE PARK

The skate park is in bright sunshine.
Teenagers of various ages are skating.

LONG SHOT

In the corner of the skate park, CALLUM and
HOLLY are sitting on a bench, talking.

MID SHOT

                        HOLLY
    (Annoyed) I don't think I'll ever be able
    to do a flip. You make it look so easy.

OVER THE SHOULDER SHOT

                        CALLUM
    Are you serious? You've only been trying
    a few days. It took me a year before I
    landed my first kick flip.

CLOSE UP

                        HOLLY
    Wow. I didn't think it would
    take that long.

                                        CUT TO:

INT. SCHOOL - DAY

LONG SHOT
```

Locations

Information about locations is given at the start of a scene.

EXT. means **exterior** (outside).

INT. means **interior** (inside).

Shot types

Descriptions of each shot are given with **camera angles** and **shot types**.

Dialogue

The **character name** is given in the centre of the script. The **dialogue** (words they say) then follows.

Transitions

Transitions are given on the right of the page. Common transitions are **cuts** and **fades**.

Remember

Character names, locations, shot types, camera angles and transitions are all in uppercase to make them stand out.

Did you know?

Scripts are used by **directors**, **actors** and **film crew** to help everyone know what is happening at each point in the **production** process.

1. Match each of the following words to their meanings.

INT.	A location that is outside.
EXT.	The place where a scene will take place.
Dialogue	A location that is inside.
Location	The words that actors will say.

[4]

Write your mark here

2. Look at the following excerpt from a script.

```
INT. SUPERMARKET - DAY •———— A
LONG SHOT •———— B
                    SOPHIE
      So, how's the new job going?
MID SHOT
                    ADAM •———— C
      Really well thanks. I never thought
      it would be so much fun.
                              FADE TO: •———— D
```

Match the script components below with the labels shown above.

A	Character name
B	Shot type
C	Transition
D	Location

[4]

3. Complete the table below to give the formatting commonly used for each script component.

Script component	Script formatting
Character name	
Transition	

[2]

Try it

Create a script for a scene in a film or TV programme. You may like to base the characters or scene on an existing film or TV programme that you like.

Make sure to use the correct formatting and conventions for writing the scene.

Total ☐ /10

How well do you feel you know this topic? ☺ ☐ 😐 ☐ ☹ ☐

TOPIC 18.3

STORYBOARDING

Storyboards are created once a script has been written. The **director** and any other key people will consider each **shot** in the **production**. A **frame** will then be sketched for each shot. Other useful information will also be included.

Storyboard components

The following components are typically provided in a storyboard

- Scene number
- Shot number
- Duration of the shot
- Camera movement
- Camera angle or shot type
- Transition
- Dialogue

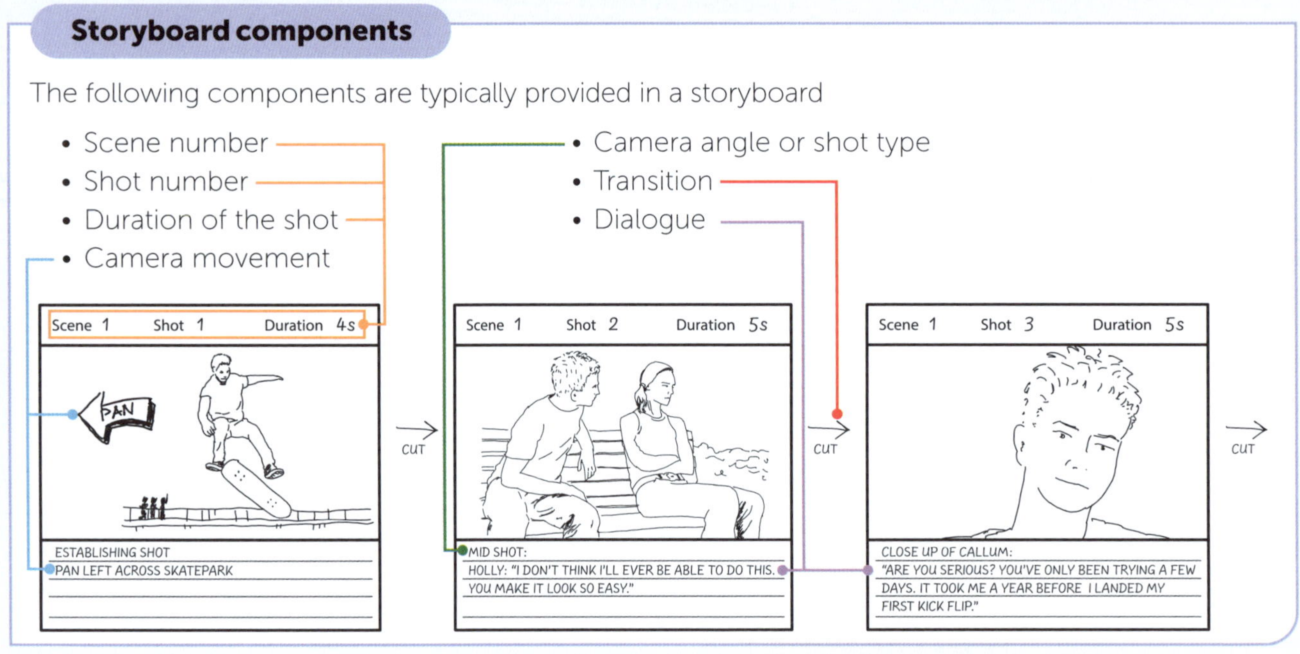
Scene 1 Shot 1 Duration 4s
PAN
ESTABLISHING SHOT
PAN LEFT ACROSS SKATEPARK
CUT
Scene 1 Shot 2 Duration 5s
MID SHOT:
HOLLY: "I DON'T THINK I'LL EVER BE ABLE TO DO THIS.
YOU MAKE IT LOOK SO EASY."
CUT
Scene 1 Shot 3 Duration 5s
CLOSE UP OF CALLUM:
"ARE YOU SERIOUS? YOU'VE ONLY BEEN TRYING A FEW
DAYS. IT TOOK ME A YEAR BEFORE I LANDED MY
FIRST KICK FLIP."
CUT

Did you know?

Scenes often use a **long shot** or **wide shot** to provide context to a scene or location. These are known as **establishing shots**. Moving to a **mid shot**, then a **close up** allows the audience to understand where the actors are before any key parts of dialogue begin.

Remember

A storyboard needs to clearly show how each shot appears. If you aren't great at sketching, stick figures are fine as long as they are clear and help people understand what you are trying to film.

Professional films and TV programmes employ a **storyboard artist** to do the sketches.

Write your mark here

1. Tick **two** of the job roles below that will usually be involved in the creation of a storyboard.

A	Director	☐	**C**	Storyboard artist	☐
B	Actor	☐	**D**	Cinema owner	☐

[2]

2. Other than a sketch, give **two** storyboard components that are often given for each frame of the storyboard.

Component 1: ....

Component 2: .... **[2]**

3. Look at the storyboard on the left.

(a) Complete the fourth frame of the storyboard (below right) for the section of the script (below left) When completing the frame, draw a sketch and write any other details.

```
CLOSE UP
                    HOLLY
          Wow. I didn't think it
        would take that long.
                                CUT TO:
```

Scene	Shot	Duration

[5]

(b) The next scene in the script starts with:

```
INT. SCHOOL - DAY

LONG SHOT
```

Give **one** reason why a long shot will be appropriate.

....

.... **[1]**

Try it

Create a storyboard for the script given in 3(b).

Now extend this further. Complete the script for the scene, then create the storyboard to match your script.

Total ☐ /10

How well do you feel you know this topic? ☐ ☐ 

TOPIC 18.4

VIDEO EDITING

When creating a film or TV programme, lots of footage will be created. This all needs to be **edited** together by an editor.

Did you know?

A **video editor** will edit video for TV programmes, whilst a **film editor** will edit films. Both roles are often referred to as just **editors**. The **director** will work with the editor to make sure their vision is produced.

Did you know?

Footage refers to clips of film or video that have been recorded. The term comes from reels of film which were originally measured in feet and frames. Editing these required physical cuts to be made in the film. The term **cut** is still used for digital video footage today.

Video editing techniques

A video editor will make use of the script and storyboard to select the best **takes** to use in the **final cut**. The following shows the **video editing software** and techniques that are commonly used.

Project files are imported so they may be dragged onto the **timeline**.

Video tracks have **video clips** in order. Video clips on a higher track will be overlayed on top of video tracks on a lower track.

Audio tracks are used for **dialogue**, **sound effects** and **background music** or a soundtrack.

The **video preview** allows the editor to view the result of their editing

The **timeline** is used to arrange the order of video and audio clips.

A **slider** indicates the frame that is currently being shown in the video preview. Moving the **slider** left and right is known as **scrubbing**.

Transitions may be applied between each shot. Here, a **cross fade** has been applied. If no transition is applied, then a **cut** occurs.

1. Match the following words with their meanings.

Scrubbing	A transition which instantly moves from one shot to another.
Timeline	Fading out one shot whilst fading in another shot.
Cross fade	An area in video editing software where video and audio clips are arranged.
Cut	Moving the slider back and forth through the timeline.

[4]

Write your mark here

2. Give **two** uses for audio tracks.

Use 1: ....

Use 2: .... **[2]**

3. The following question refers to the video editing screenshot on the left which is being used for editing a soap opera.

(a) Identify the number of video and audio clips that have currently been imported into the software for use in the timeline.

.... **[1]**

(b) Identify the number of audio and video tracks that are currently being used.

.... **[1]**

(c) Name the job role that will carry out the video editing of the soap opera.

.... **[1]**

(d) The titles for the soap opera are placed on a track below the track used for video footage. Identify the problem that will occur.

....

.... **[1]**

Try it

You may already have free video editing software such as iMovie for Apple Mac.

If you don't have any video editing software, then download OpenShot for free from:

www.openshot.org

This is available for Windows, macOS and Linux.

Total /10

How well do you feel you know this topic? ☺ ☐ 😐 ☐ ☹ ☐

TOPIC 19.1

WORD PROCESSING

Word processors are used to create, edit and print documents.

Formatting features

Formatting features allow the **style** of the text to be changed. Some common features are given below.

- B **Bold**
- I *Italic*
- U Underline
- X_2 Subscript
- X^2 Superscript

The font style and size may also be changed.

Alignment

Text may be positioned relative to the page.

- **Right aligned**
- **Left aligned**
- **Centred**
- **Justified** (Software increases and decreases the space width so that text is aligned to the left and right of the page.)

Lists

Lists of information may be given in **numbered lists** (if there is an order to the items) or **bulleted lists** (if the list is unordered).

1. Add eggs.
2. Add milk.
3. Mix.
4. Fry pancakes.

- Dogs
- Cats
- Fish
- Hamsters

Common word-processed documents

Documents that are usually created with a word processor include:

- Business letters on headed paper
- Personal letters
- CVs (for applying for jobs)
- Essays

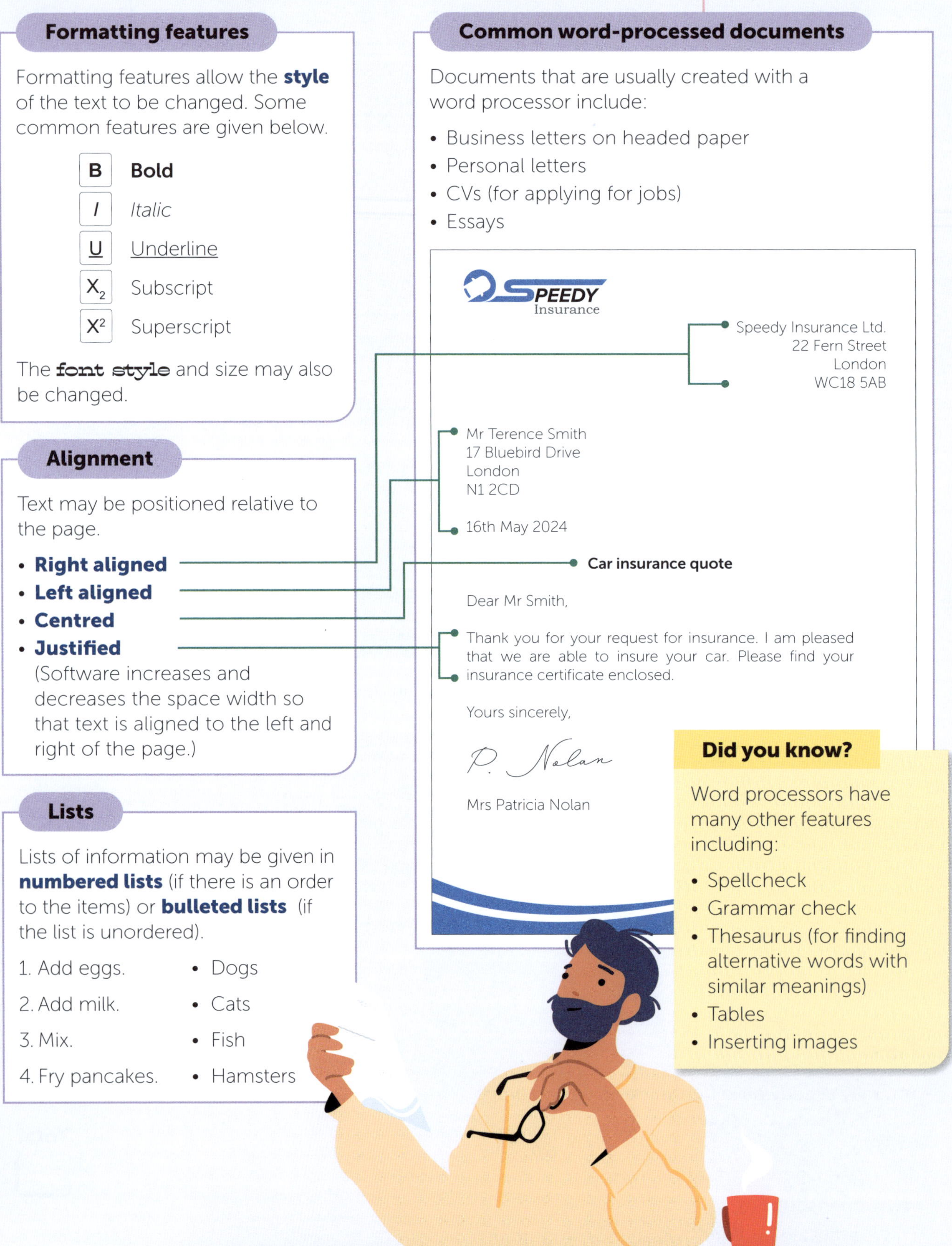

SPEEDY Insurance

Speedy Insurance Ltd.
22 Fern Street
London
WC18 5AB

Mr Terence Smith
17 Bluebird Drive
London
N1 2CD

16th May 2024

Car insurance quote

Dear Mr Smith,

Thank you for your request for insurance. I am pleased that we are able to insure your car. Please find your insurance certificate enclosed.

Yours sincerely,

P. Nolan

Mrs Patricia Nolan

Did you know?

Word processors have many other features including:

- Spellcheck
- Grammar check
- Thesaurus (for finding alternative words with similar meanings)
- Tables
- Inserting images

1. Match each item of text below to the formatting feature that has been used. One item of text may be matched to one or two features.

H_2O	Bold
For example,	Italics
<u>Urgent</u>	Underline
	Subscript

[3]

2. A school has made a document with a list of names going on a school trip.

(a) Give **one** reason why a bulleted list may be used.

....

.... **[1]**

(b) Give **one** reason why a numbered list may be used.

....

.... **[1]**

3. The letter below shows grey bars where text is placed. Complete the labels for the alignment that has been used for each area of text.

....

....

....

[3]

4. One feature found in word processors is a spell checker. Name **two** other features commonly found in word processors that aren't already given above.

Feature 1: ....

Feature 2: .... **[2]**

Write your mark here

Total /10

Try it

Your school may be able to provide you with access to an online word processor such as Google Docs or Microsoft 365 Word.

Alternatively, you may like to download LibreOffice which has an offline word processor known as Writer for Windows, MacOS and Linux.

How well do you feel you know this topic? ☺ ☐ 😐 ☐ ☹ ☐

TOPIC 19.2

DESKTOP PUBLISHING

Desktop Publishing (DTP) software is used for more complex page layouts and designs than word processing software is able to achieve. For this reason, it has more features and usually takes longer to learn how to use.

Page layouts

DTP software allows very accurate control over the **layout** of a page.

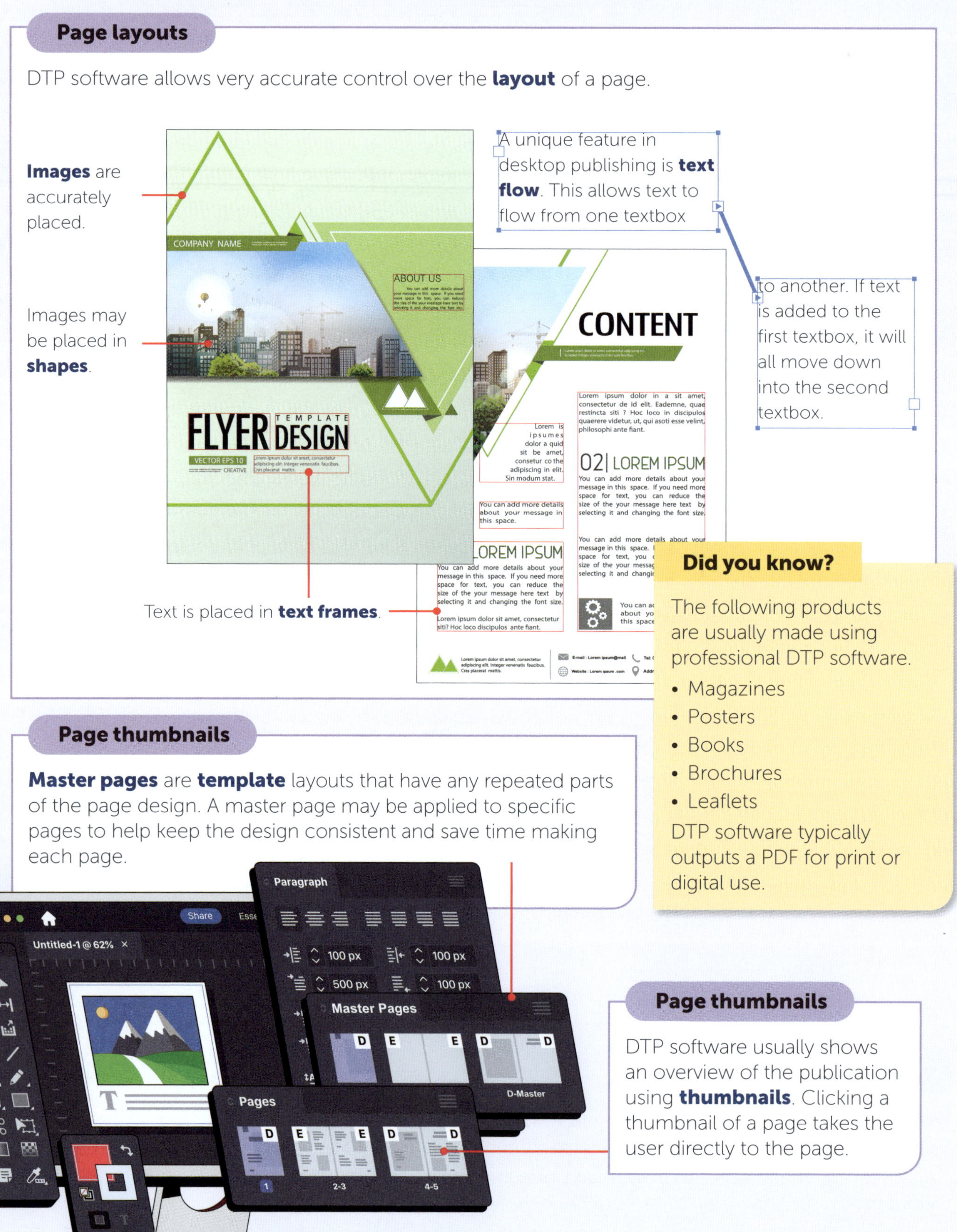

Images are accurately placed.

Images may be placed in **shapes**.

Text is placed in **text frames**.

A unique feature in desktop publishing is **text flow**. This allows text to flow from one textbox to another. If text is added to the first textbox, it will all move down into the second textbox.

Did you know?

The following products are usually made using professional DTP software.

- Magazines
- Posters
- Books
- Brochures
- Leaflets

DTP software typically outputs a PDF for print or digital use.

Page thumbnails

Master pages are **template** layouts that have any repeated parts of the page design. A master page may be applied to specific pages to help keep the design consistent and save time making each page.

Page thumbnails

DTP software usually shows an overview of the publication using **thumbnails**. Clicking a thumbnail of a page takes the user directly to the page.

1. Match the words below with their meanings.

Page layout	Text is placed around an image or shape.
Text frame	The positioning of text, images and shapes on a page.
Text wrap	Text spills from one frame to another.
Text flow	A rectangular placeholder for text.

[4]

Write your mark here

2. Name **three** products that are often produced using desktop publishing software.

① ....

② ....

③ .... **[3]**

3. Give **one** way that page thumbnails help a designer when creating a book in DTP.

....

.... **[1]**

4. Explain how master pages could help a designer working on a magazine.

....

....

....

.... **[2]**

Try it

Professionals often use Adobe InDesign for desktop publishing. Other paid for alternatives include Serif Affinity Publisher and Microsoft Publisher.

Alternatively, you might like to download Scribus which is a free alternative.

wiki.scribus.net

Total /10

How well do you feel you know this topic?    

TOPIC 19.3

PRESENTATION SOFTWARE

Presentation software allows a number of slides to be created. Each of these is then shown in sequence by a **presenter**, **teacher** or **trainer**. When played, the presentation advances to the next slide on a key press or mouse click. Some presentations will run automatically.

Slides

An individual **slide** should be created for each topic of the presentation. Features that are often used include:

- **Background colour** or **background image**
- **Text boxes**
- **Bullet points**
- **Charts**
- **Images**
- **Videos**
- **Sound** or **music**

Make sure when creating slides that you keep the colours, backgrounds and style consistent.

A **master slide** may be made with common features such as the background colour, logo and text box layout. These are then applied to all slides so that they are consistent.

Slide 1

Slide 2

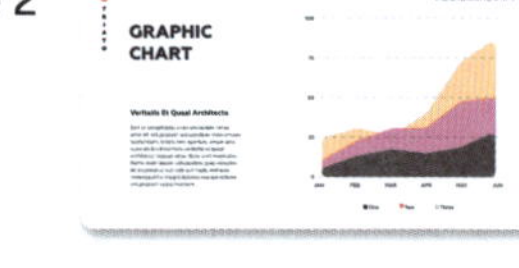

Slide 3

Slide 4

Transitions

Transitions are any effects used to change from one slide to another. Unless there is a specific reason to use a transition, keep them minimal and consistent throughout a presentation to avoid distracting the viewer.

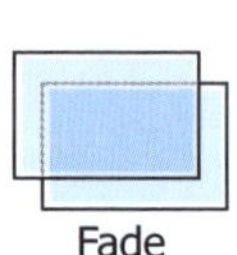

Fade

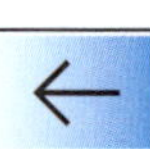

Wipe

Cube

Top tip

Don't overuse animations, transitions or other multimedia content. Some of the most effective slides simply have a title and image. This helps the audience to listen to the speaker rather than being distracted with the presentation slides.

Animations

Each object (such as text boxes or images) on the slide may have **animation** applied to it. This changes how the object appears or disappears on the slide.

Each animation may be **timed** or **triggered** by an event such as a mouse click.

Fade

Fly in

Bounce

1. Slides often use text boxes with bullet points, images and charts. Name **three** other types of content that could be added to a slide.

Write your mark here

① ....

② ....

③ .... **[3]**

2. Once a presentation is playing, give **one** way that the presenter advances to the next slide.

.... **[1]**

3. Match each of the words below with their meaning.

Animation	A visual effect that is applied when moving from one slide to the next.
Transition	Control the duration of an animation, transition or delay needed before a slide is advanced.
Trigger	Slide objects may move or change appearance as they enter, are displayed or leave the screen.
Timing	The event that causes an animation to occur.

[4]

4. Give **two** pieces of advice for someone creating an effective presentation.

① ....

....

② ....

.... **[2]**

Try it

Commonly available presentation software includes Keynote® for MacOS, Microsoft PowerPoint for Windows and Google Slides. There are also free alternatives you may like to try such as:

- Canva® (online) **canva.com**
- Libre Office Impress (offline) **libreoffice.org**

Total /10

How well do you feel you know this topic?   

ANSWERS

Topic 1.1

1. (a) School work.[1] [1]

(b) Art[1], Computing,[1] English.[1] [2]

(c) English homework – business letter.[1] *[Or something similar that is meaningful.]* [1]

(d) Create a new folder named Year 7.[1] Create a new folder names Year 8.[1] Move all the folders and files in the School Work folder into the Year 7 folder[1] then start using a Year 8 folder.[1] *Other ways of organising these folders are also possible.* [2]

2. (a) If the files are accidentally deleted / the hard drive breaks[1] then they will want to retrieve the work they have spent time doing.[1] [2]

(b) Highlight the files to backup[1] then press CTRL+C to copy them.[1] Select the backup location[1] then press CTRL+V to save them.[1] [2]

Topic 1.2

1.

Search query	Meaning
"Well done is better than well said"	Searches for the exact phrase.[1]
beach filetype:pdf	Finds PDF files that contain the word beach in them.[1]
fruit -apple	Finds web pages that have the keyword fruit in, but not the keyword apple.[1]
map inurl:emilycollege.sch.uk	Searches for web pages/files containing the keyword map and contain queenemilycollege.sch.uk in the web address.[1]

[4]

2. Check the URL,[1] check for a padlock next the web address,[1] confirm information with other websites you respect,[1] check the published date.[1] [3]

3. (a) Bing,[1] DuckDuckGo,[1] Yahoo![1] *[There are also other search engines]* [2]

(b) CTRL + D .[1] [1]

Topic 1.3

1.

Scenario	Action to reduce the risk or deal with the situation
Adam is playing an online game when a stranger asks to chat privately. They keep on asking despite being told no.	• Report to CEOP[1] • Tell someone you trust such as a parent or teacher[1] • Block the user[1] • Report the user to the game publisher or website owner[1]
A friend has received emails that are upsetting them.	• Block the sender[1] • Tell someone you trust[1] • Don't reply[1] • Save any evidence[1]
Freya has seen an image online which has upset her.	• Report to the website owner[1] • Tell someone you trust[1] • Talk to Childline[1] • For certain images, report to CEOP[1]

[6]

2. **B** National Crime Agency (NCA)[1] [1]

3. (a) Examples include: name,[1] age,[1] address,[1] interests,[1] posts made,[1] medical information,[1] financial information[1] and many more. [2]

(b) Alter the privacy settings[1] so that posts are restricted to certain friends/groups.[1] *[There are other ways to improve online privacy. The most effective is to not upload certain information in the first place.]* [1]

Topic 1.4

1. (a) Use passwords that are at least 12 characters long.[1] Use at least one special character.[1] Use at least one number.[1] Use a mixture of uppercase and lowercase letters.[1] [3]

(b) *Any two from* !"£$%^&*()}{][~@#':;?></., [2]

2. (a) The spam should be moved to a spam folder.[1]
Block or report as spam.[1] [1]

(b) Clicking a link contained in the spam email.[1] Replying to the spam email.[1] [2]

3. (a) It prevents someone from misusing it / deleting files / sending something in your name / damaging the data on it.[1] It helps to match any misuse to the correct user that did it.[1] [1]

(c) Windows: WINDOWS + L[1], CTRL + ALT + DEL[1]

Mac: Control + Command + Q[1] [1]

Topic 2.1

1. (a)

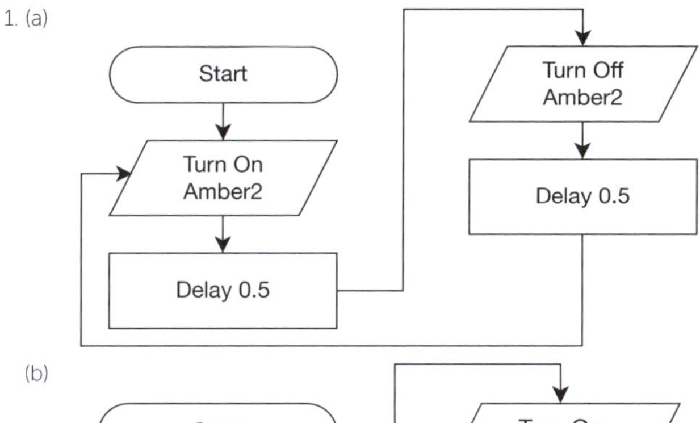

Allow solutions which flash the lights once, then stop. [3]

(b)

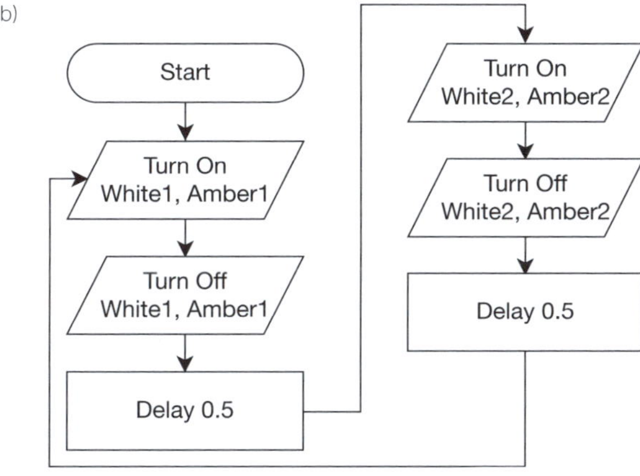

[7]

Topic 2.2

1.

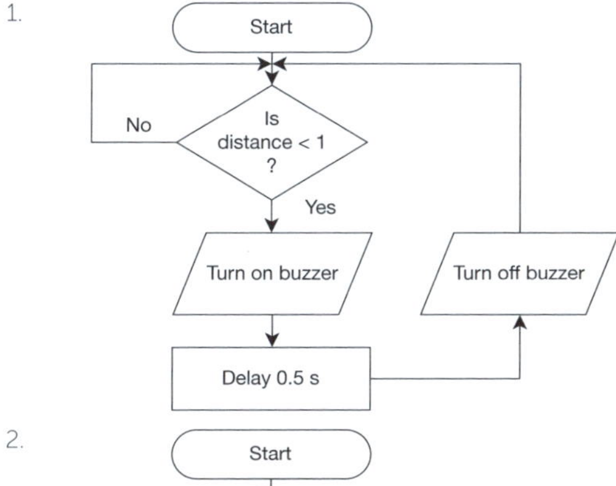

[1 mark for the decision symbol, 1 mark for the condition (distance < 1 or something similar), 1 mark for labelling correcting with Yes and No arrows]

[3]

2.

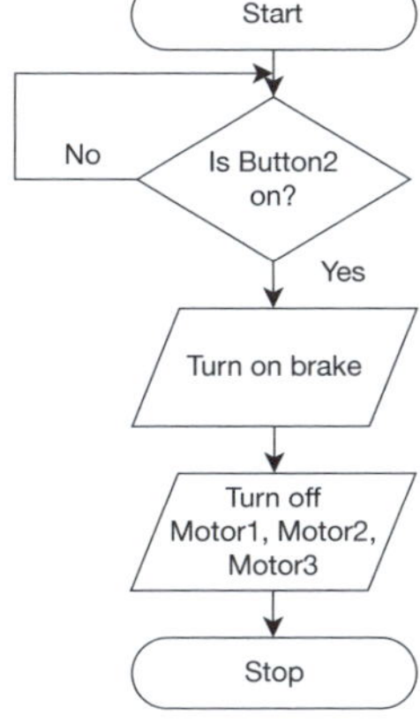

[1 mark for start symbol, 1 mark for decision symbol, 1 mark for condition, 1 mark for Yes and No labels, 1 mark for turning on the brake, 1 mark for turning off the motors, 1 mark for stop symbol.] [Note: the motors could be turned off before turning on the brake. Each motor could also be in its own output symbol.]

[7]

Topic 2.3

1. (a)

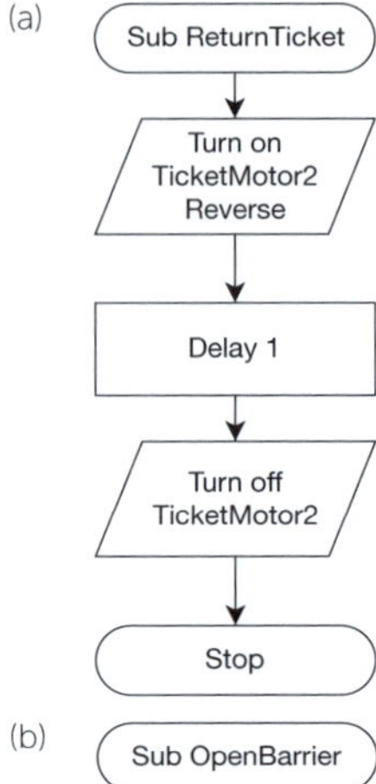

[3]

(b)

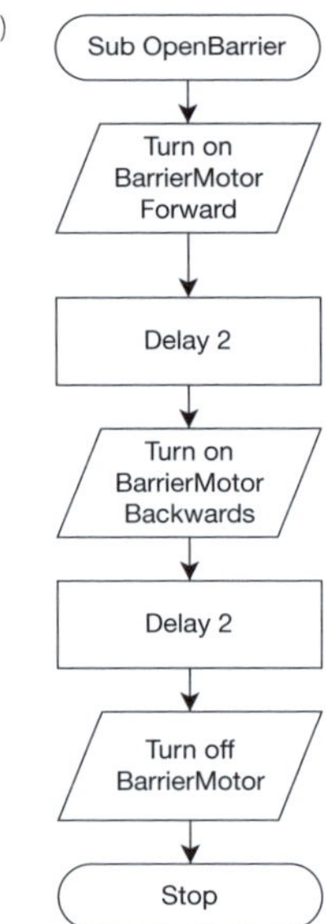

[7]

Topic 2.4

1. (a) 9[1] [1]

(b) Add a process box containing:

average = total / 3[1]

Then add an output symbol containing:

OUTPUT average[1] [2]

2.

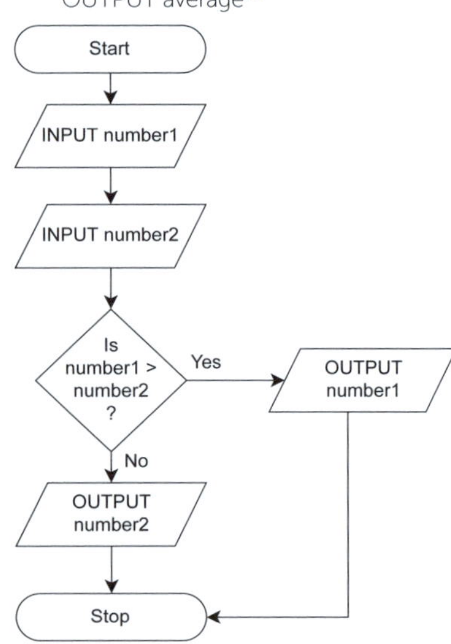

[One mark for each symbol that is correctly connected.] [7]

Topic 3.1

1. Algorithmic thinking[1], abstraction[1], decomposition[1]. [3]

2.

Name	Star (✓)	Planet (✓)	Moon (✓)
TRAPPIST-1	✓ [1]		
TRAPPIST-1b		✓ [1]	
TRAPPIST-1c		✓ [1]	

[3]

3. (a)
```
IF inCar OR[1] inTaxi THEN
        mustUseSeatBelt()
```
[1]

(b)
```
IF schoolAge AND[1] NOT[1] sick THEN
        mustGoToSchool()
```
[2]

(c)
```
IF NOT[1] gameOver THEN
        playGame()
```
[1]

Topic 3.2

1.

Logic gate	Symbol
AND gate	
OR gate	
NOT gate	

[3]

2.

A	B	Output
1	1	1
1	0	1
0	1	1
0	0	0

[4]

3. ON 1, ON 1, ON 1; OR gate output 1; NOT gate output 0; AND gate output 0

[1 mark for the output of each logic gate.] [3]

Topic 3.3

1.

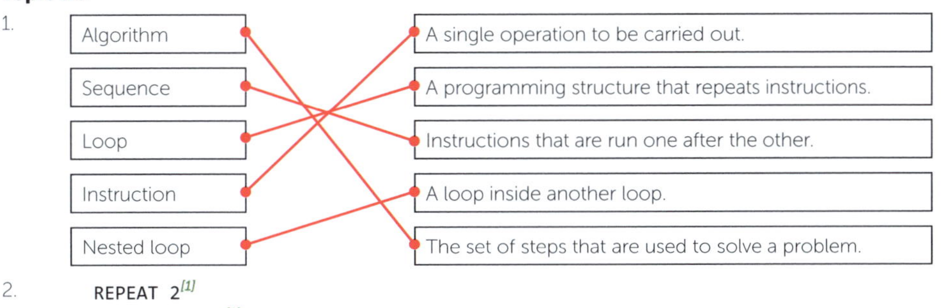

Algorithm
Sequence
Loop
Instruction
Nested loop
A single operation to be carried out.
A programming structure that repeats instructions.
Instructions that are run one after the other.
A loop inside another loop.
The set of steps that are used to solve a problem.

[5]

2.
```
REPEAT 2[1]
  forward(8)[1]
  right(90)[1]
  forward(2)  ⎤
  right(90)   ⎦ [1]
  forward(8)  ⎤
  left(90)    ⎥
  forward(2)  ⎥ [1]
  left(90)    ⎦
END REPEAT
```

Award max 4 marks for correct algorithm without the repeat loop [5]

Topic 3.4

1. Abstraction is the removing/hiding of unnecessary details[1] (to help solve a Computing problem). [1]

2.

Question	Answer
Give a route to get from A to D.	A, B, C, D[1]
Give an alternative route to get from A to D.	A, B, G, E, C, D[1]
Give a route to get from H to A.	H, G, B, A[1]

[3]

3. (a)

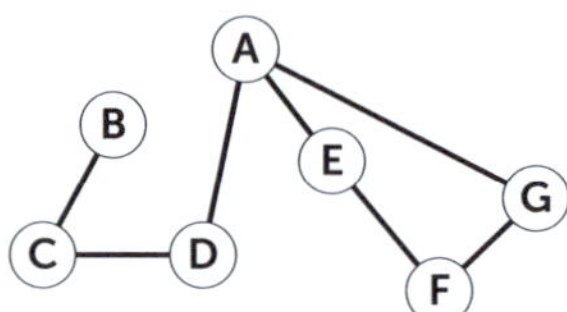

Connecting A-D[1]
Connecting A-E and A-G[1]
All other connections correct[1] [3]

(b) A-D-C-B[1]
Allow error carried forward from 3. (a) [1]

(c) A-E-F[1]
A-G-F[1]
Allow error carried forward from 3. (a) [2]

Topic 3.5

1. Breaking down a problem into smaller problems[1] (that are easier to solve). [1]

2. An example of a structure diagram:

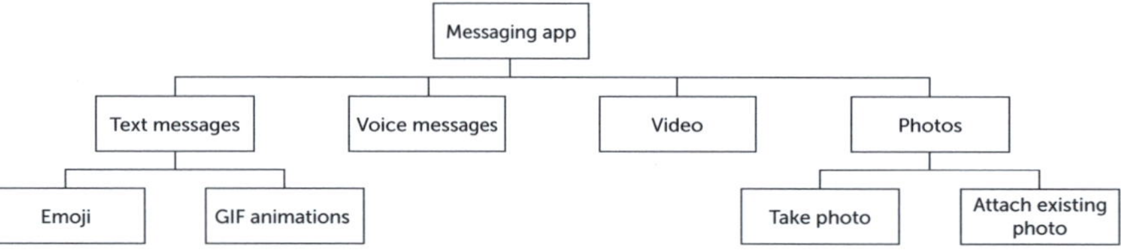

A maximum of 5 marks from:

- Starting with Messaging app at the top.[1]
- Having the boxes get more specific as they get lower[1] and having at least three levels.[1]
- Up to three marks: a useful part of a messaging app[1]. [5]

3.

```
MoveCarRight():
IF inLeftLane THEN[1]
    MoveToCentreLane()[1]
ELSE IF inCentreLane THEN[1]
    MoveToRightLane()[1]
ENDIF
```

[4]

Topic 3.6

1. 5 comparisons.[1] (5, 6, 8, 15, 23) [1]

2. (a)

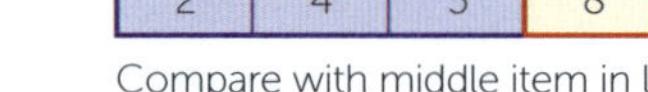

Compare with middle item in list. 5 < 8, so search the left of 8.[1]

Compare with middle item in list. 5 > 4, so search the right of 4.[1]

5

= 5. Item found.[1] [3]

(b) 1 comparison.[1] [If the item is 5.] [1]

(c) 3 comparisons.[1] [If the item is 8.] [1]

3. Algorithm: Linear search.[1]
Reason: Because the list is unsorted.[1] [2]

4. Algorithm: Binary search.[1]
Reason: Because it will be much faster.[1] [The number of words halves with each comparison. So it will take a maximum of 14 comparisons to search the whole dictionary. Using a linear search would require 10 000 comparisons in the worst case, and 5 000 comparisons on average. [2]

Topic 3.7

1. (a)

8	5	7	3		(swap 8,5)
5	8	7	3	[1]	(swap 8,7)
5	7	8	3	[1]	(swap 8,3)
5	7	3	8	[1]	

[3]

(b) When a full pass has happened and no swaps are made[1] the list will be sorted. [1]

2.

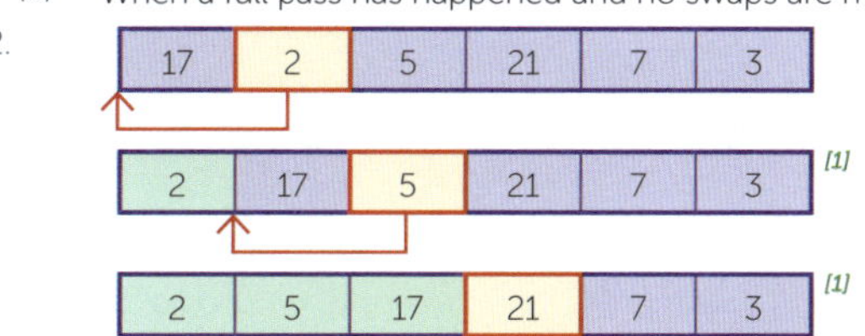

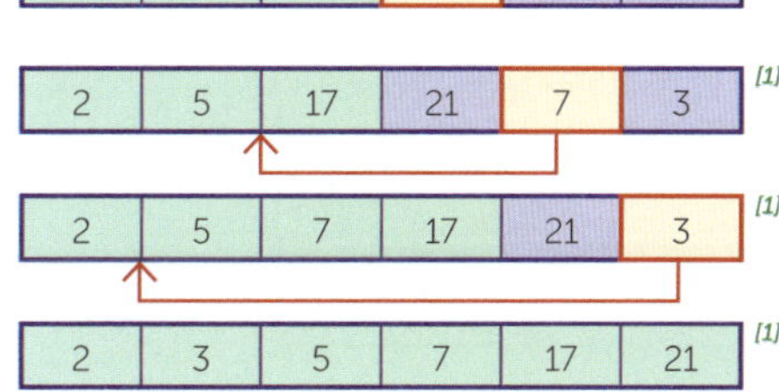

[5]

3. The insertion sort is usually faster than the bubble sort to sort a list.[1] [1]

Topic 4.1

1.

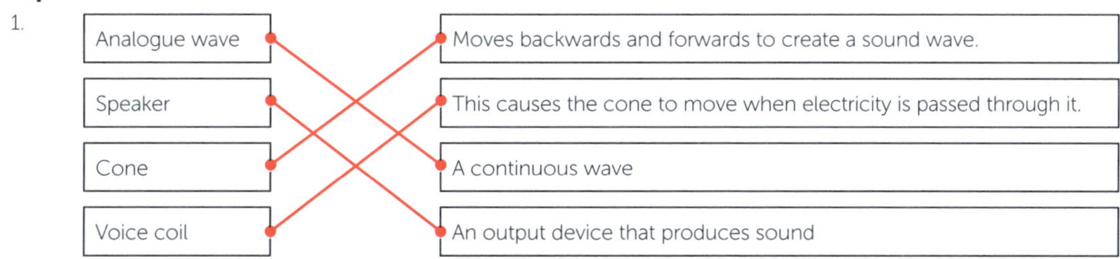

[4]

2. (a) There will be 44 100 samples of the wave position[1] taken each second.[1] [2]

(b) The bit depth position of the sample will correspond to the position of the speaker cone.[1] If there is a higher bit depth, there will be more positions[1] which will make the movement of the cone more precise[1] and improve the sound quality.[1] [2]

(c) Reducing the sample rate will decrease the sound quality[1] and reduce the file size.[1] [2]

Topic 4.2

1. (a)

Echoes are being heard in the interview.	Use sound proofing / acoustic foam.[1]
Whenever someone says a word with 'p' or 'b', a loud sound is heard on the recording.	Use a pop filter[1].
The microphone stand is on a table. If someone touches the table, a bang is heard on the recording.	Use a shock mount[1].

[3]

(b) Fade / Fade out[1] [1]

(c) Noise reduction[1] [1]

(d) A cut could be made[1] either side of the mistake[1] then the clip could be removed[1] and the rest of the track dragged so that it fills in the gap.[1] [2]

(e) The two microphone recordings would each be on their own separate track.[1] [1]

(f) Audio technician.[1] [1]

(g) Sound editor.[1] [1]

Topic 5.1

1. (a) Games controller,[1] joystick,[1] steering wheel,[1] pedals,[1] keyboard,[1] mouse.[1] [4]

(b) Display/monitor.[1] [1]

(c) Speakers / headphones.[1] [1]

2.

Computer product	Hardware (✓)	Software (✓)
Graphics tablet	✓	
Microsoft Windows		✓
Webcam	✓	
Racing game		✓

[4]

Topic 5.2

1. (a)

Computer product	Solid state (✓)	Magnetic (✓)	Optical (✓)
Blu-ray disc			✓
Hard disk drive		✓	
Memory card	✓		
DVD			✓

[4]

(b) Compact Disc.[1] [1]

(c) Digital Versatile Disc.[1] [1]

2. A spinning platter[1] has a magnetic coating[1] which stores the data.[1] A drive head[1] moves to the correct track on the disk[1] and waits for the platter to spin to the location containing the data.[1] [2]

3. It has no moving parts[1] which makes read/write access faster[1] and it also has lower power usage.[1] Both these reasons make it more suitable for portable battery operated devices.[1] [2]

Topic 5.3

1.

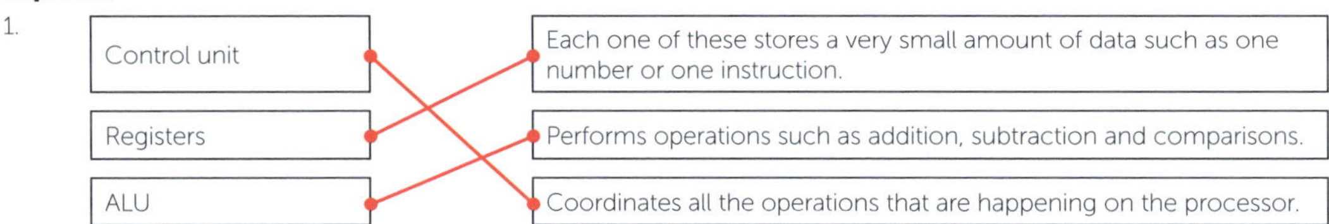

Control unit
Registers
ALU
Each one of these stores a very small amount of data such as one number or one instruction.
Performs operations such as addition, subtraction and comparisons.
Coordinates all the operations that are happening on the processor.

[3]

2. 1 Fetch the instruction[1] (from main memory/RAM/ROM).
   2 Decode the instruction[1] (the control unit decodes the instruction).
   3 Execute the instruction[1] (the ALU does this). [3]

3. Making a video requires lots of processing[1] which means the CPU has to do more work, so it gets hotter[1]. The fan spins quickly to help cool the computer[1] (this is the sound that is heard). [2]

4. (a) The 4 GHz processor is faster[1] (it's the same as 4 000 MHz). [1]

(b) (The CPU clock speed is the number of instructions / fetch-decode-execute cycles that occur each second.[1] [1]

Topic 5.4

1. (a)

Type of main memory	Volatile (✓)	Non-volatile (✓)
RAM	✓	
ROM		✓

[2]

(b) RAM[1] [1]

(c)

Computer product	RAM (✓)	Hard drive (✓)
A running program's instructions.	✓	
The data being used in a running program.	✓	
A program that isn't running.		✓

[3]

2.

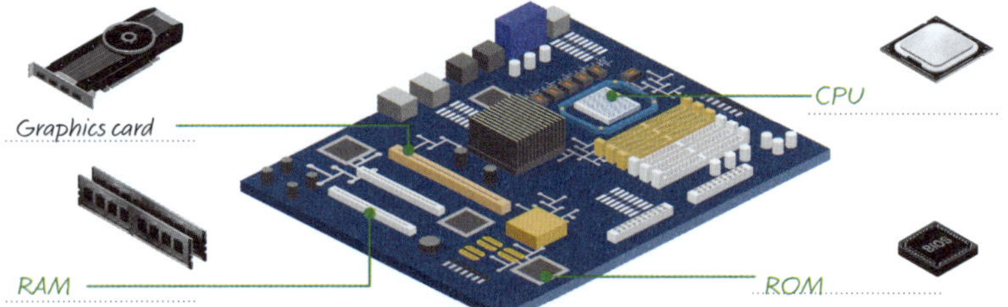

[4]

Topic 5.5

1. (a) 1, 0[1] [1]

(b) 1011[1] [1]

2. (a) 16+4+2+1 = 23[1] [1]

(b) 64+8+2[1]=74[1] [2]

3. (a)

	128	64	32	16	8	4	2	1	
	0	0	0	1	0	0	1	0	[1]
Remainder				2					[1]

[2]

(b)

	128	64	32	16	8	4	2	1	
	0	1	1	0	0	0	1	1	[1]
Remainder		35	3						[1]

[2 marks if the correct answer 01100011 is given.] [2]

4. 255[1] [1]

Topic 5.6

1. (a) 10[1] [1]

(b) 11[1] [1]

2. (a)

	128	64	32	16	8	4	2	1	
	0	1	0	1	0	1	0	1	
	1	0	1	0	1	0	1	0	
Carry									+
	1	1	1	1	1	1	1	1	

[1]

(b)

	128	64	32	16	8	4	2	1	
	0	0	1	0	1	0	1	0	
	0	1	0	0	1	0	1	1	
Carry				1		1			+
	0	1	1	1	0	1	0	1	

[1] [2]

3. (a)

	128	64	32	16	8	4	2	1	
	0	1	1	0	1	1	0	0	
	0	1	0	0	1	0	1	1	
Carry	1			1					+
	1	0	1	1	0	1	1	1	

[1]

(b)

	128	64	32	16	8	4	2	1	
	0	1	0	1	1	1	0	1	
	0	1	0	1	1	1	0	1	
Carry	1		1	1	1		1		+
	1	0	1	1	1	0	1	0	

[1] [2]

4. (a)

	128	64	32	16	8	4	2	1	
	0	0	1	1	0	0	1	1	
	1	0	1	0	1	0	1	0	
Carry		1				1			+
	1	1	0	1	1	1	0	1	

[1]

[1 mark for correctly laying out the column titles and carry row. 1 mark for the answer. If the correct answer is given give 2 marks]

(b)

	128	64	32	16	8	4	2	1	
	0	1	0	1	1	0	1	0	
	0	1	1	1	1	1	1	1	
Carry	1	1	1	1	1	1			+
	1	1	0	1	1	0	0	1	

[1]

[1 mark for correctly laying out the column titles and carry row. 1 mark for the answer. If the correct answer is given give 2 marks] [4]

Topic 5.7

1. (a) American Standard Code for Information Interchange.[1] [1]

(b) 8 bits.[1] [1]

(c)

Character	ASCII code in decimal
b	98
k	107
r	114
Space	32
Full stop	46

[4]

(d)

c	a	l	l
0110 0011	0110 0001	0110 1100	0110 1100

[Space]	m	e	.
0010 0000	0110 1101	0110 0101	0010 1110

[1 mark for each two correct boxes.] [4]

Topic 6.1

1.

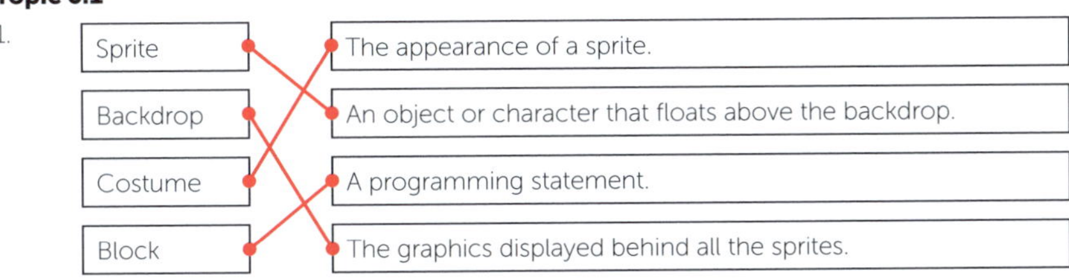

Sprite
Backdrop
Costume
Block
The appearance of a sprite.
An object or character that floats above the backdrop.
A programming statement.
The graphics displayed behind all the sprites.

[4]

2. **B** When the green flag is pressed.[1]

D When a key is pressed.[1] [2]

3.

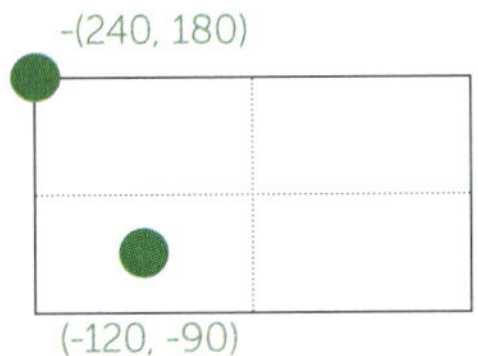

[2]

4. 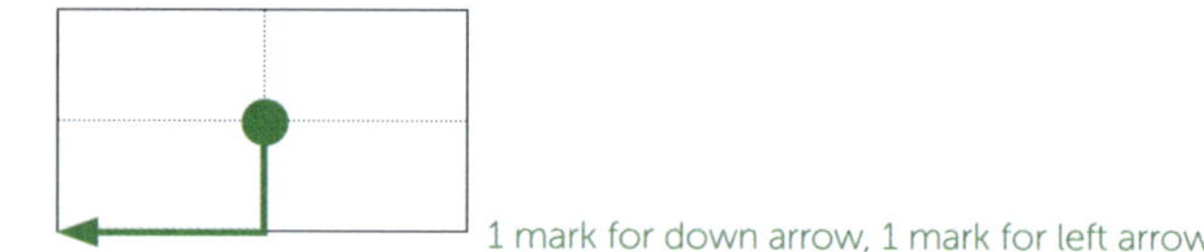 1 mark for down arrow, 1 mark for left arrow. [2]

Topic 6.2

1. (a)

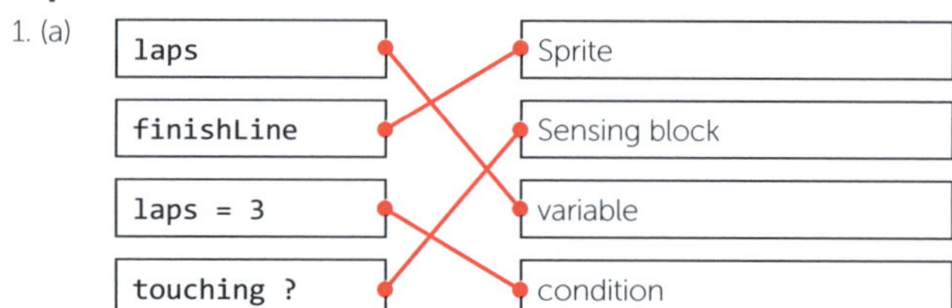

[4]

(b) Blue car output: You win.[1] [Note that the variable blueCarLaps is currently set to 3]
Yellow car output: Keep going.[1] [2]

(c)

Current variable name	The problem with the variable name	New suggested variable name
`time to complete lap`	It is too long and contains spaces. [1]	`lapTime` [1]
`p1name`	It isn't obvious what 'p' means. [1]	`player1Name` [1]

[4]

Topic 6.3

1. (a) **A** repeat <number>[1] **D** repeat until <condition>[1] **E** forever[1] [3]

2.

Code	when clicked; set counter to 0; repeat 3; change counter by 2; say counter for 1 seconds	when clicked; set counter2 to 0; repeat 3; repeat 3; change counter2 by 1; say counter2 for 1 seconds
Number of repetitions	3[1]	9[1]
Output	6[1] [Note: the counter variable is increased by 2 each time the loop happens]	9[1]

[4]

3. The code starts when the green flag is clicked[1]. It then repeats the first say block / says "Catch me"[1] until the mouse pointer touches the sprite[1]. It then says "You win"[1]. [3]

Topic 7.1

1. Operating systems[1]
Websites[1]
[Note: Computer software or applications are also correct answers. These are often also referred to as 'apps' these days.] [2]

2.

Wireframe component	Name
☒	Images[1] / Photos[1]
▶	Video player[1]
☰	Text[1] / paragraph of text[1]
▭	Button[1]

[4]

3. Marks for:

- Title of the ride attraction[1]
- A wireframe box for the photo[1]
- Lines for the other information[1]
- The current queue time[1]. [This is more meaningful with a title. The time itself could be written, in a box, or as a line if it is just text.]

[4]

Topic 7.2

1.

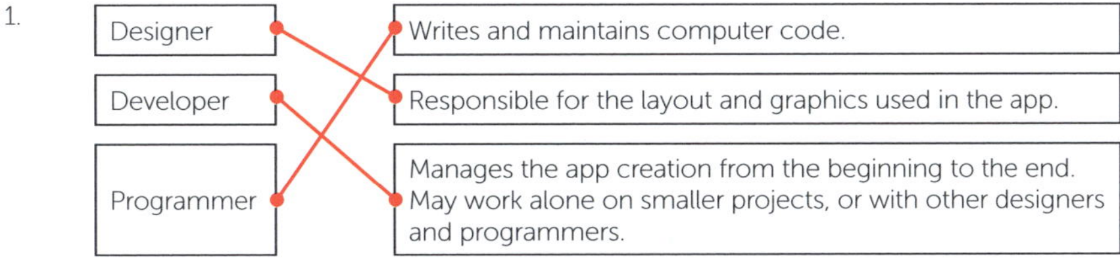

[3]

2. (a) Helps to show the user that the app is loading.[1]
Shows the user the logo/name of the app.[1] [2]

(b) Photos[1], illustrations[1], videos[1], sound effects[1], audio clips.[1] [2]

(c) Testing.[1] [1]

(d) They distribute the app to users[1] and bill customers / take payment for the app.[1] [2]

Topic 8.1

1. (a) 5 fields[1] [1]

(b) 7 records[1] [1]

(c) The title (name) of a column (field)[1] [1]

(d) The unique[1] field[1] that holds a unique value for each record[1] making each record unique.[1] [2]

(e) 7,6,5,4,3,2,1 [1] [This is because the population is ascending, so starts with the lowest] [1]

(f) 7,1,5,2,4,6,3 [1] [1]

(g) Viewing the data is easier[1] as only one record is displayed[1]. Buttons help the user to save the record / add a new record[1]. The form can be made more attractive[1] using formatting (such as background colour)[1] or altering the layout.[1] [3]

Topic 8.2

1. (a) <[1] [1]

(b) >=[1] [1]

(c) =[1] [1]

2.

Criteria for the Area field	Records returned from query
>6	2
<2	3 [Note: The criteria is <2, so doesn't include 2]
<=2	4
=0.4	1

[4]

3. SQL / Structured Query Language[1] [1]

4. Better presentation of the results[1] including improved/altered formatting[1] and layout[1]. [Other answers could include specific improvements such as adding a background colour, images or text colour.] [2]

Topic 9.1

1.

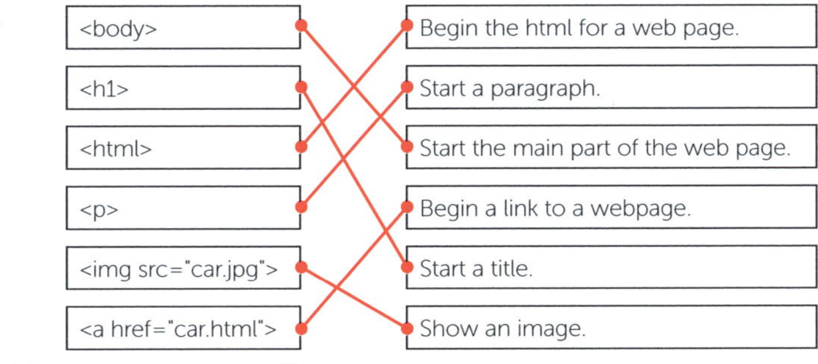

[6]

2. (a) <img src="dog.jpg"> [1] [1]

(b) <a href="dogs.html">All about dogs</a>
[1 mark for <a href="dogs.html">, 1 mark for </a>, 1 mark for appropriate text between the start and end tag.] [3]

Topic 9.2

1. Cascading Style Sheets.[1] [1]
2. center[1] [1]
3.

color	The colour of text.
background-color	The colour behind the text.
text-align	Make the text move to the left, centre or right.
border	Set the border width, style and colour.

[4]

4.

```
P {
  color : white;
  background-color: blue;
  border: 3px solid red;
  text-align: center;
    }
```

[4]

Topic 9.3

1.

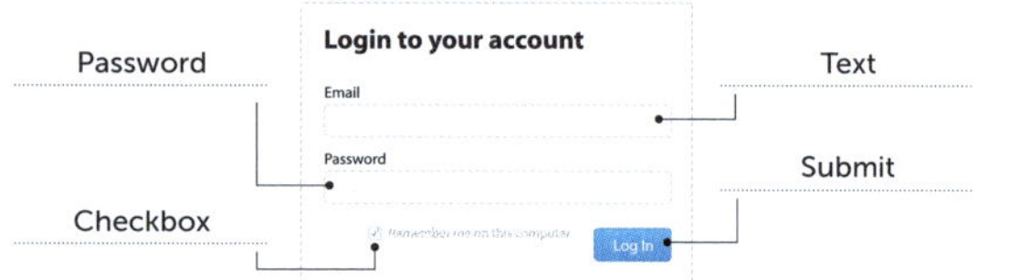

[4]

2. Only one radio button in a group can be selected at a time[1] whilst any number of checkboxes can be selected at the same time.[1] Checkboxes have a tick in a square box[1] whilst radio buttons have a dot in a circle.[1] [2]
3.

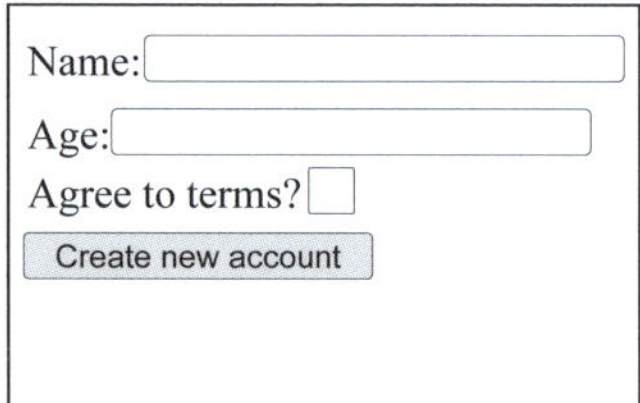


```
<form action="page_to_process">
  Name:<input type="....submit....."><br>
  Age:<input type="text"><br>
  Agree to terms and conditions?
  <input type=....."checkbox"><br>
  <input value....="Create new account">
</form>
```

[4]

Topic 10.1

1.

	Cable(s)	Terminators	Switch
Bus network	✓	✓	
Star network	✓		✓

1 mark for each correct row. [2]

2. Bus network: If the cable is cut, all computers lose their access to the network.[1] [Unless it's the cable from the PC to the backbone.]
Star network: If a cable is cut, only the one computer connected with that cable will lose access to the network.[1] [2]
3.

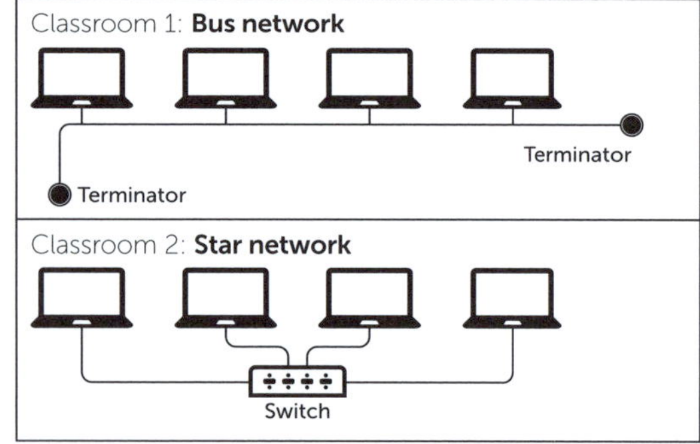

One cable for the bus network.[1]
Each computer connects to the one cable.[1]
A terminator is placed at either end of the cable.[1]
[The exact positioning of the cable doesn't matter.]

One cable to each computer.[1]
One central switch.[1]
Each cable connects to the switch.[1]
[The exact positioning of the cables and switch don't matter.]

[6]

Topic 10.2

1.

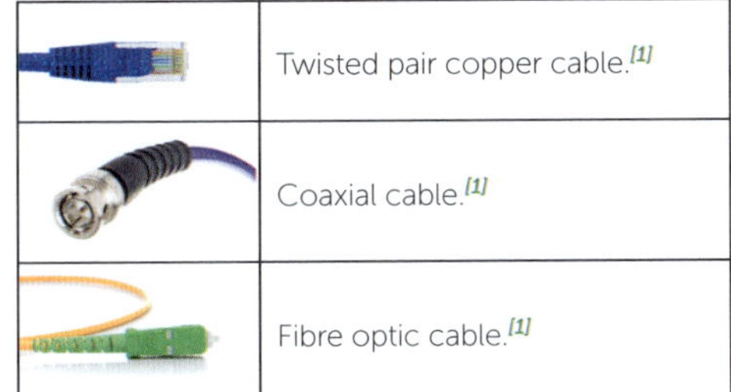

	Twisted pair copper cable.[1]
	Coaxial cable.[1]
	Fibre optic cable.[1]

[3]

2.

Situation	Connection type	Reason for your choice
To connect a PC to a school network.	Twisted pair copper cable.[1]	It is used for star networks[1]. It is relatively fast.[1] Most PCs come with a port for this type of connection[1].
To connect a smartphone to a home network.	Wireless [1] / Wi-Fi[1]	It allows the device to be portable / it doesn't require a cable / smartphones don't have a network cable port[1].

[4]

3. File size = 100 megabyte x 8 = 800 megabits [1]
800 megabits ÷ 20 megabits per second [1] = 40 seconds [1] [3]

Topic 10.3

1. (a) HTTP / Hypertext Transfer Protocol[1] or HTTPS / Hypertext Transfer Protocol Secure[1] [1]
(b) social[1] [1]
(c) pgexd.com[1] [1]
(d) profile[1] [1]

2.

IP address	✓/×
74.6.143.26	✓[1]
185.15.590.226	×
13.107.21.200	✓[1]
151.101.128.144.22	×

[2]

3. The information is broken down into smaller amounts[1] called packets.[1] Each packet contains a packet number[1] and destination address.[1] The packets can take different routes to the destination.[1] Once at the destination the packets are put back into order.[1] [3]

4. The world wide web is one service that makes use of the Internet.[1] [1]

Topic 10.4

1.

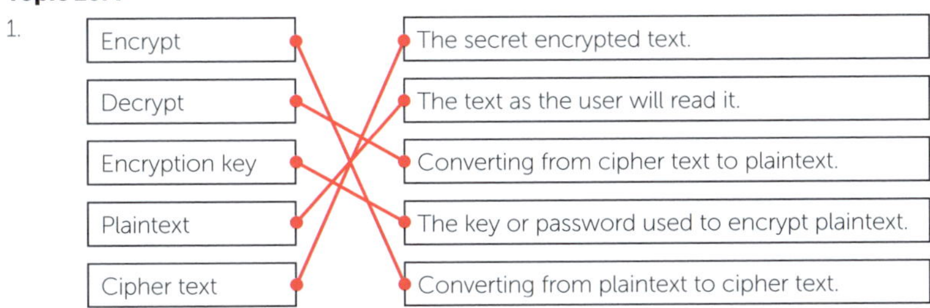

Encrypt
Decrypt
Encryption key
Plaintext
Cipher text
The secret encrypted text.
The text as the user will read it.
Converting from cipher text to plaintext.
The key or password used to encrypt plaintext.
Converting from plaintext to cipher text.

[5]

2. (a) (i) MJ[1]
(ii) LEH[1]
(iii) JIIH[1] [3]
(b) FAB CHEF BIG BEACH [1] [1]

3. The green padlock means that the web page is encrypted/secure[1] (when data is transmitted between the user's computer and the web server). [1]

Topic 11.1

1. (a) *[1] [1]
(b) /[1] [1]

2. (a) £15.00[1] [1]
(b) D7[1] [1]
(c) =B2[1]*C2[1] [2]
(d) =B3[1]*C3[1] [2]
(e) =D2+[1]D3+D4+D5[1] OR =SUM[1](D2:D5) [1] [2]

Topic 11.2

1. (a) 4[1] [1]
(b) =AVERAGE(C2:C8)[1] [1]
(c) =MAX(B2:B8)[1] [1]

(d) =MAX(C2:C8)[2] [2]

(e) =MIN(C2:C8)[2] [2]

(f) =COUNT(B2:B8)[2] [2]

(g) 28[1] [1]

Topic 11.3

1. A (dotted) border.[1]
(orange) text colour.[1]
(light green) fill colour.[1] [3]

2.

Merge cells	Make the text thicker.
Insert image	Combine two or more cells so they act as one cell.
Bold	Add a picture, photo or illustration.

[3]

3. (a) Conditional formatting alters the formatting of each cell[1] based on the values that each cell contains.[1] [2]

(b) There are many examples, for example, prices of sweets,[1] number of children in each class.[1] [1]

4. Fill the cells with white.[1] Alternatively press ALT + W, V, G or go to View > Show > deselect gridlines checkbox. [1]

Topic 11.4

1. (a) £2,000[1] [1]

(b) =B5*E3[2]
1 mark for =B5* 1 mark for E3 [2]

(c) =B15*E3[2]
1 mark for =B15 1 mark for the rest of the formula [2]

(d) =SUM(C4:C15)[2]
1 mark for =SUM( ) 1 mark for C4:C15 [2]

(e) £144,000[1] [1]

(f) It makes the cell reference an absolute cell reference[1] which means that it won't change when it is copied and pasted to another cell.[1] [1]

(g) It is only a prediction[1] so it could lead to incorrect results[1] which cause people to make the wrong/poor decisions.[1] [1]

Topic 11.5

1. (a) Line chart[1] [1]

1. (b)

A	Key
B	x-axis label
C	y-axis label
D	Title

[4]

(c) Height increases with age.[1]
Boys keep growing until around 17[1] whilst girls keep growing until around 16.[1]
Boys and girls have similar heights until around age 14[1] when boys become slightly taller. [2]

(d) A pie chart cannot represent both boys and girls data[1] (two pie charts would need to be used to do this).
As all the heights are very similar, it would be very hard to see the trend/differences in a pie chart.[1]
A pie chart isn't appropriate as it is normally used to show a proportion of the total amount.[1] The total height from all year's measurements makes no sense.[1] [2]

2. People have less money in January (after spending at Christmas) so this could result in lower sales.[1]
People often diet in January, so this could affect fast food sales.[1]
Accept other reasonable reasons for low January sales. [1]

Topic 12.1

1. (a)

Syntax	Carry out the instructions in a program.
Line numbers	The order in which words and symbols are correctly placed in a programming language.
Run	Lines of code run in order, one after the other.
Sequence	A unique number given to each line of code.

[4]

(b) `print("Game Over!")`[1] [1]

(c) `print("Instructions")`[1]
`print("------------")`[1] [2]

(d) `input(`[1]`"Press enter for the next level")`[1] [2]

(e) F5[1] [1]

Topic 12.2

1. When a program is running it needs to store values for later use. Each value is stored in a variable.[1] Values could be a string[1] (e.g. "Hello"), integer (e.g. 47) or floating point number (e.g. 8.72). In programming the = symbol is known as the assignment[1] operator when it is putting a value into a variable. [3]

2.

Item of data	Suggested variable name
A score in a game.	`score`
The length of time to complete one lap around a racetrack.	`lapTime` [1]
A password to log in to a website.	`loginPassword` [1]
Player 1 in a two player game.	`player1` [1]

[3]

3. Enter pet name:[1] Rocky
Hello
Rocky[1] [2]

4.

```
city =[1] input("What is the capital of Italy?")
print("You said")
print(city[1]) [Note: "City" in quotes is incorrect as this is using a variable not a string]
print("The correct answer is Rome")
```

[2]

Topic 12.3

1.

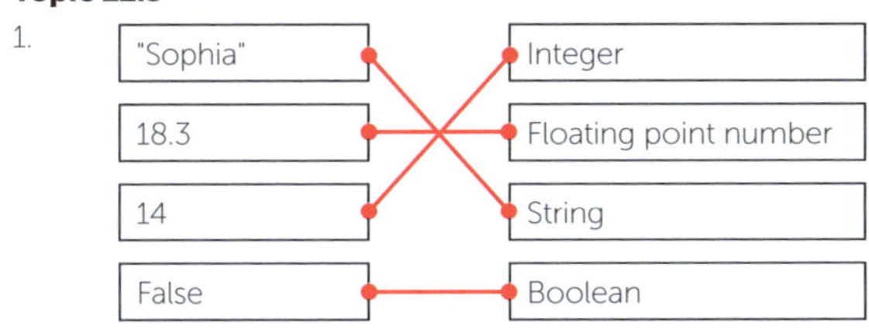

[4]

2. Concatenate operator / joining two strings together [1].
Addition / adding two numbers together [1]. [2]

3. `float("5.0")`[1]

4.

```
seconds = input[1] ("Enter your race time in seconds")
seconds = int[1] (seconds)
minutes = seconds / 60
print("Your race time was " + string[1] (minutes))
```

[4]

Topic 12.4

1. 12[1]
27[1]
3[1]
25[1] [4]

2. Program 1: +[1]
Program 2: –[1] [2]

3. Program 1: 100[1]
Program 2: 2.0[1]
Program 3: 8[1]
Program 4: 120.0[1] [4]

Topic 12.5

1.

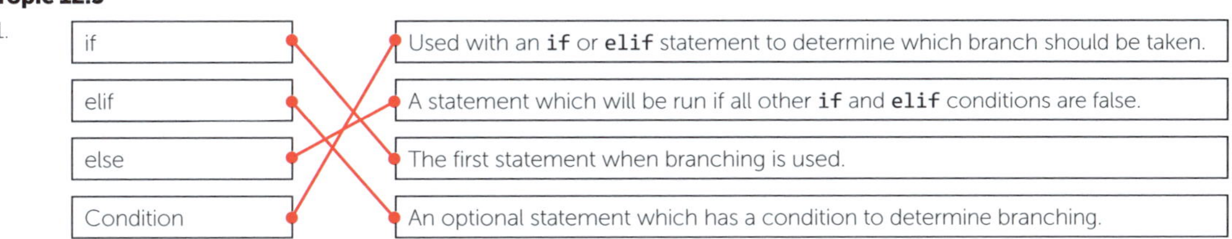

[4]

2.

```
password = input("Please enter your password: ")
if password ==[1] "monster15":
  print("Welcome")
else[1]:[1]
  print("Incorrect password")
```

[3]

3.

```
quantity = int(input("How many apples would you like? "))
if quantity < 1:
  print("You must buy at least 1")

elif quantity >= 1 and quantity < 9:
  print("Buy individually")
else:
  print("Buy in bulk")
```

1 mark for: `quantity >= 1` or `quantity > 0`
1 mark for: `and`
1 mark for: `quantity < 9`
Only 2 marks for: `quantity >= 1 and <9` as this won't run. [3]

Topic 12.6

1. **B** For loop.[1]
   F While loop.[1] [2]

2. 1 x 6 = 6[1] [1 mark for have two rows of output (due to two repetitions)]
   2 x 6 = 12[1] [1 mark for the correct style of output] [2]

3. (a)

Input guess	Output
17	Too low. [1]
-1	Too low. [1]
33	Too high. [1]
32	You got it! [1]

[4]

(b) Before the user enters anything[1] the program will output "Too low."[1]. This is because the guess is initially -1.[1] An elif should be used instead of the else statement[1] with the code:

```
elif guess < target and guess != -1:
```
[2] [2]

Topic 13.1

1.

Car detection and probability	Car action
School: 100%	Drive at 20mph or less[1]
Slow sign: 100%	Reduce speed (below 20mph)[1]
Girl: 90% **AND** Zebra crossing: 60%	Stop[1]
Zebra crossing: 100% **AND** girl: 0% **AND** boy: 0%	Drive at 10mph[1]

[4]

2. If there is furniture in front, turn left/right.[1]
   If there is a person/animal in front, turn left/right.[1]
   If there is a wall in front, turn left/right.[1]
   If cannot move forward (e.g. too steep / a rug stops the wheels turning), reverse.[1]
   (There are many other rules that could be used here.) [2]

3. The use of AI could free people from the easier parts of the job[1] so that they focus on the more interesting/difficult problems to solve[1]. However, the use of AI in this way could mean that jobs are lost.[1] If the AI system has any biases/mistakes in it,[1] then these would continue to be given in the output text.[1] The company that develops the AI[1] will control the output[1] which could result in it serving the agenda of just a few people/large companies[1] rather than the general population.[1] [4]

Topic 13.2

1.

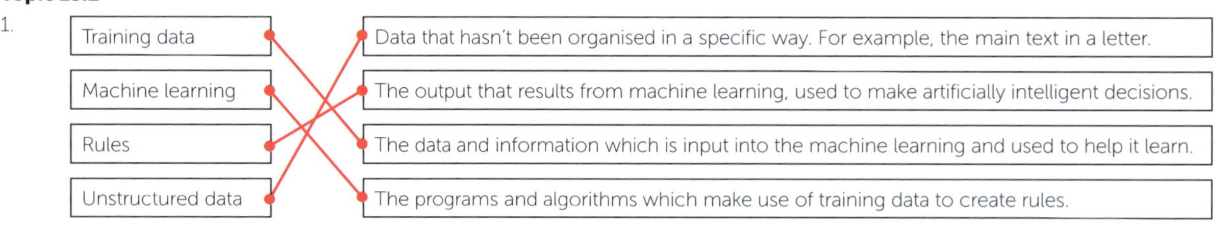

Training data
Machine learning
Rules
Unstructured data
Data that hasn't been organised in a specific way. For example, the main text in a letter.
The output that results from machine learning, used to make artificially intelligent decisions.
The data and information which is input into the machine learning and used to help it learn.
The programs and algorithms which make use of training data to create rules.

[4]

(a) The rules say that a cat must have two open eyes[1] but the cat shown has closed eyes.[1] As all the training data had cats with open eyes[1] the rule was (incorrectly) created that cats must have open eyes.[1] [2]

(b) A larger amount of training data could be used[1] which includes cats with closed eyes[1] and other animals with open/closed eyes.[1] This would give the machine learning system more opportunity to learn what a cat with closed eyes looks like.[1] [2]

(c) Machine learning could be given training data of x-rays of lots of arms[1]. Both broken and unbroken arms would be given.[1] The arms would be classified as broken and unbroken.[1] The machine learning algorithm/program would then create a set of rules[1] to determine if another x-ray/image of an arm was broken or not.[1] [2]

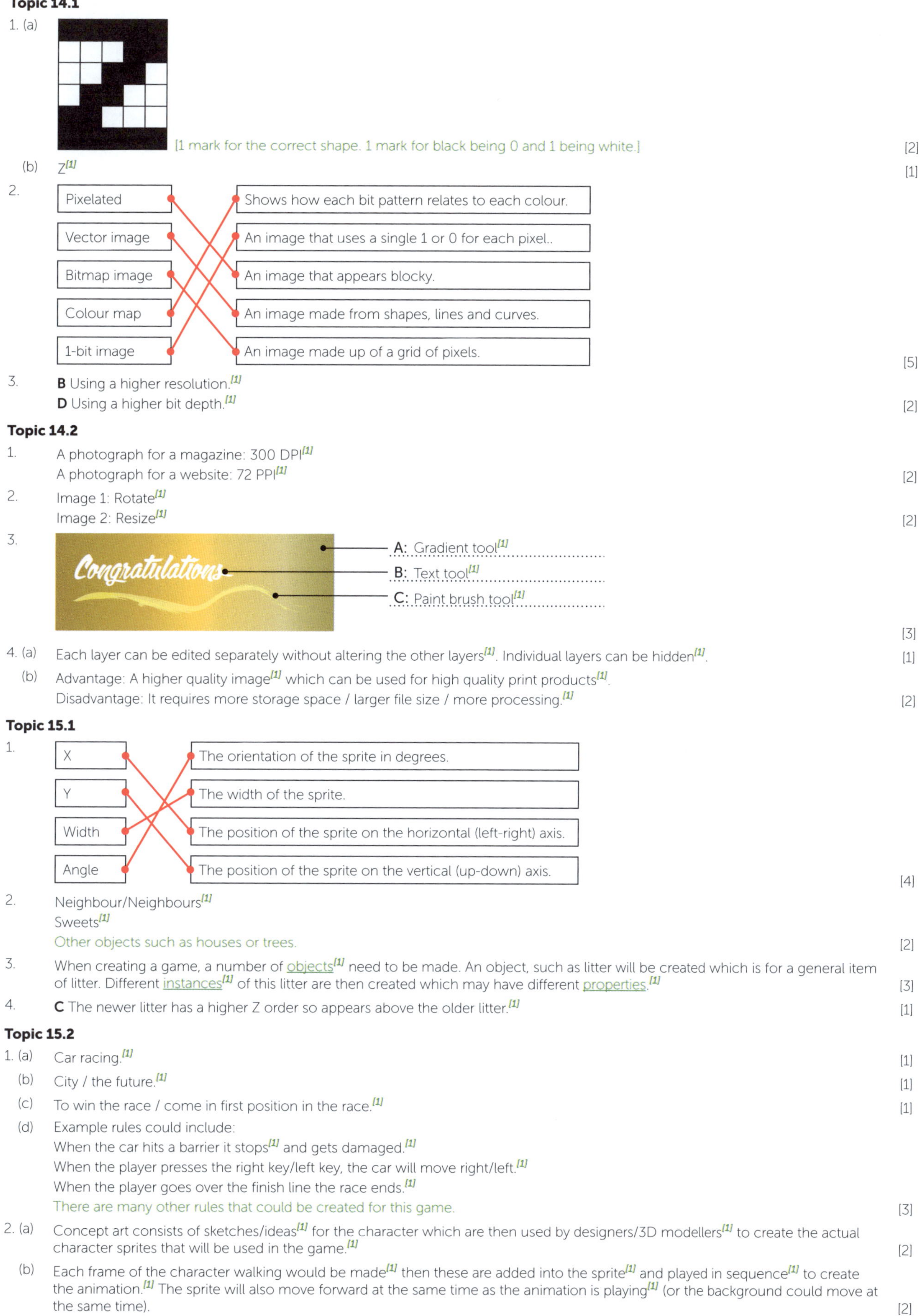

Topic 14.1

1. (a) [1 mark for the correct shape. 1 mark for black being 0 and 1 being white.] [2]

   (b) Z[1] [1]

2.

Pixelated	Shows how each bit pattern relates to each colour.
Vector image	An image that uses a single 1 or 0 for each pixel..
Bitmap image	An image that appears blocky.
Colour map	An image made from shapes, lines and curves.
1-bit image	An image made up of a grid of pixels.

[5]

3. **B** Using a higher resolution.[1]
   D Using a higher bit depth.[1] [2]

Topic 14.2

1. A photograph for a magazine: 300 DPI[1]
   A photograph for a website: 72 PPI[1] [2]

2. Image 1: Rotate[1]
   Image 2: Resize[1] [2]

3. Congratulations

   A: Gradient tool[1]
   B: Text tool[1]
   C: Paint brush tool[1] [3]

4. (a) Each layer can be edited separately without altering the other layers[1]. Individual layers can be hidden[1]. [1]

   (b) Advantage: A higher quality image[1] which can be used for high quality print products[1].
   Disadvantage: It requires more storage space / larger file size / more processing.[1] [2]

Topic 15.1

1.

X	The orientation of the sprite in degrees.
Y	The width of the sprite.
Width	The position of the sprite on the horizontal (left-right) axis.
Angle	The position of the sprite on the vertical (up-down) axis.

[4]

2. Neighbour/Neighbours[1]
   Sweets[1]
   Other objects such as houses or trees. [2]

3. When creating a game, a number of objects[1] need to be made. An object, such as litter will be created which is for a general item of litter. Different instances[1] of this litter are then created which may have different properties.[1] [3]

4. **C** The newer litter has a higher Z order so appears above the older litter.[1] [1]

Topic 15.2

1. (a) Car racing.[1] [1]

   (b) City / the future.[1] [1]

   (c) To win the race / come in first position in the race.[1] [1]

   (d) Example rules could include:
   When the car hits a barrier it stops[1] and gets damaged.[1]
   When the player presses the right key/left key, the car will move right/left.[1]
   When the player goes over the finish line the race ends.[1]
   There are many other rules that could be created for this game. [3]

2. (a) Concept art consists of sketches/ideas[1] for the character which are then used by designers/3D modellers[1] to create the actual character sprites that will be used in the game.[1] [2]

   (b) Each frame of the character walking would be made[1] then these are added into the sprite[1] and played in sequence[1] to create the animation.[1] The sprite will also move forward at the same time as the animation is playing[1] (or the background could move at the same time). [2]

Topic 15.3

1.

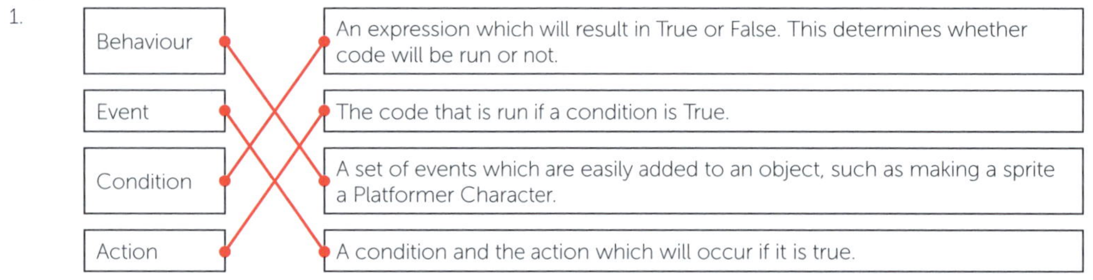

Behaviour
Event
Condition
Action
An expression which will result in True or False. This determines whether code will be run or not.
The code that is run if a condition is True.
A set of events which are easily added to an object, such as making a sprite a Platformer Character.
A condition and the action which will occur if it is true.

[4]

2. (a) When the dinosaur falls below the bottom of the screen[1] (from falling off a platform) they are sent back to the starting position.[1]
OR
When the position of Dino is greater/lower than the window/screen height[1] change the x,y coordinates of Dino to (250,288).[1] [2]

(b) **B** Platformer character.[1] [1]

(c)

Event	
Condition	Action
Dino is in collision with Enemy[1]	Change the x position of Dino: set to 450[1] Change the y position of Dino: set to 288[1]

[3]

Topic 16.1

1.

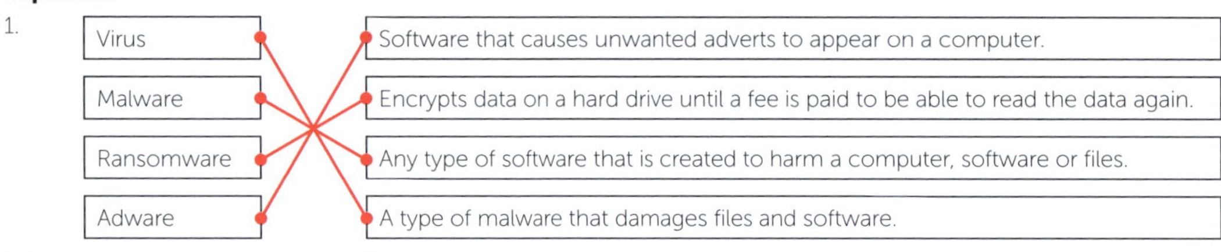

Virus
Malware
Ransomware
Adware
Software that causes unwanted adverts to appear on a computer.
Encrypts data on a hard drive until a fee is paid to be able to read the data again.
Any type of software that is created to harm a computer, software or files.
A type of malware that damages files and software.

[4]

2. (a) **A** maGazine4tooth&queen[1]
B fq=FNrTThi+5 [1] [2]

(b) Update software/apps,[1] virus checkers.[1]
Only download files from websites you trust.[1]
Never visit/download from illegal sites.[1]
Be careful when opening email attachments.[1] [2]

3. It only has 9 characters.[1] (A strong password should have 10 or more characters.)
It doesn't have any numbers.[1]
It doesn't have any special characters.[1]
It is made up of recognisable words.[1] [2]

Topic 16.2

1. © Copyright Sam Heath 2024
©[1]
Copyright[1]
2024[1]
Alternative order such as Copyright © 2024 Sam Heath is acceptable. [3]

2. **A** A film[1]
D A book[1] [2]

3. Copyright, Designs and Patents Act.[1] [1]

4. Scenario 1: 70 years[1] after the author's death.[1]
Scenario 2: 50 years[1] (from the date it is first broadcast). [3]

5. **B** This is illegal.[1] (This is because Anika only has a licence for the music for personal use. She would need a different licence or permission to use the soundtrack in a video that she provides for public use). [1]

Topic 16.3

1. (a) Blue light can keep you up / disrupt sleep patterns.[1] [1]

(b) Night time settings / night shift settings (iPhone) / night light settings (Windows) / eye comfort settings (Android) are used to reduce blue light.[1] [1]

(c) **A** The display doesn't have any reflections on it.[1]
D The display can be tilted up and down.[1]
E The display doesn't flicker.[1] [3]

2. Elbow angle between 90-120° (here it is about 80°).[1]
Wrist support not being used for the keyboard.[1]
No lumbar support on the chair.[1]
Feet aren't touching the floor / no footrest.[1]
The user is hunched over / doesn't have a straight back.[1] [4]

3. Training in how to use equipment safely.[1]
Correct lighting.[1]
Removing trip hazards.[1]
Regular electrical testing.[1]
Suitable fire extinguishers.[1]
Access to fire escapes.[1] [1]

Topic 17.1

1. `names = ["Olivia", "Noah", "Ali"]`
1 mark for each name being in speech marks/quote marks (to make them strings).
1 mark for the use of square brackets.
1 mark for each string separated by a comma. [3]

2.

Line of code	Output
`print(results[0])`	`8`
`print(results[3])`	`10`
`print(results)`	`[8, 7, 9, 10, 6]`

[3]

3.

```
results = [8, 7, 9, 10, 6]
total = 0
for i in range(0,5):
    total = total + results[i]
average = total / 5
print(average)
```

1 mark for range( ).
1 mark for the correct range as 0,5.
1 mark for results[ ].
1 mark for using i inside the square brackets. [4]

Topic 17.2

1.

Question	Answer
Give the reason why **pyramidVolume** is a function not a procedure.	It returns volume / returns a value. (Procedures don't return anything).
How many arguments does **pyramidVolume** have?	Three.
Give the output from the program.	6.0 (accept 6).
Give the result of the following function call: `pyramidVolume(3, 1, 1)`	1.0 (accept 1).
Give the result of the following function call: `pyramidVolume(5, 3, 2)`	10.0

[5]

2. (a)

```
def average(a, b):
    result = (a + b) / 2
    return result
print(average(10,2))
```

1 mark for **a, b** in the brackets.
1 mark for return
1 mark for result [3]

(b) 6.0[1] [accept 6]. [1]

(c) `average(15, 5)`[1].
Accept `print(average(15,5)`.
Accept `average(5,15)`. [1]

Topic 18.1

1.

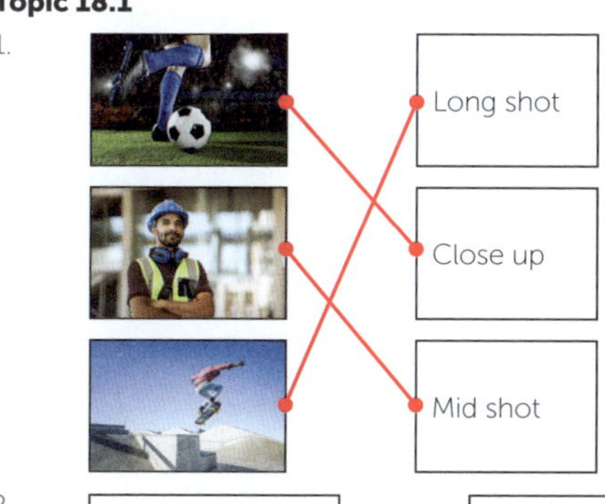

[3]

2.

Pan	Move the camera up and down.
Tilt	Move the camera side to side.
Tracking	Move the camera along a predefined route.

[3]

3. Shot type: Close up.[1] Reason for choice: It helps to show the joy in the teenager's face.[1]
Shot type: Mid shot.[1] Reason for choice: The teenager's expressions in arm movements could also be seen.[1] The bike could also be in shot.[1]
Accept other shot types or camera angles if they have an appropriate reason. [2]

4. Camera angle: High angle.[1] Reason for choice: This angle helps to show someone as weak/vulnerable[1] (which matches the situation).
Accept other camera angles/reasons if they match the scenario. [2]

Topic 18.2

1.

INT.	→	A location that is inside.
EXT.	→	A location that is outside.
Dialogue	→	The words that actors will say.
Location	→	The place where a scene will take place.

[4]

2.

A	→	Location
B	→	Shot type
C	→	Character name
D	→	Transition

[4]

3.

Script component	Formatting that is usually used
Character name	Uppercase/Capital letters[1]/Centred[1]
Transition	Uppercase/Capital letters[1]/Right-aligned[1]

A maximum of one mark for Uppercase/Capital letters. [2]

Topic 18.3

1. **A** Director[1]
C Storyboard artist[1] [2]

2. Scene number,[1] shot number,[1] duration,[1] camera movement,[1] camera angle,[1] shot type,[1] transition,[1] dialogue.[1] [2]

3. Scene 1 Shot 4 Duration 4s

CLOSE UP.
HOLLY – "WOW. I DIDN'T THINK IT WOULD TAKE THAT LONG."

→ CUT

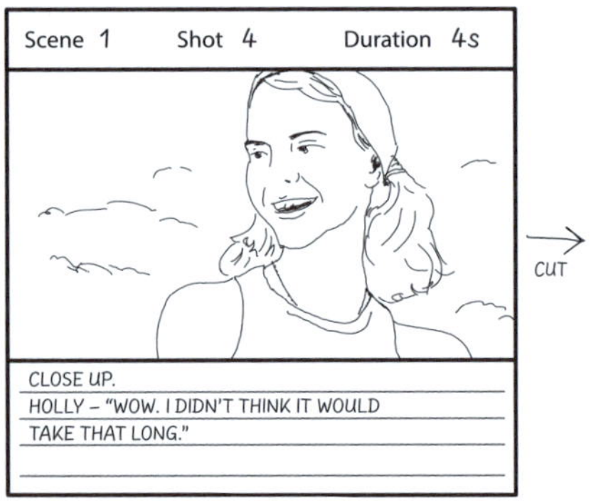

Scene 1.[1]
Shot 4.[1]
Sensible duration.[1]
Close up (either written or obvious from the sketch drawn).[1]
Sketch shows holly.[1]
She is facing Callum (who is on the left of the shot).[1]
Description shows the dialogue for the shot.[1]
Transition shown[1]
Award an additional mark for well-drawn sketches.[1]

[5]

4. The long shot will allow the viewer to know they are watching a new setting/location.[1] This will work well as an establishing shot.[1] [1]

Topic 18.4

1.

Scrubbing	→	Moving the slider back and forth through the timeline.
Timeline	→	An area in video editing software where video and audio clips are arranged.
Cross fade	→	Fading out one shot whilst fading in another shot.
Cut	→	A transition which instantly moves from one shot to another.

[4]

2. Background music / soundtrack.[1]
Sound effects.[1] [2]

3. (a) 5.[1] [1]
(b) 3.[1] [1]
(c) Editor / video editor.[1] [Not film editor as this isn't a film]. [1]
(d) The titles will not be seen / be obscured by the video footage in the track.[1] [1]

Topic 19.1

1.

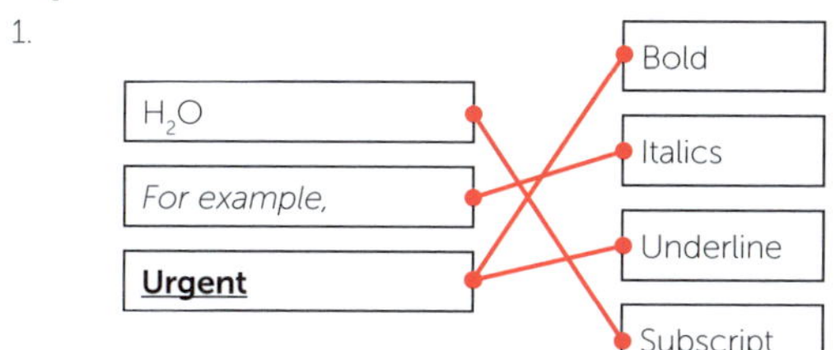

[3]

2. (a) The names don't need to be in order / numbered lists are used for items that need to be ordered.*[1]* [1]

(b) It's easy to see exactly how many students are on the list. *[1]* [1]

3.

Centred[1]

Justified[1]

Right aligned[1]

[3]

4. Superscript*[1]*. Grammar check*[1]*. Thesaurus*[1]*. Tables*[1]*. (inserting) images*[1]*.

Accept other features that are commonly used in word-processors such as word count, index, contents page, page numbering and styles. [2]

Topic 19.2

1.

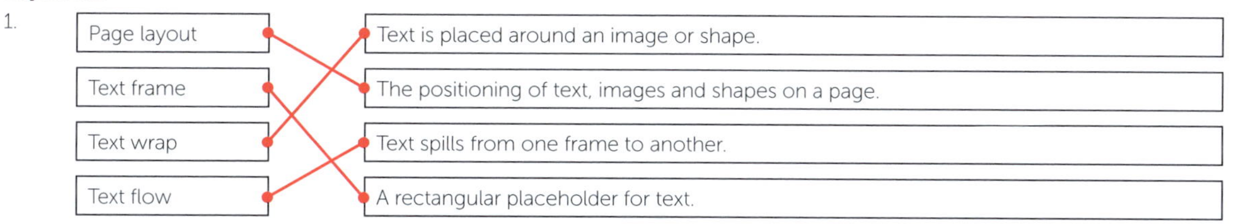

Page layout — The positioning of text, images and shapes on a page.
Text frame — A rectangular placeholder for text.
Text wrap — Text is placed around an image or shape.
Text flow — Text spills from one frame to another.

[4]

2. Magazines,*[1]* posters,*[1]* books,*[1]* brochures,*[1]* leaflets.*[1]*

Accept other products likely to use DTP such as CD inlays, DVD inlays, Bus wraps. [3]

3. Page thumbnails give a designer the ability to see/scroll through many pages at once.*[1]* This enables them to quickly find a page.*[1]* By clicking/selecting the thumbnail of a page, the page will appear ready for editing.*[1]* [1]

4. The designer makes one or more master pages that contain features that will be the same on many pages*[1]*. They then apply the master page to many pages.*[1]* The layout/common features of these pages are then automatically completed*[1]* which will save the designer time.*[1]* If a change is made to the master, then it will be applied to all pages that use it*[1]* which will save the designer time.*[1]* Improved design consistency.*[1]* [2]

Topic 19.3

1. Background colour.*[1]*
Background image.*[1]*
Videos.*[1]*
Sound/music.*[1]*

Accept other common features such as shapes, icon or tables. [3]

2. (left) mouse click,*[1]* press a key/space/right cursor key/down cursor key.*[1]* [1]

3.

Animation	Slide objects may move or change appearance as they enter, are displayed or leave the screen.
Transition	A visual effect that is applied when moving from one slide to the next.
Trigger	The event that causes an animation to occur.
Timing	Control the duration of an animation, transition or delay needed before a slide is advanced..

[4]

4. Consistent transitions,*[1]* consistent colour/background/style,*[1]* use master slides*[1]* to save time and create consistent slides, don't overuse animation/transitions/multimedia content,*[1]* consider having minimal content to allow the audience to focus on the speaker.*[1]* [2]

USEFUL INFORMATION

Shortcuts

Shortcut	Meaning
CTRL + C	Copy
CTRL + V	Paste
CTRL + X	Cut
DEL	Delete
F2	Edit/rename
WIN + E	Windows Explorer
CTRL + D	Bookmark a web page
CTRL + H	Show web history
WINDOWS + L	Lock computer

Flowchart symbols

Symbol	Meaning
Start	Start / stop
Delay 1	Delay, processing
Turn On Amber	Turn on / off, input/output
Is button 1 ON? Yes / No	Decision
Sub OpenBarrier	Subroutine
→	Direction of flow

Logic gates

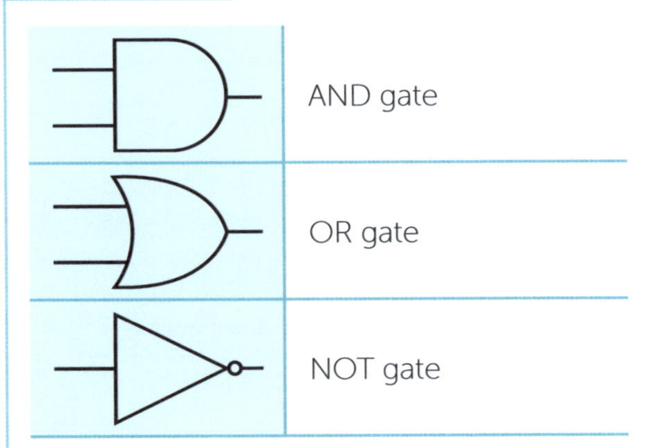

AND gate

OR gate

NOT gate

Wireframe components

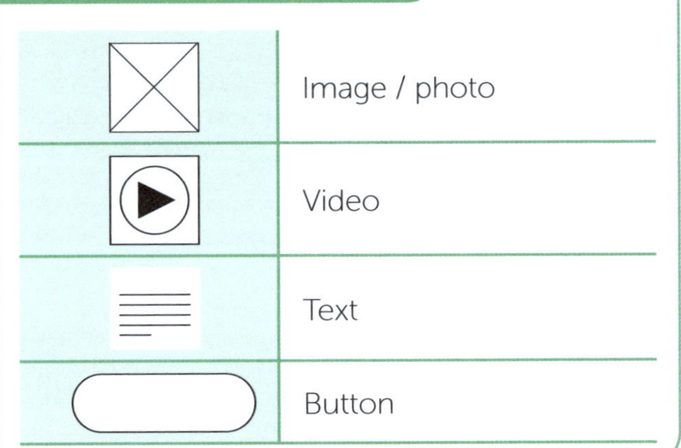

Image / photo

Video

Text

Button

Units

Prefix	Symbol	Meaning
Kilo	k	1 000
Mega	M	1 000 000
Giga	G	1 000 000 000
Tera	T	1 000 000 000 000

	Symbol	Meaning
Bit	b	1, 0 (binary digit)
Nibble		4 bits
Byte	B	8 bits
hertz	Hz	Frequency (cycles per second). Used in recordings or CPU speed.

Spreadsheet functions

`=AVERAGE(A1:A5)`	Find the average from cells A1 to A5.
`=SUM(A1:A5)`	Adds all the numbers from cells A1 to A5.
`=MIN(A1:A5)`	Finds the minimum number from cells A1 to A5.
`=MAX(A1:A5)`	Finds the maximum number from cells A1 to A5.
`=COUNT(A1:A5)`	Counts how many cells contain values from cells A1 to A5.

Python

`score = 5`	Assignment
`input("Age: ")`	Get user input
`print("Hello")`	Output "Hello"
`int()`	Convert to integer
`float()`	Convert to floating point number
`str()`	Convert to string

`if score == 10:`
`  print("Perfect")`
`elif score >= 8:`
`  print("Well done")`
`else:`
`  print("Keep trying")`
	If, else if and else statement

`while lives > 0:` `  #play game`	While loop
`for i in range(1,11):` `  print(i)`	For loop that outputs 1 to 10
`scores = [8, 7, 8, 9]`	Create a list with four numbers.
`print(scores[0])` `print(scores[1])`	Output 8 then 7 (remember lists start at 0)
`def add(a, b):` `  return a + b`	Make a function which adds two numbers
`add(3, 5)`	Call the **add** function. 8 Will be returned.

Comparison operators

Operator	Meaning
<	Less than
<=	Less than or equal to
>	Greater than
>=	Greater than or equal to
==	Equal to
!=	Not equal to

Arithmetic operators

Operator	Meaning
+	Addition
-	Subtraction
*	Multiplication
/	Division
**	Exponent (power)

ASCII table

Code	Char	Code	Char	Code	Char	Code	Char
00 ↓ 31	Control characters	53	5	78	N	103	g
		54	6	79	O	104	h
		55	7	80	P	105	i
		56	8	81	Q	106	j
32	Space	57	9	82	R	107	k
33	!	58	:	83	S	108	l
34	"	59	;	84	T	109	m
35	#	60	<	85	U	110	n
36	$	61	=	86	V	111	o
37	%	62	>	87	W	112	p
38	&	63	?	88	X	113	q
39	'	64	@	89	Y	114	r
40	(	65	A	90	Z	115	s
41	)	66	B	91	[	116	t
42	*	67	C	92	\	117	u
43	+	68	D	93	]	118	v
44	,	69	E	94	^	119	w
45	-	70	F	95	_	120	x
46	.	71	G	96	`	121	y
47	/	72	H	97	a	122	z
48	0	73	I	98	b	123	{
49	1	74	J	99	c	124	|
50	2	75	K	100	d	125	}
51	3	76	L	101	e	126	~
52	4	77	M	102	f	127	DEL

Binary and hexadecimal

Denary	Binary	Hexadecimal
0	0	0
1	1	1
2	10	2
3	11	3
4	100	4
5	101	5
6	110	6
7	111	7
8	1000	8
9	1001	9
10	1010	A
11	1011	B
12	1100	C
13	1101	D
14	1110	E
15	1111	F

NOTES, DOODLES AND TESTS

Year 7

Target grade:

....

End of year grade/result:

....

Test dates

Year 7: ....

Year 8: ....

Year 9: ....

Year 8

Target grade:

....

End of year grade/result:

....

Year 9

Target grade:

....

End of year grade/result:

....

ANSWER CONTINUATION SHEETS

INDEX

MAPPING TO THE NATIONAL CURRICULUM

The following shows how each of the sections of this book cover the subject content in the Computing programme of study for the Key Stage 3 National Curriculum.

	1	2	3	4	5	6	7	8	9	10	11	12	13	14	15	16	17	18	19
Design, use and evaluate computational abstractions that model the state and behaviour of real-world problems and physical systems.		✓	✓							✓	✓		✓		✓		✓		
Understand several key algorithms that reflect computational thinking [for example, ones for sorting and searching]; use logical reasoning to compare the utility of alternative algorithms for the same problem.			✓									✓	✓				✓		
Use two or more programming languages, at least one of which is textual, to solve a variety of computational problems; make appropriate use of data structures [for example, lists, tables or arrays]; design and develop modular programs that use procedures or functions.		✓				✓						✓			✓		✓		
Understand simple Boolean logic [for example, AND, OR and NOT] and some of its uses in circuits and programming; understand how numbers can be represented in binary, and be able to carry out simple operations on binary numbers [for example, binary addition, and conversion between binary and decimal].			✓		✓							✓					✓		
Understand the hardware and software components that make up computer systems, and how they communicate with one another and with other systems.		✓			✓					✓									
Understand how instructions are stored and executed within a computer system; understand how data of various types (including text, sounds and pictures) can be represented and manipulated digitally, in the form of binary digits.				✓	✓									✓					
Undertake creative projects that involve selecting, using, and combining multiple applications, preferably across a range of devices, to achieve challenging goals, including collecting and analysing data and meeting the needs of known users.	✓			✓		✓	✓	✓	✓		✓			✓	✓			✓	✓
Create, re-use, revise and re-purpose digital artefacts for a given audience, with attention to trustworthiness, design and usability.	✓			✓			✓		✓		✓			✓	✓	✓		✓	✓
Understand a range of ways to use technology safely, respectfully, responsibly and securely, including protecting their online identity and privacy; recognise inappropriate content, contact and conduct and know how to report concerns.	✓									✓						✓			

New titles coming soon!

Revision, re-imagined

These guides are everything you need to ace your exams and beam with pride. Each topic is laid out in a beautifully illustrated format that is clear, approachable and as concise and simple as possible.

- Hundreds of marks worth of examination style questions
- Answers provided for all questions within the books
- Illustrated topics to improve memory and recall
- Specification references for every topic
- Examination tips and techniques
- Free Python solutions pack (CS Only)

Absolute clarity is the aim.

Explore the series and add to your collection at **www.clearrevise.com**

Available from all good book shops

PG ONLINE
2021 Winner 2022 Winner 2023 Winner
ClearRevise
Illustrated revision and practice
OCR
Creative iMedia
Levels 1/2
J834 (R093, R094)

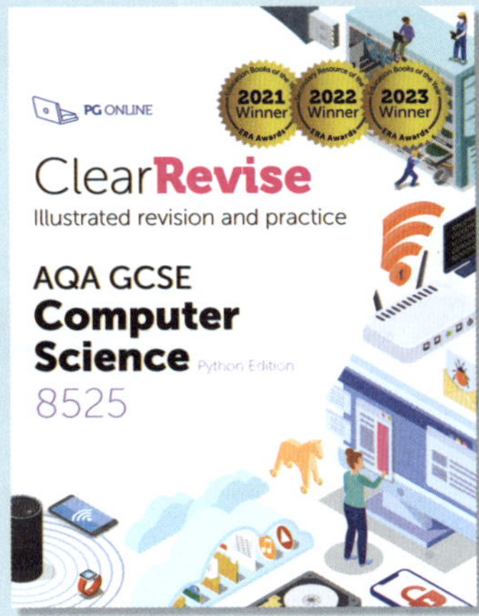

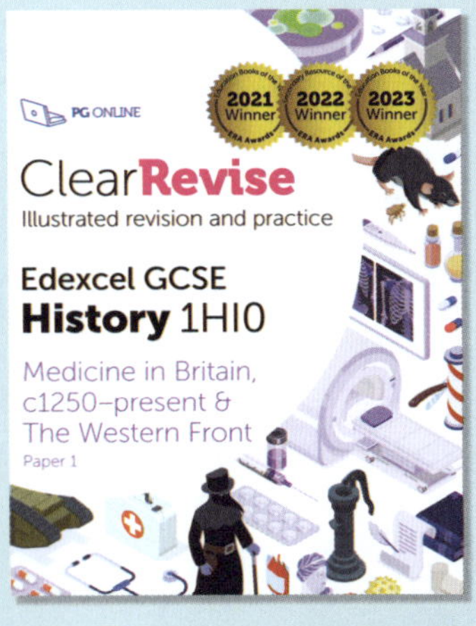

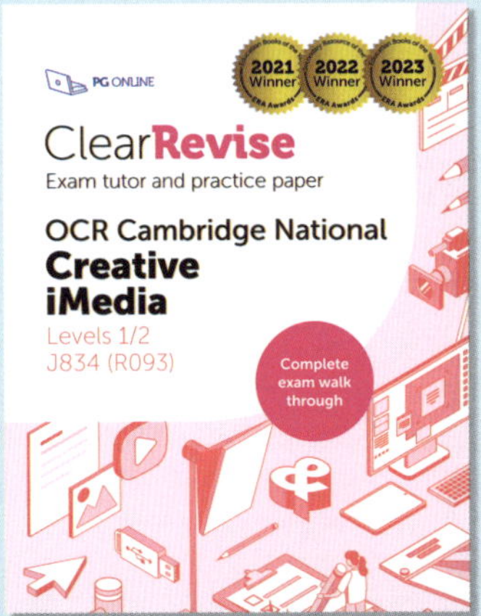

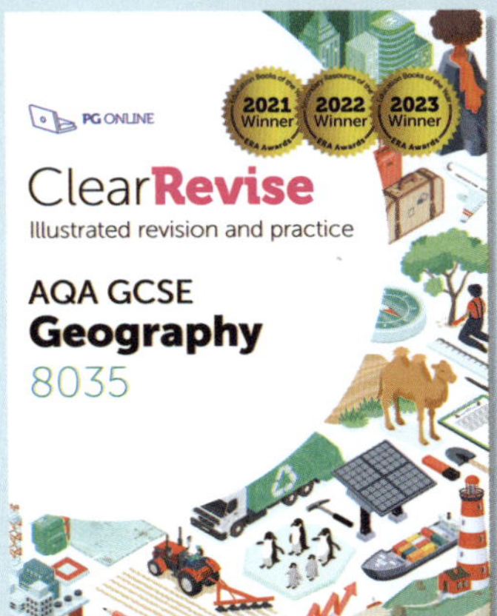

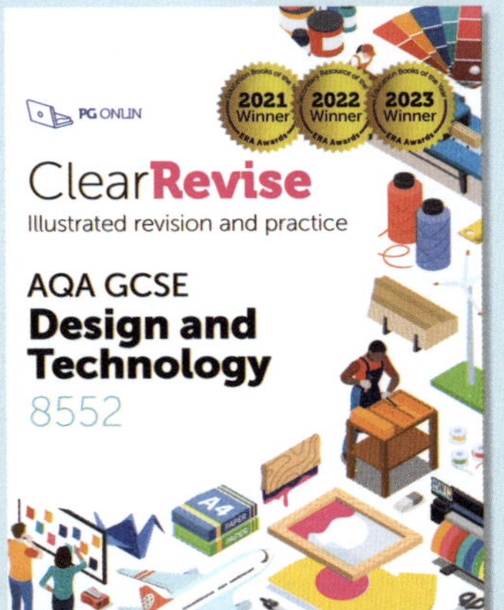